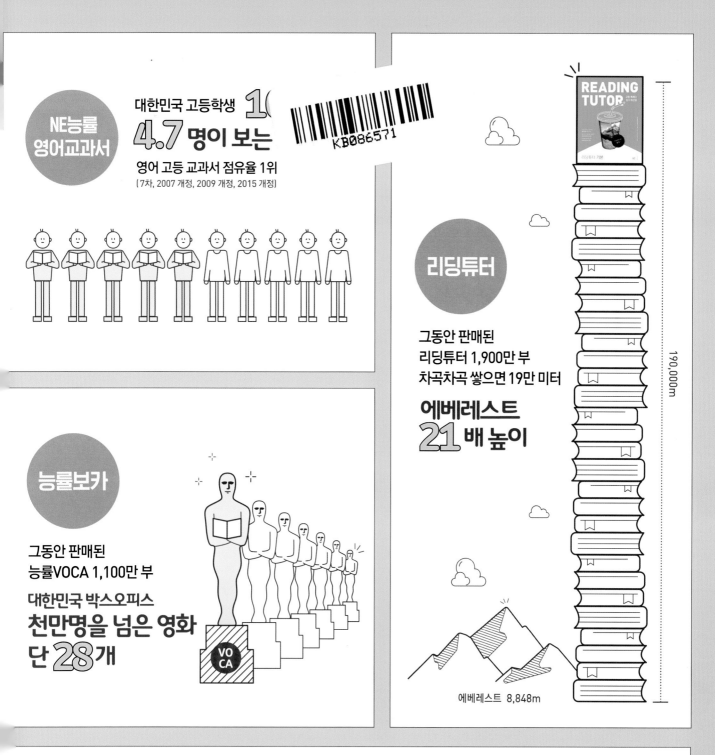

NE능률 영어교과서

대한민국 고등학생
4.7 명이 보는

영어 고등 교과서 점유율 1위
(7차, 2007 개정, 2009 개정, 2015 개정)

KB086571

리딩튜터

그동안 판매된
리딩튜터 1,900만 부
차곡차곡 쌓으면 19만 미터

에베레스트
21 배 높이

190,000m

에베레스트 8,848m

READING
TUTOR

능률보카

그동안 판매된
능률VOCA 1,100만 부

대한민국 박스오피스
천만명을 넘은 영화
단 28개

VO CA

그래머존

그동안 판매된 450만 부의 그래머존을 바닥에 쭉 ~ 깔면
1000km 서울-부산 왕복가능

서울

부산

READING
Inside

LEVEL 3

지은이	NE능률 영어교육연구소
선임연구원	조은영
연구원	이지영, 이희진
영문교열	Curtis Thompson, Angela Lan, Olk Bryce Barrett
디자인	김연주
내지 일러스트	최주석, 한상엽, 김동현
맥편집	김선희
영업	한기영, 이경구, 박인규, 정철교, 김남준, 이우현
마케팅	박혜선, 남경진, 이지원, 김여진

NE능률이
미래를
창조합니다.

건강한 배움의 고객가치를 제공하겠다는 꿈을 실현하기 위해
40년이 넘는 시간 동안 열심히 달려왔습니다.

앞으로도 끊임없는 연구와 노력을 통해
당연한 것을 멈추지 않고

고객, 기업, 직원 모두가 함께 성장하는 NE능률이 되겠습니다.

KB124528

READING
Inside

LEVEL 3

STRUCTURES

● This shows how each reading passage is related to the topic and the school subject.

● Reading Comprehension

The students' understanding of the passage is checked through a series of multiple-choice and descriptive questions. This also helps to strengthen students' reading accuracy.

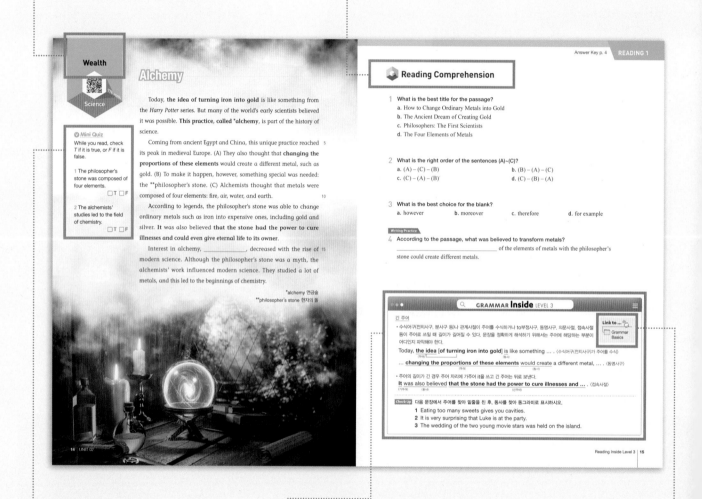

● Mini Quiz

While learners are reading the passage, they are asked to do some simple tasks. Through these simple activities, students can understand the information in the passage more easily and get ready to answer the Reading Comprehension questions.

● GRAMMAR Inside

This helps learners grasp the key structures of sentences and strengthens their understanding of the passage. It is also related to the best-selling grammar series *Grammar Inside*.

📁 From the **Link to…** , ●

learners can see which chapter and unit of the *Grammar Inside* series are directly related to this section.

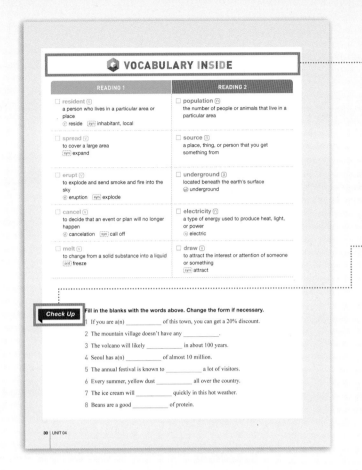

VOCABULARY INSIDE

This presents come content words in context and provides synonyms, antonyms, related parts of speech, and idioms to improve students' vocabulary. Learners should check if they know the words first before proceeding with the further learning.

Through **Check Up**,

students can better understand the practical usage of words by filling in the blanks with words from the chart.

Workbook

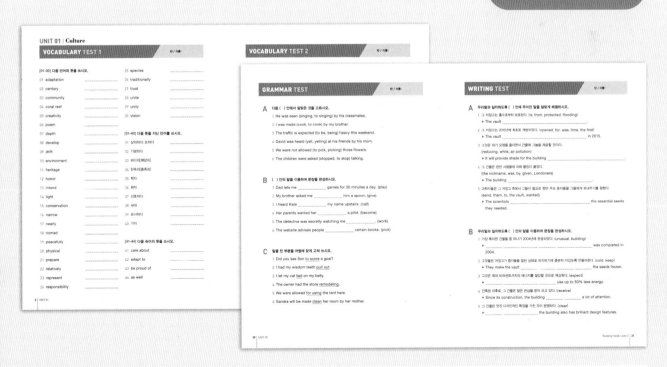

The workbook, which is composed of four pages of vocabulary tests, grammar tests, and writing tests, helps reinforce what students have learned in the main text.

CONTENTS

Link to GRAMMAR Inside

UNIT
01 | Culture

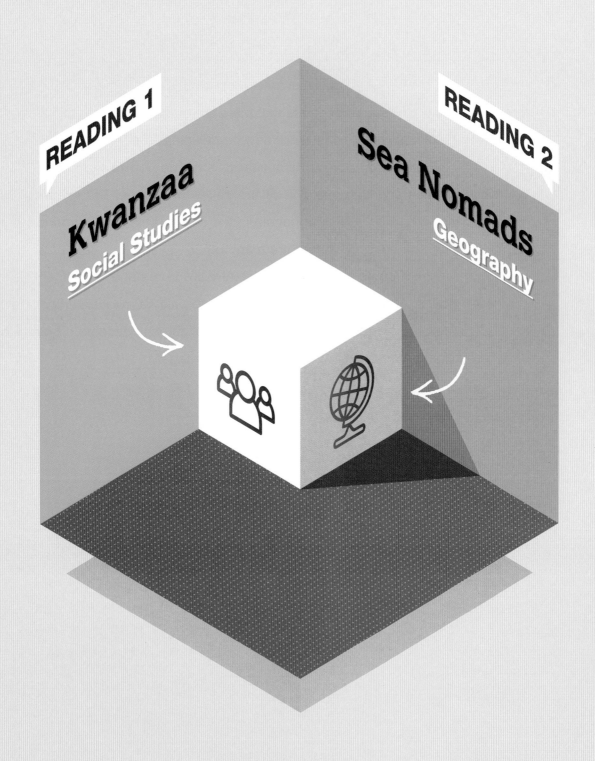

READING 1
Kwanzaa
Social Studies

READING 2
Sea Nomads
Geography

Kwanzaa

Every year, African Americans celebrate a holiday called Kwanzaa from December 26 to January 1. Dr. Maulana Karenga, an African-American scholar, began this holiday in 1966 to unite African Americans. Dr. Maulana wanted them to care about their heritage. After researching African celebrations, he created the holiday and named it 5 with a Swahili word that means "harvest."

Kwanzaa includes seven principles: unity, choice, responsibility, teamwork, purpose, creativity, and trust. Dr. Maulana chose these values because he believed they could improve the African-American community. During Kwanzaa, people prepare seven candles called 10 Mishumaa Saba. Three are red, three are green, and one is black. Each candle represents one of the seven principles.

Every night during Kwanzaa, **it** is a tradition **to light** one of the candles and **discuss** one of the seven principles. For example, on the first night, the black candle in the center is lit, and the principle of 15 unity is discussed. There are many other ways Kwanzaa is celebrated as well. People make music with African drums and read poems and stories. Also, the whole family gathers to enjoy a meal together. As Dr. Maulana intended, this relatively new holiday has become a great way to help African Americans honor their heritage. 20

ⓥ Mini Quiz

While you read, check *T* if it is true, or *F* if it is false.

1 Kwanzaa lasts for about a week.

☐ T ☐ F

2 During the period of Kwanzaa, people light seven colored candles.

☐ T ☐ F

Reading Comprehension

1　What is the best title for the passage?

　　a. Ethnic Holidays in the US

　　b. Kwanzaa: An Ancient African Festival

　　c. An American Holiday Comes to Africa

　　d. Celebrating African Heritage in America

2　What was the purpose of creating Kwanzaa?

　　a. to remind African Americans of their heritage

　　b. to get African Americans to help each other

　　c. to introduce African culture to other people

　　d. to promote African-American art

3　What is NOT mentioned about Kwanzaa?

　　a. when it starts and finishes each year

　　b. the meaning of the word in Swahili

　　c. what the colors of the Mishumaa Saba are

　　d. why unity is discussed on the first night

Writing Practice

4　According to the passage, why did Dr. Maulana choose the seven values?

　　because he believed they could _____

⊙ ⊙ ⊙　　🔍 **GRAMMAR Inside** LEVEL 3　　≡

가주어 it과 to부정사구 주어

• 주어로 쓰인 to부정사의 길이가 길어질 경우 가주어 it을 쓰고 to부정사는 뒤로 보낸다. 이때 뒤로 이동한 to부정사를 진주어라고 하고, it을 '그것'이라고 해석하지 않는다.

…, **it** is a tradition **to light** one of the candles and **(to) discuss** one of the seven
　(가주어)　　　　　　　　　촛불 중 하나에 불을 붙이고 일곱 개의 원칙 중 한 가지에 관하여 논의하는 것은 (진주어)
principles.

• to부정사의 의미상의 주어는 to부정사가 뜻하는 동작이나 상태의 주체가 되며, 대개 「for + 목적격」으로 나타낸다.

It was exciting **for her to see** the rock band's performance.
　(가주어)　　　그녀가 (의미상의 주어)　　그 록밴드의 공연을 보는 것은 (진주어)

Link to ... 👆
　📁 Chapter 04
　📁 Unit 01, 03

Check Up 두 문장의 의미가 같도록 빈칸에 알맞은 말을 쓰시오.

　　To complete this crossword puzzle is difficult.

　　→ _____ is difficult _____ _____ this crossword puzzle.

Sea Nomads

Although nearly half of all species on Earth live in the ocean, most people probably prefer to live on land. The Sama-Bajau people of Southeast Asia, however, are different. They call the ocean their home.

The Sama-Bajau are an ethnic group who has lived at sea for centuries. Traveling the waters of Indonesia, Malaysia, and the Philippines, they have deep links to the ocean. The Sama-Bajau are proud of their *nomadic lifestyle. Traditionally, they live on long, narrow boats called lepa-lepa and drift with the **currents. This has led some people to describe the Sama-Bajau as "sea nomads."

Over generations, the Sama-Bajau have even developed physical adaptations to marine environments. When hunting for fish, they can free dive to great depths. They also can stay there for long periods on a single breath. Sama-Bajau children have strong underwater vision because their eyes have adapted to salt water. Plus, since the Sama-Bajau spend so much time at sea, they sometimes feel "landsick" when they step on the ground.

Recently, some Sama-Bajau people have begun to move onto the land because they find **it** too difficult **to live** at sea. However, you can still find the traditional Sama-Bajau boats peacefully floating among the coral reefs today.

5

10

15

20

*nomadic 유목의, 방랑의
**current 해류

Mini Quiz

Read and underline the answers in the passage.

Paragraph 2

1 Which countries can the Sama-Bajau be found near?

Paragraph 2

2 What does "This" refer to in the passage?

Reading Comprehension

1 **What is the passage mainly about?**
   a. how to survive in the ocean
   b. the marine lifestyle of an ethnic group
   c. the importance of marine conservation
   d. the advantages of living near water

2 **What are true about the Sama-Bajau? (Choose two.)**
   a. The Sama-Bajau are proud of how they live.
   b. The Sama-Bajau don't use their boats when they move.
   c. The Sama-Bajau survive by fishing and farming at sea.
   d. Some Sama-Bajau people have moved onto land.

3 **What is NOT included in the underlined part?**
   a. The Sama-Bajau are able to free dive deep underwater.
   b. The Sama-Bajau can stay underwater for a long time.
   c. Sama-Bajau children use their good vision to find salt.
   d. Stepping on the ground sometimes makes the Sama-Bajau feel sick.

Writing Practice
4 **According to the passage, why do the Sama-Bajau feel sick on land?**
   because they _____

GRAMMAR Inside LEVEL 3

가목적어 it과 to부정사구 목적어
목적어로 쓰인 to부정사의 길이가 길어질 경우 가목적어 it을 쓰고 to부정사는 뒤로 보낸다. 이때 뒤로 이동한 to부정사를 진목적어라고 하고, it을 '그것'이라고 해석하지 않는다.

… because they find **it** too difficult **to live** at sea.
        (가목적어)   바다에 사는 것을 (진목적어)

We thought **it** impossible **for the children to win** the competition.
       (가목적어)   그 아이들이 (의미상의 주어)   그 대회에서 이기는 것 (진목적어)

Link to …
Chapter 04
Unit 01, 03

Check Up 다음 문장을 우리말로 해석하시오.
   I found it impossible to persuade my parents.
   → _____

VOCABULARY INSIDE

READING 1	READING 2
☐ **celebrate** ⓥ to do something on a special day ⓝ celebration	☐ **ethnic** ⓐ related to a certain race or people
☐ **unite** ⓥ to join together to achieve a certain goal ⓝ unity [syn] cooperate	☐ **generation** ⓝ a group of people in society who are born and live around the same time ⓥ generate
☐ **principle** ⓝ a basic law or rule that is followed by people	☐ **adaptation** ⓝ a change in something that makes it more suitable for its environment ⓥ adapt
☐ **responsibility** ⓝ something that is your job or duty to take care of ⓐ responsible [ant] irresponsibility	☐ **breath** ⓝ the air that goes in and out of your lungs ⓥ breathe
☐ **discuss** ⓥ to talk about something ⓝ discussion [syn] debate	☐ **float** ⓥ to stay or move on the surface of a liquid [syn] sail, drift

Check Up **Fill in the blanks with the words above. Change the form if necessary.**

1 This _____ group has a unique culture.

2 We _____ my father's birthday in this hotel every year.

3 The nations _____ and fought back against the enemy.

4 Yesterday, we _____ Chinese history in class.

5 Monkeys have many _____ that help them live in trees.

6 The leaves are _____ on the river.

7 The present _____ enjoys different lifestyles from the previous one.

8 The main _____ of equality is that all people have the same rights.

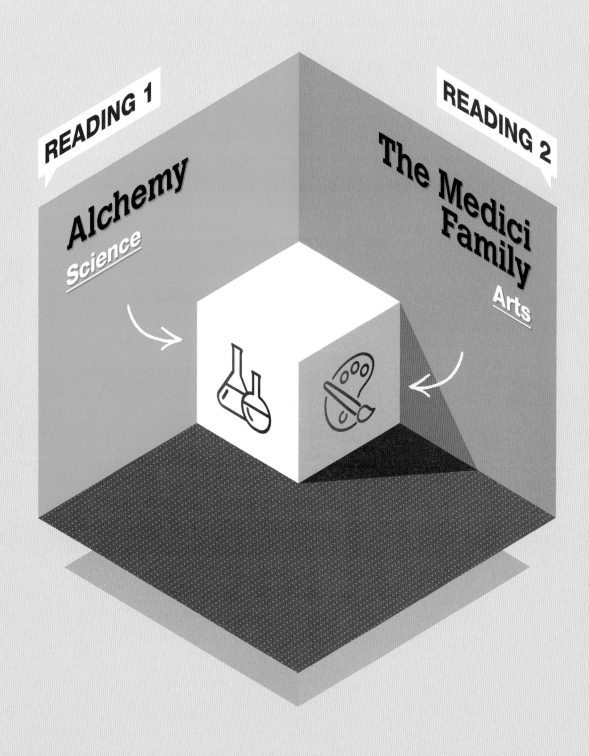

READING 1

Alchemy
Science

READING 2

The Medici
Family
Arts

Alchemy

Today, **the idea of turning iron into gold** is like something from the *Harry Potter* series. But many of the world's early scientists believed it was possible. **This practice, called *alchemy**, is part of the history of science.

Coming from ancient Egypt and China, this unique practice reached 5 its peak in medieval Europe. (A) They also thought that **changing the proportions of these elements** would create a different metal, such as gold. (B) To make it happen, however, something special was needed: the **philosopher's stone. (C) Alchemists thought that metals were composed of four elements: fire, air, water, and earth. 10

According to legends, the philosopher's stone was able to change ordinary metals such as iron into expensive ones, including gold and silver. **It** was also believed **that the stone had the power to cure illnesses and could even give eternal life to its owner.**

Interest in alchemy, _____, decreased with the rise of 15 modern science. Although the philosopher's stone was a myth, the alchemists' work influenced modern science. They studied a lot of metals, and this led to the beginnings of chemistry.

*alchemy 연금술
**philosopher's stone 현자의 돌

ⓥ Mini Quiz

While you read, check *T* if it is true, or *F* if it is false.

1 The philosopher's stone was composed of four elements.
☐ T ☐ F

2 The alchemists' studies led to the field of chemistry.
☐ T ☐ F

Reading Comprehension

1 **What is the best title for the passage?**
   a. How to Change Ordinary Metals into Gold
   b. The Ancient Dream of Creating Gold
   c. Philosophers: The First Scientists
   d. The Four Elements of Metals

2 **What is the right order of the sentences (A)~(C)?**
   a. (A) – (C) – (B)　　　　　　b. (B) – (A) – (C)
   c. (C) – (A) – (B)　　　　　　d. (C) – (B) – (A)

3 **What is the best choice for the blank?**
   a. however　　　b. moreover　　　c. therefore　　　d. for example

> **Writing Practice**

4 **According to the passage, what was believed to transform metals?**
   _____ of the elements of metals with the philosopher's
   stone could create different metals.

Q GRAMMAR Inside LEVEL 3 ☰

긴 주어
• 수식어구(전치사구, 분사구 등)나 관계사절이 주어를 수식하거나 to부정사구, 동명사구, 의문사절, 접속사절
  등이 주어로 쓰일 때 길이가 길어질 수 있다. 문장을 정확하게 해석하기 위해서는 주어에 해당하는 부분이
  어디인지 파악해야 한다.

Link to ...
📁 Grammar
   Basics

Today, **the idea [of turning iron into gold]** is like something ... . 〈수식어구(전치사구)가 주어를 수식〉
　　　　(주어) └──────────┘　　(동사)

... **changing the proportions of these elements** would create a different metal, ... 〈동명사구〉
　　(주어)　　　　　　　　　　　　　　　　(동사)

• 주어의 길이가 긴 경우 주어 자리에 가주어 it을 쓰고 긴 주어는 뒤로 보낸다.
It was also believed **that the stone had the power to cure illnesses and ...** . 〈접속사절〉
(가주어)　(동사)　　　　　　　　　(진주어)

Check Up 다음 문장에서 주어를 찾아 밑줄을 친 후, 동사를 찾아 동그라미로 표시하시오.
   1 Eating too many sweets gives you cavities.
   2 It is very surprising that Luke is at the party.
   3 The wedding of the two young movie stars was held on the island.

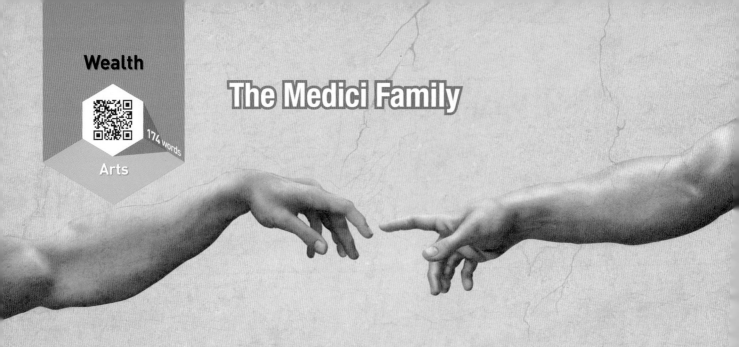

The Medici Family

⊙ Mini Quiz

Read and underline the answers in the passage.

Paragraph 2

1 What famous building was built with the support of the Medici family?

Paragraph 3

2 How could Galileo study the universe?

The Renaissance period began in the 1300s in Florence, Italy. The power of wealthy families was essential in its development—the Medicis were one of these families.

At that time, artists needed **the help of financial supporters** so that they could focus on their work without worrying about money. The Medici family supported Renaissance masters such as Michelangelo, Leonardo da Vinci, and Botticelli. Because of the family's support, Michelangelo was able to paint the Sistine Chapel. It also allowed famous buildings to be constructed, including the Milan Cathedral.

5

▲ Galileo Galilei (1564-1642)

10

In addition to the arts, science was of great interest to the Medici family. (①) They supported many scientists, such as da Vinci and Galileo. (②) Galileo was able to study the universe with the money 15 he earned from teaching the Medici children. (③) Moreover, the family established **a science academy that attracted many scientists to Florence.** (④) They also helped scholars study ancient texts and sponsored schools and libraries. Without the family's love for arts, science, and culture, the history of the arts would be a lot different 20 today.

Reading Comprehension

1　What is the passage mainly about?
　a. how the Medici family became wealthy and powerful
　b. a wealthy family that supported artists and scientists
　c. reasons why the Renaissance began in the 1300s
　d. famous works of art created in Florence

2　What is NOT true about the Medici family?
　a. They were one of the wealthy families in Italy.
　b. Michelangelo was able to paint the Sistine Chapel because of their help.
　c. They established a science academy in the Milan Cathedral.
　d. They helped scholars study ancient texts.

3　Where would the following sentence best fit?

> He even named some of the stars he found after the children of the family.

　a. ①　　　　　b. ②　　　　　c. ③　　　　　d. ④

Writing Practice

4　According to the passage, why did the artists need the help of supporters?
　Because with their help, the artists could _____
　without _____.

🔍 **GRAMMAR Inside** LEVEL 3

긴 목적어

to부정사구, 동명사구, 의문사절, 접속사절이 목적어로 쓰이거나, 수식어구 혹은 관계사절이 목적어를 수식할 때 목적어의 길이가 길어질 수 있다.

I just avoided **going to the mountain alone at night.** 〈동명사구〉
I didn't know **that you liked snowboarding.** 〈접속사절〉
…, the family established **a science academy [that attracted …].** 〈관계사절이 목적어 수식〉

Link to …
　Grammar
　Basics

· ·

Check Up　다음 문장에서 목적어를 찾아 밑줄을 친 후, 우리말로 해석하시오.

　1 Did you notice that Amy had her hair cut?
　　→ _____

　2 I saw the action movie you recommended yesterday.
　　→ _____

VOCABULARY INSIDE

READING 1	READING 2
☐ **practice** (n) something that is routinely done as a habit or custom	☐ **financial** (a) related to money (n) finance
☐ **element** (n) a basic substance that can't be split into something simpler [syn] component	☐ **support** (v) to help someone succeed (n) support, supporter
☐ **cure** (v) to make a disease go away and make someone healthy [syn] heal, make better	☐ **earn** (v) to receive money as payment for work that you do (n) earnings [syn] be paid
☐ **eternal** (a) continuing or existing forever [syn] everlasting, endless [ant] temporary	☐ **establish** (v) to set up a business or organization [syn] set up
☐ **interest** (n) the feeling of wanting to be involved with something or to discover more about it (a) interesting, interested	☐ **attract** (v) to cause someone to be interested in something (a) attractive (n) attraction [syn] draw

Check Up   **Fill in the blanks with the words above. Change the form if necessary.**

1 What are the main _____ of coal?

2 They're developing a new medicine to _____ cancer.

3 I believe that our love is _____ .

4 Anna had _____ problems, so she borrowed some money.

5 The organization was established to _____ poor families.

6 I'd recommend this film to anyone who has a(n) _____ in food.

7 It's common _____ in the US to tip your server.

8 I don't expect to _____ a living from my paintings.

UNIT
03 | Shapes

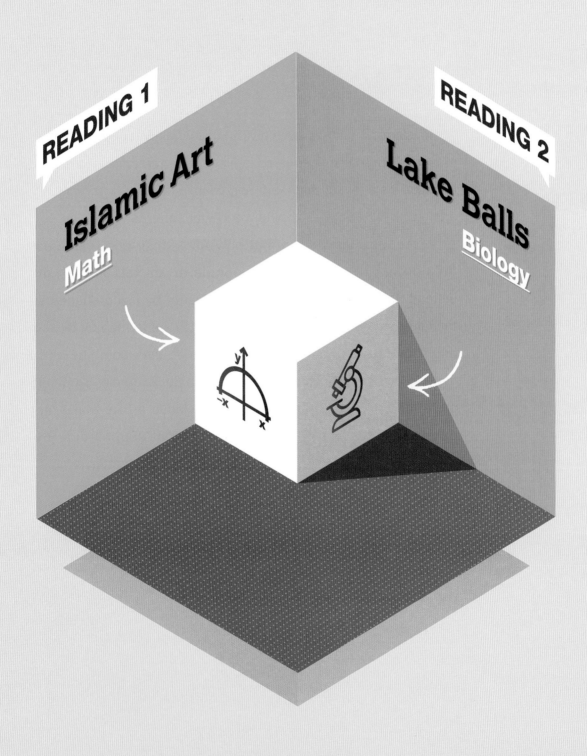

READING 1

Islamic Art
Math

READING 2

Lake Balls
Biology

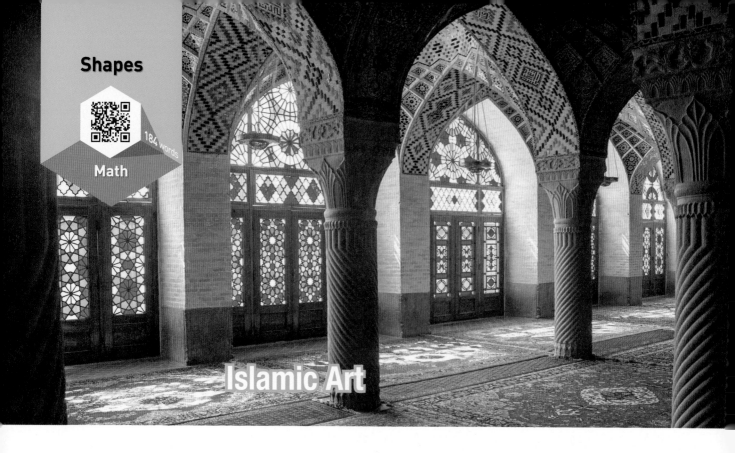

Sholes

Math

184 words

Islamic Art

ⓥ Mini Quiz

While you read, check *T* if it is true, or *F* if it is false.

1 Muslims use geometric shapes to show beauty.
☐ T ☐ F

2 Many drawing tools are needed to make Islamic patterns.
☐ T ☐ F

In Islamic countries such as Türkiye, you'll find ceilings and floors of mosques and palaces covered in elegant patterns. Islamic art is unique because it's a mix of math, art, and Islamic culture. In particular, Islamic artists are proud of developing wonderful patterns.

Since Muslims believe that only Allah, their god, can create life, 5 they do not depict images of people or animals in their artwork. Instead, Islamic artists **try to show** beauty by using shapes such as triangles, squares, and pentagons. (A) They are formed by two squares, one rotated by 45 degrees. (B) Moreover, they combine and rotate them to create more complex shapes. (C) For example, 8-pointed stars 10 are often used in their artwork. Then Islamic artists make repeating patterns of the stars, laying thousands of shapes side by side. Surprisingly, the artists can create the complex patterns only with a ruler and a pair of compasses.

Repeating geometric shapes in Islamic art have a deep meaning. For Muslims, repetitive mathematical patterns describe the infinite nature of Allah. Islamic art shows that art is a great way to represent how people see the world.

15

20

Reading Comprehension

1 **What is the best title for the passage?**
   a. Allah in Famous Islamic Artworks
   b. Patterns: A Key Element in Islamic Art
   c. The Origins of Art in Islamic Countries
   d. The Meanings of Different Shapes in Islam

Writing Practice

2 **According to the passage, why don't Muslims draw people or animals in their artwork?**
   Because they think _____

3 **What is the right order of the sentences (A)~(C)?**
   a. (A) – (C) – (B)   b. (B) – (A) – (C)
   c. (B) – (C) – (A)   d. (C) – (B) – (A)

4 **Which CANNOT be answered based on the passage?**
   a. Where can you find Islamic patterns?
   b. What kinds of shapes do Muslims use?
   c. What does the number 8 mean in Islamic art?
   d. What do the repetitive patterns in Islamic art represent?

GRAMMAR Inside LEVEL 3

동명사와 to부정사를 모두 목적어로 취하는 동사

동명사와 to부정사를 모두 목적어로 취하면서 의미 차이가 거의 없는 동사가 있는 반면, 무엇을 목적어로 취하느냐에 따라 의미가 달라지는 동사들이 있다.

Link to ...
Chapter 05
Unit 02

• 의미 차이가 거의 없는 경우: like, love, hate, begin, start, continue 등
  My sister **likes baking[to bake]** in her free time.

• 의미 차이가 있는 경우: remember, forget, try 등
  remember[forget] v-ing: (과거에) ~했던 것을 기억하다[잊다]   try v-ing: (시험 삼아) ~해보다
  remember[forget] to-v: (앞으로) ~할 것을 기억하다[잊다]   try to-v: ~하려고 노력하다

  Jamie **tried opening** the drawer, but it was locked.
         열려고 해봤다
  Instead, Islamic artists **try to show** beauty by using shapes … .
                            보여주려고 노력한다

Lake Balls

Have you ever visited a freshwater aquarium? If so, you **may have seen** some green velvety balls floating in the water. Known as Marimo moss balls, these small unusual balls are not actually moss. In fact, they are made of algae, a kind of freshwater plant. As the algae grow, they produce *filaments. These become tangled at the bottom of lakes 5 and rivers. Over time, they form into the shape of a ball.

Look closely at the water balls. You **might have noticed** that they float during the day and sink at night. (①) The secret to this behavior is **photosynthesis. (②) When the balls get sunlight, they give off tiny bubbles of oxygen. (③) The bubbles 10 soon disappear as the light fades, causing the balls to sink. (④)

Marimo balls were easy to find several decades ago. However, their population has decreased. The use of fertilizers in agriculture has increased the number of rival species of algae. These plants cover 15 the surface of the water and block out the light for photosynthesis. As a result, today Marimo balls are seen only in Japan.

*filament 가는 실
**photosynthesis 광합성

Reading Comprehension

1 **What is the passage mainly about?**
   a. how lake balls float in water
   b. the characteristics of lake balls
   c. the life cycle of underwater plants
   d. why algae cannot survive in freshwater

2 **Where would the following sentence best fit?**

> These bubbles become trapped in the filaments and push the balls up to the surface.

   a. ①   b. ②   c. ③   d. ④

3 **What can be answered based on the passage?**
   a. Which countries were lake balls found in previously?
   b. What kind of fertilizer is needed to grow lake balls?
   c. What animal feeds on lake balls?
   d. Why did Marimo balls start to disappear?

Writing Practice

4 **According to the passage, how do other types of algae stop the photosynthesis of lake balls?**

_____ on land has helped rival species of algae.

These plants _____ by covering the surface of the water.

○○○ ○   🔍 **GRAMMAR Inside** LEVEL 3   ☰

「조동사 + have v-ed」

「조동사 + have v-ed」는 과거의 일에 대한 의심, 후회, 유감, 추측 등을 나타낸다.

He **can't have forgotten** my name. (과거의 일에 대한 강한 의심: ~이었을 리가 없다)
I **should have gone** to bed early last night. (과거의 일에 대한 후회나 유감: ~했어야 했다)
She **must have met** them before at school. (과거의 일에 대한 강한 추측: ~이었음에 틀림없다)
You **may[might] have seen** some green velvety balls … . (과거의 일에 대한 약한 추측: ~이었을지도 모른다)

Link to ... 👆
📁 Chapter 02
📁 Unit 02

Check Up 다음 문장을 우리말로 해석하시오.

I might have left my umbrella in the café.

→ _____

◆ VOCABULARY INSIDE

READING 1	READING 2
☐ **depict** ⓥ to show something in a picture [syn] illustrate	☐ **sink** ⓥ to move down below the surface of water ⓝ sink [syn] submerge
☐ **rotate** ⓥ to move or turn something in a circle ⓝ rotation [syn] spin	☐ **behavior** ⓝ a certain way of acting ⓥ behave
☐ **combine** ⓥ to mix things together to form a single substance ⓝ combination [syn] mix [ant] separate	☐ **disappear** ⓥ to move somewhere else and no longer be seen ⓝ disappearance [ant] appear
☐ **complex** ⓐ having a lot of details and small parts ⓝ complexity [syn] complicated [ant] simple	☐ **decrease** ⓥ to become less in number or amount ⓝ decrease [syn] reduce [ant] increase
☐ **infinite** ⓐ having no end in space or time ⓝ infinity [syn] limitless, endless [ant] limited	☐ **agriculture** ⓝ the practice or science of farming ⓐ agricultural [syn] farming

Check Up Fill in the blanks with the words above. Change the form if necessary.

1 _____ all the ingredients and mix them.

2 The boat will _____ if water keeps flowing into it.

3 The forest was cut down, and then the land was used for _____.

4 This puzzle is too _____ for young children.

5 In our solar system, eight planets _____ around the sun.

6 You can see that the picture _____ a landscape in bright colors.

7 His rude _____ at dinner is unforgivable.

8 The demand for travel has _____ sharply due to the pandemic.

UNIT
04 | Nature

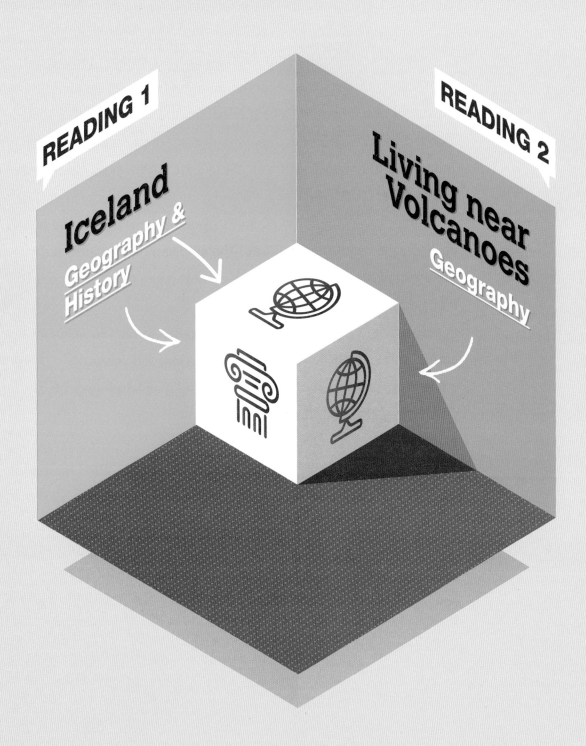

READING 1

Iceland
Geography &
History

READING 2

Living near
Volcanoes
Geography

Nature

Geography & History

200 words

Iceland

⊙ Mini Quiz

Find the answers from the passage and write them.

Paragraph 2

1 Find the word in the passage that has the given meaning.

| having existed for a long time |

→ _____

Paragraph 4

2 What have the melted glaciers formed in Iceland?

→ _____

_____

Iceland is a country that makes every visitor fall in love with its breathtaking landscapes. According to legend, a wizard turned into a whale and swam toward Iceland to control it with his magic. But he was stopped by the island's spirits, who bravely protected their homeland. Today, you may not meet those same spirits. However, Iceland's huge 5 volcanoes and grand glaciers will surely make you believe in magic.

The island was created 20 million years ago when magma bubbled up along the *Mid-Atlantic Ridge. The smoking ground and lava looked like a battlefield of the gods, so the earliest residents of Iceland thought they **had found** an ancient land. 10

Even now, the land is still being formed. About 130 volcanoes are spread across the island, erupting twice every ten years. _____(A)_____ some eruptions are not that big, others release large amounts of lava. Of all the volcanoes, Grímsvötn is the most active. _____(B)_____ its eruption in 2011, 900 flights were canceled. 15

▲ an example of fjord

Ice is another natural force that is shaping Iceland. Over the past 7,000 years, glaciers on the island have melted away and formed the beautiful **fjords and valleys of Iceland. These 20 glaciers still cover nearly ten percent of the country.

*Mid-Atlantic Ridge 대서양 중앙 해령
**fjord 피오르드 지형

Reading Comprehension

1 **What is the passage mainly about?**
a. the natural features of Iceland
b. a legend about the origin of Iceland
c. how volcanoes were formed in Iceland
d. problems caused by melting glaciers in Iceland

2 **What is NOT mentioned in the passage?**
a. why the wizard went to Iceland
b. when Iceland was created
c. which volcano is the most active
d. how many glaciers there are in Iceland

3 **What is the best choice for blanks (A) and (B)?**

(A)	(B)		(A)	(B)
a. Though	– Due to		b. However	– Before
c. Because	– After		d. Even though	– Despite

Writing Practice
4 **According to the passage, why did the earliest residents of Iceland think it was an ancient land?**
because the smoking ground and lava looked like _____

🔍 **GRAMMAR Inside** LEVEL 3　　☰

과거완료
과거완료는 「had v-ed」의 형태로 과거의 어느 시점 이전에 완료되었거나 그 시점까지 지속되었던 일을 나타낼 때 쓰며, 동작이나 상태의 〈완료, 결과, 경험, 계속〉 등의 의미를 나타낸다.

… the earliest residents of Iceland thought they **had found** an ancient land. 〈완료〉
The car **had broken** down, so I took the subway. 〈결과〉
I **had** never **been** to Europe before I went as an exchange student. 〈경험〉
This house **had been** empty for a year before I moved in. 〈계속〉

Link to ... 👆
　📁 Chapter 01
　　📁 Unit 02

Check Up 우리말과 일치하도록 ( ) 안의 말을 이용하여 문장을 완성하시오.

그녀는 새로운 직업을 시작하기 전에 조종사로 일했었다. (work)
→ She _____ _____ as a pilot before she started her new job.

Living near Volcanoes

Mount Merapi, located in Indonesia, is **one of the world's most active volcanoes**. Surprisingly, there are about one million people who live within 20 miles of it. And the local population is growing. Why would so many people live near something so dangerous? Believe it or not, _____.   5

First, the soil around volcanoes is rich in minerals, so it provides plants with nutrients. Also, many volcanic products are actually quite useful. For example, *sulphur can be used as an ingredient in medicine or matches. Other valuable materials including gold, silver, and diamonds are also found near volcanoes. For this reason, mining towns 10 are often built near volcanoes.

In countries such as Iceland and New Zealand, volcanoes are used as a source of **geothermal energy. People use steam heated by underground magma to drive engines in power stations. This produces electricity that can be used in homes and factories.   15

In addition, volcanoes draw a lot of tourists, who come to see volcanic features such as hot springs. In Hawaii, tourists can even visit exotic beaches whose black sand is made from volcanic rocks. And all of these attractions create jobs for local people. Now, do you see why so many people live near volcanoes?   20

*sulphur 황, 유황
**geothermal energy 지열 에너지

V Mini Quiz

While you read, check *T* if it is true, or *F* if it is false.

1 A lot of valuable materials can be found near volcanoes.
☐ T ☐ F

2 Local people benefit from the tourists who visit volcanic areas.
☐ T ☐ F

Reading Comprehension

1 **What is the best title for the passage?**

 a. Countries with Amazing Volcanoes

 b. Why People Live Close to Volcanoes

 c. Why Tourists Enjoy Visiting Volcanoes

 d. Mt. Merapi: The World's Most Active Volcano

2 **What is the best choice for the blank?**

 a. people are always prepared for an emergency

 b. volcanoes have not erupted for a long time

 c. living near a volcano has many benefits

 d. people try to overcome their fears there

Writing Practice

3 **According to the passage, how is steam heated by magma used?**

 It _____ in power stations and _____

 for homes and factories.

4 **What can be answered based on the passage?**

 a. Why is volcanic soil rich with minerals?

 b. What kinds of materials can be found in volcanic soil?

 c. How do people make medicine with sulphur?

 d. How many people visit the exotic beaches of Hawaii?

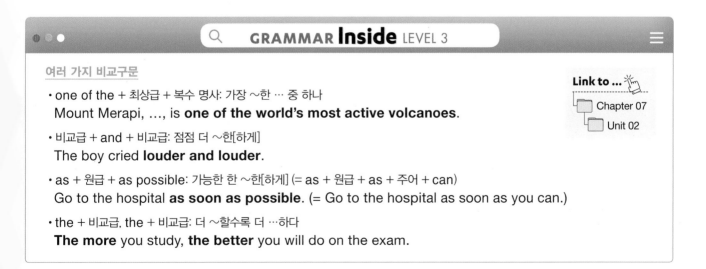

● ● ●   Q   GRAMMAR **Inside** LEVEL 3   ≡

여러 가지 비교구문

• one of the + 최상급 + 복수 명사: 가장 ~한 … 중 하나
 Mount Merapi, …, is **one of the world's most active volcanoes**.

• 비교급 + and + 비교급: 점점 더 ~한[하게]
 The boy cried **louder and louder**.

• as + 원급 + as possible: 가능한 한 ~한[하게] (= as + 원급 + as + 주어 + can)
 Go to the hospital **as soon as possible**. (= Go to the hospital as soon as you can.)

• the + 비교급, the + 비교급: 더 ~할수록 더 …하다
 The more you study, **the better** you will do on the exam.

Link to ...
Chapter 07
Unit 02

VOCABULARY INSIDE

READING 1	READING 2
☐ **resident** Ⓝ a person who lives in a particular area or place Ⓥ reside [syn] inhabitant, local	☐ **population** Ⓝ the number of people or animals that live in a particular area
☐ **spread** Ⓥ to cover a large area [syn] expand	☐ **source** Ⓝ a place, thing, or person that you get something from
☐ **erupt** Ⓥ to explode and send smoke and fire into the sky Ⓝ eruption [syn] explode	☐ **underground** Ⓐ located beneath the earth's surface ⓐd underground
☐ **cancel** Ⓥ to decide that an event or plan will no longer happen Ⓝ cancelation [syn] call off	☐ **electricity** Ⓝ a type of energy used to produce heat, light, or power ⓐ electric
☐ **melt** Ⓥ to change from a solid substance into a liquid [ant] freeze	☐ **draw** Ⓥ to attract the interest or attention of someone or something [syn] attract

Check Up   Fill in the blanks with the words above. Change the form if necessary.

1 If you are a(n) _____ of this town, you can get a 20% discount.

2 The mountain village doesn't have any _____.

3 The volcano will likely _____ in about 100 years.

4 Seoul has a(n) _____ of almost 10 million.

5 The annual festival is known to _____ a lot of visitors.

6 Every summer, yellow dust _____ all over the country.

7 The ice cream will _____ quickly in this hot weather.

8 Beans are a good _____ of protein.

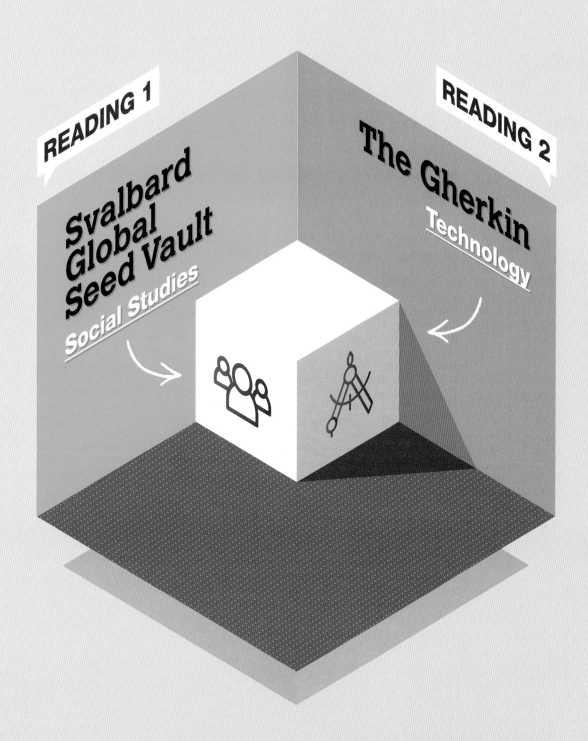

READING 1

Svalbard Global Seed Vault

Social Studies

READING 2

The Gherkin

Technology

Buildings

Social Studies

210 words

Svalbard Global Seed Vault

▼ The Arctic Circle

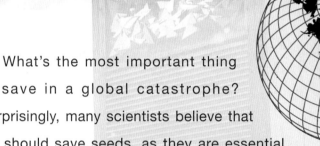

ⓥ Mini Quiz

Find the answers from the passage and write them.

Paragraph 1

1 Where is the Svalbard Global Seed Vault located?

→ _____

_____

_____

Paragraph 3

2 When was the seed vault in South Korea built?

→ _____

What's the most important thing to save in a global catastrophe? Surprisingly, many scientists believe that we should save seeds, as they are essential for producing food. For this reason, the Norwegian government built 5 the world's largest seed *vault in 2008. It is located in a mountain of the **Arctic Circle and was named the Svalbard Global Seed Vault. Its primary purpose is to store seeds and protect them from regional or global crises that threaten the Earth's plants.

(①) Actually, there are other seed vaults around the world, but 10 many have been destroyed by wars or natural disasters. (②) The mountain's ice and rock make the vault cold enough to keep the seeds frozen without electricity. (③) In addition, the vault is protected from flooding, as it's placed well above sea level. (④)

The vault was opened for the first time in 2015 to help an 15 agricultural research center in Syria. Due to a civil war, scientists from the center had to move to a safer place. To continue their research, they **wanted** the Svalbard Vault **to send** them the essential seeds they needed. This incident showed the importance of the vault. In 2016, another vault was built in South Korea. It has nearly 100,000 seeds 20 from over 4,000 different wild plant species.

*vault 저장고

**Arctic Circle 북극권

Reading Comprehension

1 What is the best title for the passage?
a. Keep Seeds in Case of a Civil War
b. The Perfect Vault for Storing Seeds
c. The Safest Place for Humans to Live
d. Why Seeds Are Our Most Valuable Resource

2 What is NOT mentioned about the Svalbard Global Seed Vault?
a. when it was built
b. what the primary mission of it is
c. how many seeds it has
d. why it is protected from flooding

3 Where would the following sentence best fit?

> The Svalbard Vault, however, is protected by its isolated and chilly location.

a. ①   b. ②   c. ③   d. ④

Writing Practice

4 According to the passage, why was the Svalbard Vault opened in 2015?
_____ in Syria

Q GRAMMAR Inside LEVEL 3 ≡

목적격 보어의 여러 형태

목적격 보어는 목적어를 보충 설명하는 말로, 동사에 따라 여러 형태로 나타낼 수 있다. 그중 목적격 보어가
부정사인 경우는 다음과 같다.

Link to ...
Chapter 04
Unit 04

• 목적격 보어가 to부정사인 경우: want, expect, tell, ask, allow, order, advise 등
  ..., they **wanted** the Svalbard Vault **to send** them the essential seeds they needed.
  _{스발바르 저장소가 보내주기를 원했다}

• 목적격 보어가 동사원형인 경우
  (1) 지각동사가 올 때: see, watch, look at, listen to, hear, feel 등 (~가 …하는 것을 보다, 듣다, 느끼다)
      I **felt** somebody suddenly **push[pushing]** me. 〈목적격 보어로 동사원형, 현재분사 모두 가능〉
      _{누군가 갑자기 떠미는 것을 느꼈다}
  (2) 사역동사가 올 때: make, have, let (~가 …하게 하다)
      Many parents don't **let** their children **play** online games at night. 〈목적격 보어로 동사원형만 가능〉
      _{자신들의 아이들이 놀게끔 하다}

• 지각동사와 사역동사의 목적격 보어가 수동의 의미를 나타낼 때는 과거분사를 쓴다.
  Layla **had** her hair **cut**.
  _{그녀의 머리카락이 잘리게 했다}

Buildings

214 words

Technology

The Gherkin

V Mini Quiz

While you read, check *T* if it is true, or *F* if it is false.

1 The Gherkin was completed in 2004 and has 41 floors.

☐ T ☐ F

2 People working in the Gherkin are required to use 50% less energy.

☐ T ☐ F

From Big Ben to the London Eye, London is home to a lot of great architecture. One of the most unusual buildings in London's skyline was completed in 2004, standing 180 meters tall with 41 floors. The building was given the nickname "the Gherkin" by Londoners because it looks like a pickle. 5

In addition to the Gherkin's unusual shape, its unique design has many practical features. Firstly, its curved shape allows the wind to flow smoothly around the building. This reduces pressure on it and decreases the amount of strong wind for pedestrians near the building. Secondly, its

▲ upper side of the Gherkin

floor-to-ceiling windows capture natural light and lessen the need for artificial lighting. Thirdly, there are plans to add a new "green wall" to the Gherkin. ① Over time, plants such as grass will grow across parts 15 of the building. ② This wall will provide shade and *insulation for the building while reducing air pollution. ③ Over 35 km of steel will be used to construct the Gherkin. ④ With its innovative design, the Gherkin **is expected to use** up to 50% less energy than ordinary office buildings.

Since its construction, the Gherkin has received a lot of attention 20 because of its unique appearance. But it's clear that the building also has brilliant design features that work in harmony with its environment.

*insulation 단열 처리

Reading Comprehension

1 What is the best title for the passage?
   a. A Unique and Comfortable Building
   b. The Origin of the Name "the Gherkin"
   c. The Most Popular Buildings in London
   d. The Gherkin: An Attractive and Innovative Building

Writing Practice
2 According to the passage, why did the Gherkin get its nickname?
   because _____

3 Which sentence is NOT needed in the passage?
   a. ①   **b.** ②   **c.** ③   **d.** ④

4 Match the design feature of the building to its benefit.
   (1) curved shape   •   • **a.** to lessen the need for artificial light
   (2) floor-to-ceiling windows •   • **b.** to provide insulation for the building
   (3) green wall   •   • **c.** to decrease the amount of strong wind
                                                       for pedestrians

---

🔍 **GRAMMAR Inside** LEVEL 3 ≡

5형식 문장의 수동태

5형식 문장을 수동태로 바꿀 때는 목적격 보어가 보통 그대로 쓰이지만, 지각동사나 사역동사가 있을 때는
목적격 보어의 형태가 바뀐다.

…, people expect <u>the Gherkin</u> to use up to 50% less energy … .
                  (목적어)   (목적격 보어)
→ …, the Gherkin **is expected to use** up to 50% less energy (by people) … .

Link to …
Chapter 03
Unit 02

• 지각동사의 목적격 보어는 수동태 문장에서 현재분사나 to부정사로 바뀐다.
  He saw Maria <u>get</u> on the bus. → Maria **was seen getting[to get]** on the bus (by him).
              (목적어) (목적격 보어)
• 사역동사(have, let, make) 중에서는 make만 수동태로 쓰이며, 목적격 보어로 쓰인 동사원형은 수동태 문장에서
  to부정사로 바뀐다.
  My mom made me <u>learn</u> taekwondo. → I **was made to learn** taekwondo by my mom.
                (목적어) (목적격 보어)

⬡ VOCABULARY INSIDE

READING 1	READING 2
☐ **government** ⓝ the group of people who officially control a country ⓥ govern	☐ **architecture** ⓝ the art or science of designing and building structures ⓝ architect
☐ **primary** ⓐ the most important ⓐⓓ primarily syn chief, main, first	☐ **pressure** ⓝ the force created by pressing on or against something ⓥ pressure
☐ **destroy** ⓥ to damage something so badly that it cannot be used or repaired syn ruin ant improve	☐ **pedestrian** ⓝ a person walking on the street
☐ **flooding** ⓝ a large amount of water covering a place that is typically dry ⓥ flood	☐ **artificial** ⓝ unnatural; produced by humans ant natural
☐ **incident** ⓝ an event that is either unpleasant or unusual syn event	☐ **brilliant** ⓐ outstanding or impressive syn bright

Check Up — **Fill in the blanks with the words above. Change the form if necessary.**

1 A car hit a(n) _____ last night.

2 Scientists made _____ rain.

3 My _____ concern is my happiness.

4 The tornado _____ several buildings in the town.

5 The doctor applied _____ to my arm to stop the bleeding.

6 The police officer is searching for people who witnessed the _____.

7 Heavy rain causes _____ in Korea every summer.

8 The US _____ is expected to announce a new tax policy.

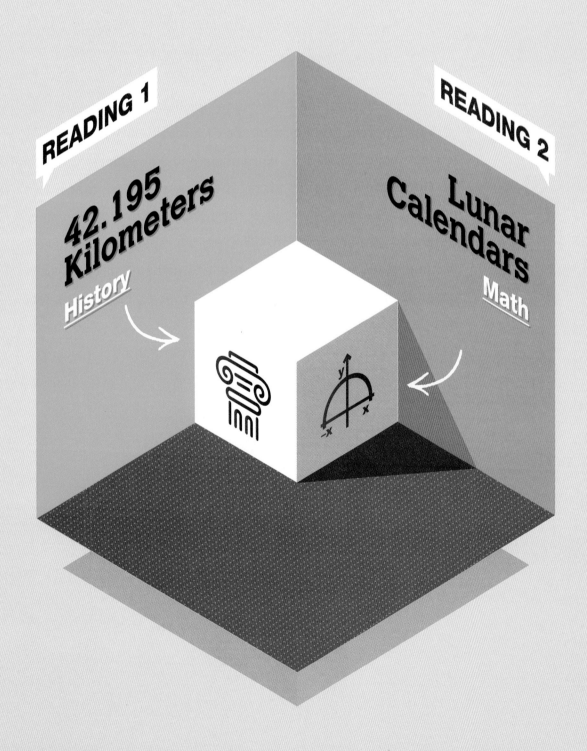

READING 1

42.195 Kilometers

History

READING 2

Lunar Calendars

Math

42.195 Kilometers

The long-distance race called the marathon has been run since ancient times. According to Greek historians, a messenger ran 40 kilometers to share news of a Greek victory before dying of exhaustion. This tale inspired the modern marathon, which is why the distance was initially 40 kilometers. Then, at the 1908 London Olympics, the length 5 was increased to **what** it is today: 42.195 kilometers.

So what happened in 1908? ① Some say Queen Alexandra demanded that Windsor Castle's lawn be the starting line of the marathon, not the stadium at the 1908 Olympics in London. ② Windsor Castle is one of the oldest castles in London. ③ She wanted the royal 10 kids to watch the race from home. ④ She also requested that the race end in front of the viewing box for royalty at the stadium. These requests added another 2.195 kilometers to the distance.

But there's another story about how this distance became permanent. During the race at the London Olympics, Italian runner 15 Dorando Pietri struggled to finish. He fell repeatedly but never gave up. Impressed with his efforts, referees helped him up when he fell down. Eventually, Pietri won the race. However, because he received help, he was disqualified and another runner was named the winner. Nevertheless, the media focused on Pietri's strong will, making him an 20 international star. People say that this story might have influenced the officials' decision to keep the distance at 42.195 kilometers.

Mini Quiz

Find the answers from the passage and write them.

Paragraph 2

1 What does "the distance" refer to in the passage?

→ _____

Paragraph 3

2 How was Pietri able to finish the race?

→ _____
_____
_____

Reading Comprehension

1 What is the best title for the passage?

a. Athletes Who Have Won in the Olympics

b. Changes in the Rules of the Olympic Marathon

c. Stories Related to the Distance of the Marathon

d. The Marathon: A Method Used by Political Campaigns

2 Which sentence is NOT needed in the passage?

a. ①   b. ②   c. ③   d. ④

Writing Practice

3 According to the passage, why was Pietri disqualified after the race?

because he _____ from referees to finish the race

4 What is NOT mentioned in the passage?

a. a Greek messenger running to share news of victory

b. Queen Alexandra's request to change the starting line

c. Dorando Pietri's struggles to complete the race

d. an international suggestion to keep the distance at 42.195 kilometers

---

GRAMMAR **Inside** LEVEL 3

관계대명사 what

Link to ...
Chapter 09
Unit 01

• 관계대명사 what은 '~하는 것'의 의미이며 the thing(s) that[which]로 바꿔 쓸 수 있다. 관계대명사 what이 이끄는 절은 문장에서 주어, 목적어, 보어 역할을 한다.

..., the length was increased *to* **what** it is today: 42.195 kilometers. 〈전치사의 목적어〉
                                        오늘날의 것

What scared me most at night was the shadows of the trees. 〈주어〉
        밤에 나를 가장 무섭게 한 것

• 그 자체로 선행사를 포함하므로 선행사가 있는 경우 what 대신 that이나 which 등을 써야 한다.

He gave me the picture [**that** he painted].
                         그가 그린 그림

Check Up 빈칸에 that과 what 중 알맞은 것을 쓰시오.

1 _____ is important in our lives is staying healthy.

2 I found the wallet _____ my girlfriend bought for me.

FEBRUARY

Monday	Tuesday	Wednesday	Thursday	Friday	Saturday
1	2	3	4	5	6
7	8	9	10	11	12	13
14	15	16	17	18	19	20
21	22	23	24	25	26	27
28	29				

Lunar Calendars

✓ Mini Quiz

While you read, check *T* if it is true, or *F* if it is false.

1 The lunar calendar is based on the movements of the Sun.
☐ T ☐ F

2 To balance the two calendars, about three epacts are added to the lunar calendar every three years.
☐ T ☐ F

Around the world, most people use the solar calendar to track each year. This calendar is based on the movements of the Earth around the Sun. However, there is another calendar that follows the movements of the moon. It is called the lunar calendar.

The time it takes the Earth to move around the Sun is known as 5 a solar year. A solar month is one-twelfth of every solar year. Similarly, a lunar year also has twelve months. However, each lunar month is defined as **the time the moon takes** to complete one cycle of its *phases. These phases include a new moon, a half moon, and a full moon. The whole process typically takes about 29.5 days, although the 10 period is not exactly the same every month. A lunar year has twelve of these cycles.

While a solar year lasts around 365 days, a lunar year is slightly shorter at 354 days. The term "epact" was used to describe this 11-day difference. In order to balance the two calendars, an extra month 15 is added to the lunar calendar every three years. On the solar calendar, there is **a "leap day" added** to the month of February every four years. This day falls on the 29th of February every "leap year."

*phase (형태가 변하는 달 또는 행성의) 상(相)

Reading Comprehension

1 What is the passage mainly about?
   a. how fast the Earth travels around the Sun
   b. why ancient people created the lunar calendar
   c. which calendar matches the seasons more closely
   d. how the lunar calendar differs from the solar calendar

2 Which CANNOT be answered based on the passage?
   a. How long does a lunar year last?
   b. Who came up with the term "epact"?
   c. How do we balance the two calendars?
   d. How many days are there in a leap year?

3 Fill in the blanks with Arabic numbers from the passage.

	Days	**Changes to the Calendar**
A Solar Year	(1) _____ days: the period it takes for the Earth to move around the Sun	(2) an extra day every _____ years
A Lunar Year	(3) 354 days: _____ cycles of the moon	(4) an extra month every _____ years

Writing Practice

4 According to the passage, what happens on a leap year?
   A _____ is added and the exact date is _____.

Q   **GRAMMAR Inside** LEVEL 3   ≡

관계대명사의 생략   **Link to ...** 👆

「주격 관계대명사 + be동사」는 생략할 수 있으며, 생략한 후에 남은 현재분사구나 과거분사구가 앞의 선행사를   📁 Chapter 09
수식한다. 또한, 목적격 관계대명사 who(m), which, that도 생략할 수 있다.   📄 Unit 03

The time (**which/that**) it takes the Earth to move around the Sun is known as ... .
〈목적격 관계대명사가 생략됨〉

..., there is a "leap day" (**which[that] is**) added to the month of February every four years.
〈「주격 관계대명사+be동사」가 생략되어 과거분사구 형태가 됨〉

VOCABULARY INSIDE

READING 1	READING 2
☐ **messenger** (n) someone who delivers messages or documents to people (n) message	☐ **cycle** (n) a set of actions or events that repeat in the same order
☐ **initially** (ad) at the beginning, at first (a) initial (syn) primarily	☐ **process** (n) a series of actions or steps taken to produce or achieve something (syn) procedure, course
☐ **permanent** (a) lasting or intending to last forever or for a long time (syn) eternal, everlasting, constant (ant) temporary	☐ **typically** (ad) generally or normally (a) typical
☐ **receive** (v) to be presented with or given something (syn) obtain	☐ **exactly** (ad) in an accurate or precise way (a) exact (syn) correctly, accurately
☐ **international** (a) related to or involving two or more countries (syn) global	☐ **balance** (v) to make separate things equal in amounts, length, strength, or importance (n) balance

Check Up

Fill in the blanks with the words above. Change the form if necessary.

1 I struggle to _____ my work and my social life.

2 _____, I forget to bring an umbrella on rainy days.

3 She played the trumpet _____, but she soon switched to the piano.

4 We were looking for a(n) _____ place to stay.

5 He followed the recipe _____, but the cake didn't taste good.

6 The life _____ of a grasshopper has three stages.

7 The rock band's concert was crowded with _____ fans.

8 You will _____ your tickets online.

UNIT
07 | Sports

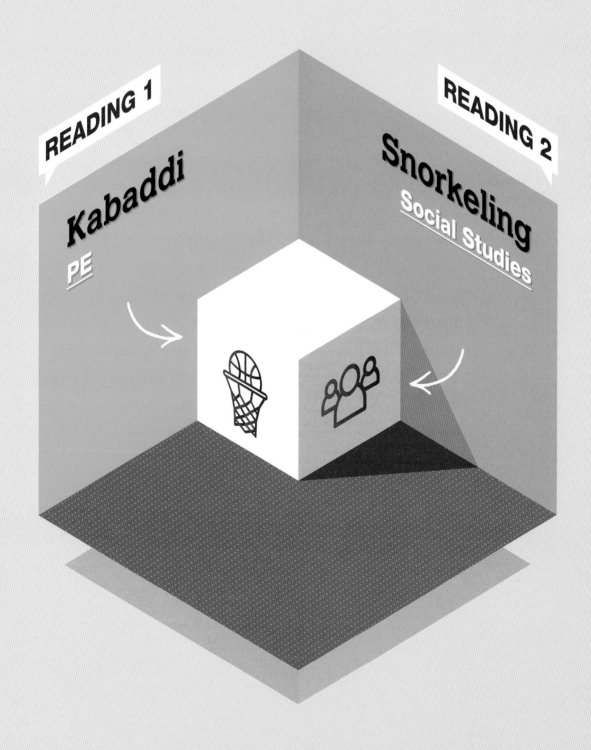

READING 1

Kabaddi
PE

READING 2

Snorkeling
Social Studies

Sports

PE

Kabaddi

⊘ Mini Quiz

Read and underline the answers in the passage.

Paragraph 1

1 Why did people in southern India practice kabaddi?

Paragraph 2

2 How can teams get a point in a kabaddi game?

If you ever watch kabaddi, you'll find it really leaves you breathless! Kabaddi originated in southern India, where it was used to practice village defense and group hunting. Later, the game evolved into an international game testing teamwork and lung power.

In kabaddi, two teams of seven each occupy one half of a small 5
court. They take turns sending an attacker into their opponents' half. The attacker must touch an opposing player and get back to his or her own side. If the attacker succeeds, the tagged opponent is out. The defenders try to catch the attacker to **prevent the player from escaping** their side. If the attacker is taken to the ground or fails to 10
tag an opponent, then he or she is out of the game. Whenever a player leaves the game, the other team gets a point.

But there's a special rule: the attacker cannot take a breath before getting back to his or her team's side! To show the attacker is not inhaling, the player must chant "kabaddi, kabaddi, kabaddi" 15
continuously. If the attacker stops chanting or takes a break, he or she must leave the game.

Kabaddi is now played in other countries such as China and Japan, and has been in the Asian Games since 1990. Do you think you could win gold for your country? 20

Reading Comprehension

1 **What is the best title for the passage?**
　a. The Origin of Kabaddi, an Asian Sport
　b. Kabaddi: A Traditional Indian Ceremony
　c. The Hunting Techniques of Ancient Indians
　d. Kabaddi: An Unusual Game with Unusual Rules

2 **When is the attacker out of the game?**
　a. when the attacker catches an opponent
　b. when the attacker is taken to the ground
　c. when the attacker escapes the defenders
　d. when the attacker gets back to his or her own side

3 **Which CANNOT be answered based on the passage?**
　a. Where did the game originate from?
　b. What do defenders do in the game?
　c. What happens if the attacker stops chanting while attacking?
　d. Which country earned the best score in kabaddi?

Writing Practice

4 **According to the passage, why does the attacker chant "kabaddi, kabaddi, kabaddi?"**

_____

● ● ●　　🔍 **GRAMMAR Inside** LEVEL 3　　　≡

주요 동명사 구문

• be worth v-ing: ~할 가치가 있다
• cannot help v-ing: ~하지 않을 수 없다
• look forward to v-ing: ~하기를 고대하다
• feel like v-ing: ~하고 싶어지다
• be busy v-ing: ~하느라 바쁘다
• be used to v-ing: ~하는 것에 익숙하다
• prevent[keep] + 목적어 + from v-ing: ~가 …하는 것을 막다

Link to ...
📁 Chapter 05
📁 Unit 02

The defenders try to catch the attacker to **prevent the player from escaping** their side.
그 선수가 탈출하는 것을 막다

We're **looking forward to meeting** you soon.
만나기를 고대하고 있다

Sports

Social Studies

Snorkeling

208 words

ⓥ Mini Quiz

While you read, check *T* if it is true, or *F* if it is false.

1 Special suits and an oxygen tank are required for snorkeling.

☐ T ☐ F

2 The first competition of Bob Snorkeling took place in 1976.

☐ T ☐ F

Every summer, people go snorkeling for fun. Snorkeling is a great way to experience the underwater world and discover its amazing wildlife. It is especially popular in tropical areas. It allows people to explore coral reefs and see a wide variety of sea creatures. Compared to scuba diving, snorkeling doesn't need a lot of equipment. Scuba 5 divers wear special suits and use an oxygen tank to go deep under the ocean. But snorkelers usually float on the surface of the ocean, so they only need a snorkeling mask and fins.

Thousands of years ago, snorkeling wasn't just a water sport. In fact, the first snorkelers were farmers in Greece. They used hollow 10 reeds to breathe underwater while collecting sea sponges. Thankfully, modern snorkel equipment has become much more effective.

Every year, there are snorkeling events held around the world. But the most popular event is the World Bob Snorkeling Championship in Wales. **Not only is it** the largest snorkeling event in the world, but it is 15 also the only competitive one. In the event, participants race against each other along a *bog trench. To win, they have to finish two lengths without swimming. The first championship took place in 1976, and it has become a popular global event.

*bog trench 습지에 판 도랑

Reading Comprehension

1 What is the passage mainly about?

 a. the characteristics of popular water sports

 b. how snorkeling has developed as a sport

 c. what makes snorkel equipment modern

 d. competitive events for snorkeling

2 What is NOT mentioned about the history of snorkeling?

 a. where the activity of snorkeling began

 b. what the farmers used for snorkeling

 c. the original reason for snorkeling

 d. who invented the modern snorkel

3 What is NOT true about the World Bob Snorkeling Championship?

 a. It is held once a year.   b. It is held in Wales.

 c. It is a unique event.   d. There are two players in a race.

Writing Practice

4 According to the passage, what should the participants do in the snorkeling race?

 The participants should complete _____.

Q   **GRAMMAR Inside** LEVEL 3   ≡

부사 및 부정어의 도치

• 장소나 방향의 부사(구)가 문장 앞으로 나오는 경우, 주어와 동사의 위치가 뒤바뀌어 「부사(구) + 동사 + 주어」
 의 어순을 갖는다.

 On top of the mountain stands a big flag.
 　　　　부사구　　　　　　　　동사　　　주어

• 부정의 의미를 지닌 부사(hardly, never, rarely, little 등)가 앞에 나올 경우, 동사의 종류에 따라 어순이 달라진다.

 (1) 조동사나 be동사가 있는 문장: 「부정의 부사 + 조동사[be동사] + 주어」

  Not only is it the largest snorkeling event in the world, … .
  　부정어구　be동사 주어

 (2) 일반동사가 있는 문장: 「부정의 부사 + do + 주어 + 동사원형」

  Never did he think of being an athlete.
  　부정어　do의　주어　동사원형
  　　　　과거형

Link to ... 👆
 📁 Chapter 12
  📁 Unit 02

....

Check Up 두 문장의 의미가 같도록 빈칸에 알맞은 말을 쓰시오.

 He could rarely decide what to do next.

 → Rarely _____ _____ _____ what to do next.

🔷 VOCABULARY INSIDE

READING 1	READING 2
☐ **opponent** ⓝ someone you are competing against ⓥ oppose [syn] rival, competitor	☐ **especially** [ad] to a great extent or more than usual [syn] remarkably, notably
☐ **succeed** ⓥ to achieve a desired result ⓝ success ⓐ successful [syn] work out, make it [ant] fail	☐ **tropical** ⓐ related to the hottest places on Earth or countries that are in the tropic regions ⓝ tropic
☐ **catch** ⓥ to take or seize someone or something with your hands [syn] capture, grab [ant] release	☐ **equipment** ⓝ a set of tools or devices needed for a particular purpose ⓥ equip [syn] tools, gear
☐ **escape** ⓥ to run away from a place or situation [syn] get away [ant] capture	☐ **collect** ⓥ to gather things of the same type and keep them for a particular reason ⓝ collection [syn] gather
☐ **inhale** ⓥ to breathe air into your lungs [syn] breathe in [ant] exhale	☐ **length** ⓝ a measurement of something from one end to the other ⓐ long, lengthy [syn] distance

Check Up **Fill in the blanks with the words above. Change the form if necessary.**

1 She likes to _____ postcards while traveling.

2 The news reported that an alligator _____ from the zoo.

3 Some kinds of fruit grow well only in _____ climates.

4 He believed that his plan would _____ .

5 Our _____ are wearing blue uniforms.

6 The movie was good, and I _____ liked the action scenes.

7 _____ a slow, deep breath before diving into water.

8 The essay is no more than 250 words in _____ .

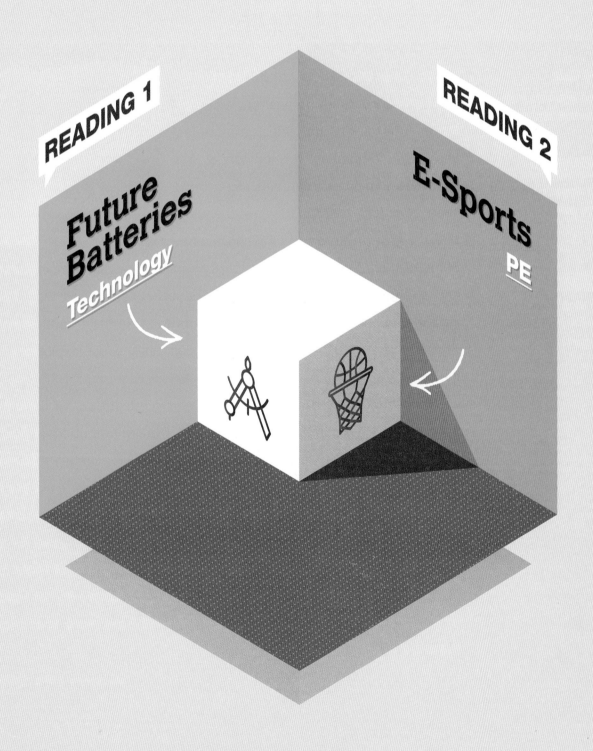

READING 1

Future Batteries
Technology

READING 2

E-Sports
PE

Future

Technology

194 words

Future Batteries

✓ Mini Quiz

Find the answers from the passage and write them.

Paragraph 1

1 What does "one" refer to in the passage?

→ _____

_____

Paragraph 2

2 How long does it take for solid-state batteries to charge?

→ _____

_____

As electric cars and consumer electronics become increasingly popular, more lithium-ion batteries are being used by companies for powering our machines. Lithium-ion batteries use a liquid *electrolyte for managing the flow of energy. There are many benefits to using <u>one</u>. 5

▲ lithium battery packs and wiring connections

Some of them include improved performance in varying temperatures and a long battery life. ① <u>They</u> have negative aspects as well. For instance, the liquid inside of ② <u>them</u> tends to make them quite heavy. 10 Furthermore, the electrolytes in ③ <u>them</u> can easily cause explosions if the battery is damaged.

Solid-state batteries can be a promising substitute for lithium-ion batteries. The main difference is that a lithium-ion battery is fluid, while a solid-state battery contains a firm electrolyte. Certain features 15 of solid-state batteries make ④ <u>them</u> powerful. First of all, solid-state batteries don't have to be recharged frequently. And they can become fully charged in less than 20 minutes. They can also be used for a long time without **being damaged**. Additionally, they are not likely to cause a fire if they are damaged. So, extra parts for safety do not need 20 to be installed. This means solid-state batteries have more space for materials that increase battery life.

*electrolyte 전해질, 전해액

Reading Comprehension

1 **What is the passage mainly about?**

a. how electrolytes affect battery life

b. why solid-state batteries are popular

c. the dangers of lithium-ion and solid-state batteries

d. a comparison of lithium-ion and solid-state batteries

2 **Among ①~④, which refers to a different thing?**

a. ①   b. ②   c. ③   d. ④

3 **Why do solid-state batteries have more space than lithium-ion batteries?**

a. They are more powerful.   b. They are heavier than lithium-ion batteries.

c. They use fewer safety parts.   d. They are made from stronger materials.

Writing Practice

4 **Fill in the blanks with words from the passage.**

	Lithium-Ion Batteries	**Solid-State Batteries**
Material	• a liquid electrolyte	• a (1) _____ electrolyte
Advantages	• improved performance in (2) _____ temperatures • a long battery life	• a powerful battery • a low risk of fire • more (3) _____ inside for other materials
Disadvantages	• heavy • a risk of (4) _____	• none

GRAMMAR Inside LEVEL 3

동명사의 수동태

동명사의 수동태는 주절의 시제를 기준으로 단순형 수동태와 완료형 수동태로 나누어 쓸 수 있다.

• 단순형 수동태(being v-ed): 동명사가 수동의 의미이고, 동명사의 시제가 문장의 시제와 같을 때 쓴다.
I don't like **being told** what to do. = I *don't like* when I'*m told* what to do.

• 완료형 수동태(having been v-ed): 동명사가 수동의 의미이고, 동명사의 시제가 문장의 시제보다 앞설 때 쓴다.
(시간상 전과 후가 명확한 경우 단순형 수동태를 쓰기도 한다.)
I admit to **having been told** the secret before anyone else.
= I *admit* that I *was told* the secret before anyone else.

Link to ...
Chapter 05
Unit 01

Future

PE

207 words

E-Sports

V Mini Quiz

Read and underline the answers in the passage.

Paragraph 1

1 Find the word in the passage that has the given meaning.

> to have something as a part of an activity, event, or situation

Paragraph 2

2 What does "this phenomenon" refer to in the passage?

Until the late 1990s, playing video games was considered to be a casual hobby. In 1997, however, it became an organized competitive sport. This was the year **when** the first major e-sports tournament was held. E-sports is short for "electronic sports," and it typically involves teams of players competing in intense competitions. The only 5 difference between e-sports and other sports is that e-sports takes place in a virtual environment rather than a physical place.

The popularity of e-sports seems to grow every year. A major reason for <u>this phenomenon</u> is because it _____ _____. Gamers don't need to be physically strong or fast, and 10 they are not limited by their age or gender. Another reason is because video games are easier to practice than other sports. All you need is a gaming system and a place **where** you can connect to the internet. Streaming is a third reason **why** e-sports is so accessible. Streaming websites give fans a way to view major tournaments from anywhere in 15 the world.

These days, the e-sports industry is starting to get the recognition it deserves. Its market value is worth more than one billion dollars, and it may be part of the Olympic Games soon. Clearly, e-sports has become a major competitive sport! 20

Reading Comprehension

1 **What is the best title for the passage?**

a. The Flourishing E-Sports Industry

b. E-Sports: A New Way of Exercising

c. The Lives of Successful E-Sports Players

d. A Comparison of E-Sports and Traditional Sports

2 **What is NOT true according to the passage?**

a. The first major competition of e-sports took place in 1997.

b. Fans can watch e-sports tournaments on the internet.

c. The e-sports industry is worth more than one billion dollars.

d. E-sports is an official competition in the Olympic Games.

3 **What is the best choice for the blank?**

a. allows for broad participation

b. provides cheap entertainment

c. has simple rules for gaming

d. helps people keep in shape

Writing Practice

4 **According to the passage, what are necessary for practicing e-sports?**

To practice e-sports, you need _____ and _____

_____.

GRAMMAR Inside LEVEL 3

관계부사

• 관계부사는 「접속사＋부사(구)」의 역할을 하며, 관계부사가 이끄는 절은 형용사처럼 선행사를 수식한다.
선행사가 시간을 나타낼 때는 관계부사 when, 장소는 where, 이유는 why, 방법은 how를 쓴다.

Link to ...
Chapter 09
Unit 02

All you need is a gaming system and a place. + You can connect to the internet at this place.

→ All you need is a gaming system and a *place* **where** you can connect to the internet. 〈장소〉

Streaming is a third reason. + E-sports is so accessible for this reason.

→ Streaming is *a third reason* **why** e-sports is so accessible. 〈이유〉

• 선행사가 place, time, reason일 때 선행사나 관계부사 중 하나가 생략될 수 있다.

I still remember the time. + At that time, there were no electric cars.

→ I still remember (*the time*) **when** there were no electric cars. 〈시간〉

◈ VOCABULARY INSIDE

READING 1	READING 2
☐ **increasingly** (ad) to a greater degree (v) increase [syn] progressively	☐ **take place** to happen [syn] happen, occur
☐ **improved** (a) better than before (n) improvement (v) improve [syn] developed, enhanced	☐ **physical** (a) having a material existence in the world (ad) physically
☐ **negative** (a) harmful or bad [ant] positive	☐ **limit** (v) to keep something within a particular range (n) limitation, limit
☐ **promising** (a) likely to be successful or have good results [syn] encouraging	☐ **industry** (n) a distinct group of companies or enterprises that produce goods or services for profit (a) industrial [syn] business
☐ **contain** (v) to have something inside or include something as a part [syn] include, hold	☐ **billion** (n) the number 1,000,000,000 (1,000 million)

Check Up

Fill in the blanks with the words above. Change the form if necessary.

1 The population of India is over 1.4 _____ .

2 Every winner has been asked to _____ their speech to three minutes.

3 The police didn't have any _____ evidence of the crime.

4 Global warming has had a(n) _____ effect on the environment.

5 Tilda's _____ grades made her friends jealous.

6 The school bazaar _____ every September.

7 My mom has been working in the computer _____ for 20 years.

8 How much water does this bottle _____ ?

READING 1

Whale Poop
Biology

READING 2

The Tragedy of
White Tigers
Social Studies
& Biology

Whale Poop

Biology

194 words

Mini Quiz

While you read, check *T* if it is true, or *F* if it is false.

1 Phytoplankton grow with the help of whale poop.

☐ T ☐ F

2 Whale hunting generates too much CO_2.

☐ T ☐ F

We all know that Earth is facing many ecological threats. However, few people know that one of them is a lack of whale poop. According to marine biologists, whale poop is essential to fighting climate change.

Unlike most marine animals, whales swim up to the surface to poop. Their poop includes important nutrients such as iron. As the 5 poop falls to the sea floor, the iron in the poop helps the growth of tiny microorganisms called *phytoplankton. In other words, the whale poop plays the role of _____ for phytoplankton.

But how does the whale poop affect climate change? **While **photosynthesizing**, phytoplankton absorb huge amounts of carbon 10 dioxide (CO_2) from the air. According to a recent study, whale poop supports enough phytoplankton to take 400,000 tons of CO_2 from the air every year.

This fact has increased concerns about whale hunting. By hunting whales, humans have decreased the amount of iron-rich whale poop 15 in oceans. As a result, we have reduced the amount of phytoplankton available to remove CO_2. This relationship shows how ecosystems work. When one part is endangered, the whole system is threatened. Now the need to protect whales seems clearer than ever!

*phytoplankton 식물성 플랑크톤
**photosynthesize 광합성하다

Reading Comprehension

1 **What is the passage mainly about?**

a. whales' unique bathroom habits

b. how whale poop prevents climate change

c. what caused whales to become endangered

d. the relationship between whales and microorganisms

2 **What is the best choice for the blank?**

a. a food to avoid

b. a toxic chemical

c. a natural fertilizer

d. a cozy place to rest

3 **What is NOT mentioned in the passage?**

a. where whales poop in the sea

b. what nutrient in whale poop helps phytoplankton grow

c. why phytoplankton absorb CO_2 when they photosynthesize

d. how much CO_2 phytoplankton remove from the air every year

Writing Practice

4 **According to the passage, how does whale hunting affect global warming?**

As whale poop decreases, the amount of _____ that can remove

_____ from the air also decreases.

Q GRAMMAR **Inside** LEVEL 3 ≡

분사구문 만드는 법

분사를 이용하여 부사절(접속사＋주어＋동사)을 분사구문으로 바꿔 쓸 수 있다.

Link to ...
Chapter 06
Unit 02

• 부사절의 주어가 주절과 같을 때, 부사절의 접속사와 주어를 생략하고 동사를 분사 형태(v-ing, v-ed)로
바꾼다.

Being very angry at him, I didn't say a word.
　　　그에게 매우 화가 나서

← **Because I** was very angry at him, I didn't say a word.

• 분사구문은 생략된 접속사의 의미에 따라 〈시간, 동시동작, 이유, 조건, 양보〉 등의 의미로 해석한다. 의미를
분명하게 하기 위해 접속사를 생략하지 않고 쓰기도 한다.

While photosynthesizing, phytoplankton absorb huge amounts of carbon dioxide ... . 〈시간〉
　　　광합성을 하는 동안

Check Up 밑줄 친 부분을 분사구문으로 바꿔 쓰시오.

While she walked her dog, she listened to music.

→ While _____ _____ _____, she listened to music.

Animals

Social Studies
& Biology

200 words

The Tragedy of White Tigers

✓ Mini Quiz

Read and underline the answers in the passage.

Paragraph 2

1 Find the word in the passage that has the given meaning.

> ordinary, not unusual; generally free from mental or physical problems

Paragraph 3

2 What do some zookeepers fool the public into thinking?

Q: _____ (A) _____

A: Kenny was rescued in 2000 from a private owner. Due to his short nose, broad face, and ugly teeth, he barely looked like a tiger. His owner said Kenny looked this way because he often hit his face against the wall. But actually, he suffered from genetic problems 5 caused by *inbreeding.

*inbreed 동족 교배[번식]시키다

Q: _____ (B) _____

A: In nature, a white tiger only occurs about once in every 10,000 births. White tigers haven't been seen in the wild since 1951. Strangely, however, there are still many white tigers. This is because 10 tigers are being bred over and over to produce the gene that creates a white coat. Unfortunately, this kind of inbreeding gives them a number of genetic problems. Almost all white tigers have the problems that Kenny had. It also shortens their life spans. Usually, only about one out of every 30 white tigers looks "normal," and the 15 rest are abandoned.

Q: _____ (C) _____

A: Some zookeepers talk **as if white tigers were** endangered. They trick the public into believing that they are helping white tigers. However, they are just using the tigers to make their zoos more 20 popular. I strongly suggest people stay away from zoos with white tigers. They should not use these animals for marketing purposes.

Reading Comprehension

1 **What is the purpose of this interview?**
   a. to discuss the serious problem of inbreeding white tigers
   b. to inform people of why white tigers are rare in nature
   c. to discuss how to protect endangered white tigers
   d. to warn people about illegal animal hunting

2 **According to the passage, what is NOT a feature of inbred white tigers?**
   a. broad faces   b. ugly teeth
   c. short life spans   d. low intelligence

3 **Match the blank to each question.**
   (1) (A) •   • a. What is the cause and effect of inbreeding?
   (2) (B) •   • b. Can you tell me the story of Kenny, the white tiger?
   (3) (C) •   • c. Why are zoos still breeding white tigers?

Writing Practice

4 **According to the passage, what is recommended for people to do to stop the inbreeding of white tigers?**

   They are recommended to _____ that own white tigers.

Q   **GRAMMAR Inside** LEVEL 3   ≡

as if 가정법

• 「as if + 주어 + 동사의 과거형」 형태의 as if 가정법 과거는 '마치 ~인 것처럼'의 의미로, 현재 사실과 반대되는 내용을 가정할 때 쓴다.
  Some zookeepers talk **as if white tigers were** endangered.
  _{백호가 멸종 위기에 처한 것처럼}

• 「as if + 주어 + had v-ed」 형태의 as if 가정법 과거완료는 '마치 ~였던 것처럼'의 의미로, 과거 사실과 반대되는 내용을 가정할 때 쓴다.
  Emily talks **as if she had met** Daniel in person.
  _{그녀가 대니얼을 직접 만났던 것처럼}

Link to ...
  Chapter 10
  Unit 02

Check Up 주어진 문장과 의미가 비슷하도록 as if를 사용하여 빈칸에 알맞은 말을 쓰시오.

   Lily acts like my sister. In fact, she is not my sister.
   → Lily acts _____ .

VOCABULARY INSIDE

READING 1	READING 2
☐ **threat** (n) something that can cause danger or harm (v) threaten [syn] danger, hazard, peril	☐ **rescue** (v) to save something or someone from a dangerous situation [syn] save
☐ **surface** (n) the outer layer of something	☐ **barely** (ad) almost not [syn] hardly, scarcely
☐ **absorb** (v) to take in something [ant] release, emit	☐ **occur** (v) to happen or be found to exist [syn] happen
☐ **increase** (v) to become greater in amount (n) increase [syn] rise [ant] decrease	☐ **rest** (n) the people or things that remain; the others
☐ **endangered** (a) at risk of dying out or being destroyed completely (v) endanger [syn] threatened	☐ **purpose** (n) the reason for doing something or the reason that something exists [syn] aim, objective

Check Up **Fill in the blanks with the words above. Change the form if necessary.**

1 We used a helicopter to _____ her from a sinking boat.

2 We hope to _____ the number of visitors to the website.

3 The accident _____ last night.

4 I used a sponge to _____ the spilled water.

5 The species is _____ because of pollution.

6 The leaves are floating on the _____ of the lake.

7 The first question was easy, but the _____ were difficult.

8 He _____ talks to me anymore. He must be angry at me.

UNIT
10 | Stories

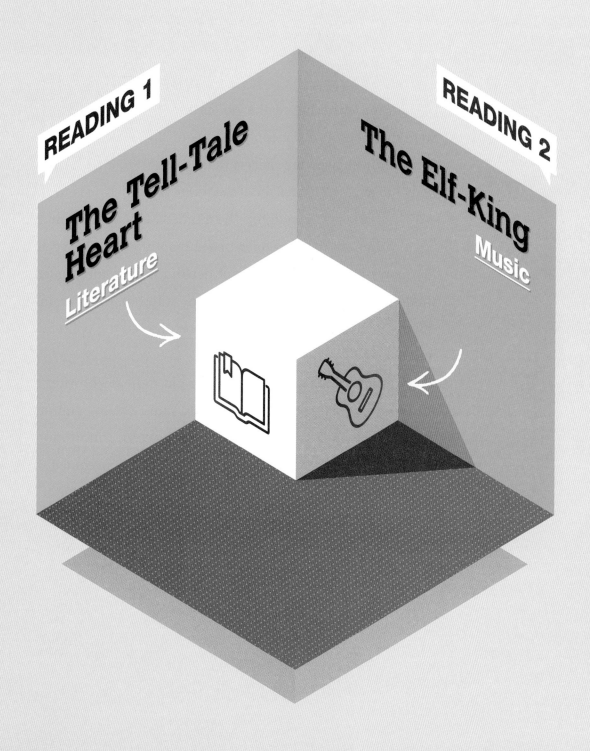

READING 1
The Tell-Tale Heart
Literature

READING 2
The Elf-King
Music

219 words

The Tell-Tale Heart

Written by Edgar Allan Poe

The Tell-Tale Heart is about a murderer **describing** his emotions in great detail. At the beginning of the story, the murderer tries to convince the reader that ① he is not mad. He confesses to **killing** an old man, but he says that it was necessary because of the old man's evil eye.

▲ Edgar Allan Poe
(1809-1849)

5

(A) Soon after, ② he heard the police **knocking** on his door. They were there because someone had heard the scream. The murderer confidently showed the officers the old man's room. With the dead 10 body hidden under the floor of the room, they continued to talk. The police didn't notice anything. The murderer enjoyed **fooling** them.

(B) Soon, however, the murderer heard a sound. It sounded like the old man's heartbeat, and it kept **getting** louder and louder. ③ He thought the police officers could hear it too, but they didn't hear 15 anything at all. Panicked, the murderer showed the police where to find the body.

(C) Every night, he secretly watched the old man sleep. After a week of **doing** this, he couldn't kill the old man. On the eighth night, however, he felt like he would finally succeed. Unfortunately, he 20 made a noise and woke the old man. The man screamed, but the murderer quickly attacked and killed ④ him. Then he hid the body under the boards of the floor.

Mini Quiz

While you read, check *T* if it is true, or *F* if it is false.

1 The story begins with the man admitting his madness.

☐ T ☐ F

2 The story ends with the murderer not being discovered.

☐ T ☐ F

Reading Comprehension

1　**What is the passage mainly about?**
a. the story of a man who committed a crime
b. a criminal's confession of his perfect crime
c. a famous criminal case that was left unsolved
d. how a stalker defends himself against another man

2　**What is the right order of the paragraphs (A)~(C)?**
a. (A) – (C) – (B)　　　　　　　b. (B) – (A) – (C)
c. (C) – (A) – (B)　　　　　　　d. (C) – (B) – (A)

3　**Among ①~④, which refers to a different person?**
a. ①　　　　b. ②　　　　c. ③　　　　d. ④

Writing Practice

4　**According to the passage, why did the man panic and show the body to the police?**
He thought that the police could _____.

GRAMMAR Inside LEVEL 3　　≡

동명사와 현재분사

동명사와 현재분사는 그 형태(v-ing)가 동일하나, 문장 내에서 어떤 역할을 하는지에 따라 쓰임이 명확히 다르다.

Link to ...
Chapter 06
Unit 01

• 현재분사: 명사를 수식하는 형용사나 보어로 사용됨
... is about *a murderer* **describing** his emotions in great detail. 〈명사를 수식하는 형용사 역할〉
Soon after, he heard *the police* **knocking** on his door. 〈목적어를 설명하는 목적격 보어〉

• 동명사: 명사로서 주어, 목적어, 보어로 사용됨
He confesses *to* **killing** an old man, ... 〈전치사의 목적어〉
The murderer *enjoyed* **fooling** them. 〈동사의 목적어〉

Check Up 다음 문장에서 밑줄 친 단어가 동명사인지 현재분사인지 쓰시오.
1 I know the old man <u>running</u> across the street. _____
2 I kept <u>running</u> along the street. _____

The Elf-King

"Elf-King," one of the best-known pieces by Franz Schubert, is based on Goethe's poem of the same title. Because Schubert admired Goethe, he borrowed the poet's legendary poem and changed it into music.

Using the poem's story, Schubert composed the music for a singer and a piano. To clearly distinguish each of the characters, he used a 5 different voice for each of them: a medium voice for the narrator, low tones for the father, high tones for the boy, and smooth, attractive tones for the Elf-King.

In the beginning, the piano imitates a running horse as the father and his son ride through the forest at night. When the father sees 10 his son trembling with fear, he **asks** the boy **why he is afraid.** Then the son **tells** his father **that he is terrified of the Elf-King.** Soon, the piano softens into a gentle melody with the Elf-King's voice. He speaks sweetly to the boy, trying to lure him away. But the boy cries out in fear. Suddenly, the pianist plays intense chords as the Elf-King tries to grab 15 the boy, who screams out in pain. The pianist plays fast while the horse runs out of the forest. Finally, the music becomes sorrowful as the father realizes his son is dead.

V Mini Quiz

Find the answers from the passage and write them.

Paragraph 2

1 Which character's voice uses high tones?

→ _____

Paragraph 3

2 How does the story of the Elf-King end?

→ _____
_____
_____

Reading Comprehension

1   What is the best title for the passage?
   a. "Elf-King," Originating from a Local Legend
   b. Goethe and Schubert: Musical Companions
   c. A Literary Analysis of the Poem "Elf-King"
   d. Schubert's Version of Goethe's Poem

2   What is true about "Elf-King"?
   a. It is based on Goethe's experience.
   b. Schubert used a medium voice for the Elf-King.
   c. The sound of a running horse is made by a singer.
   d. The piano changes its melody according to the story.

3   How does the mood of the 3rd paragraph change?
   a. noisy → impressive   b. frightening → tragic
   c. thrilling → peaceful   d. humorous → miserable

Writing Practice
4   According to the passage, why did Schubert use a different voice for each character?

_____

GRAMMAR Inside LEVEL 3

간접화법

간접화법은 다른 사람이 말한 내용을 인용부호 없이 전달하는 사람 입장에 맞게 바꿔서 전달할 때 쓴다.

Then the son **tells** his father **that** *he is* terrified of the Elf-King. 〈평서문〉
← Then the son **tells** his father, "*I'm* terrified of the Elf-King."

..., he **asks** the boy **why** *he is* afraid. 〈의문사가 있는 의문문〉
← ..., he **asks** the boy, "Why *are you* afraid?"

John **asked** me **whether**[if] *I had registered* for the swimming class. 〈의문사가 없는 의문문〉
← John **asked** me, "*Did you register* for the swimming class?"

Link to ...
Chapter 11
Unit 03

Check Up   ( ) 안에서 알맞은 말을 고르시오.
   I asked Tony (why he didn't call me / why didn't he call me) yesterday.

◆ VOCABULARY INSIDE

READING 1	READING 2
☐ **murderer** ⓝ	☐ **poem** ⓝ
someone who intentionally kills a person	a piece of writing in verse
ⓥ murder ⓝ murder [syn] killer	ⓐ poetic ⓝ poetry
☐ **describe** ⓥ	☐ **admire** ⓥ
to say or write what someone or something is like	to respect someone very much
ⓝ description [syn] report	ⓝ admiration [syn] respect
☐ **necessary** ⓐ	☐ **compose** ⓥ
so important that you must do it or have it; absolutely needed	to write music
ⓝ necessity [ant] unnecessary	ⓝ composition, composer
☐ **evil** ⓐ	☐ **imitate** ⓥ
morally bad, cruel, or very unpleasant	to behave in a similar way to someone or something else
ⓝ evil [syn] bad, wicked	ⓝ imitation [syn] copy
☐ **notice** ⓥ	☐ **scream** ⓥ
to see or become conscious of something or someone	to suddenly make a loud noise because of pain or surprise
ⓝ notice ⓐ noticeable	ⓝ scream [syn] yell

Check Up

Fill in the blanks with the words above. Change the form if necessary.

1 The police never found the _____.

2 Could you _____ who stole your bag?

3 He lacks the _____ information to complete the task.

4 Jessica waved at me, but I didn't _____ her.

5 The hunter often _____ the sound of a bird.

6 I just heard someone _____ on the street.

7 Mr. Johnson is _____ for his excellent teaching.

8 The _____ villain is responsible for the deaths of millions of people.

UNIT
11 | Psychology

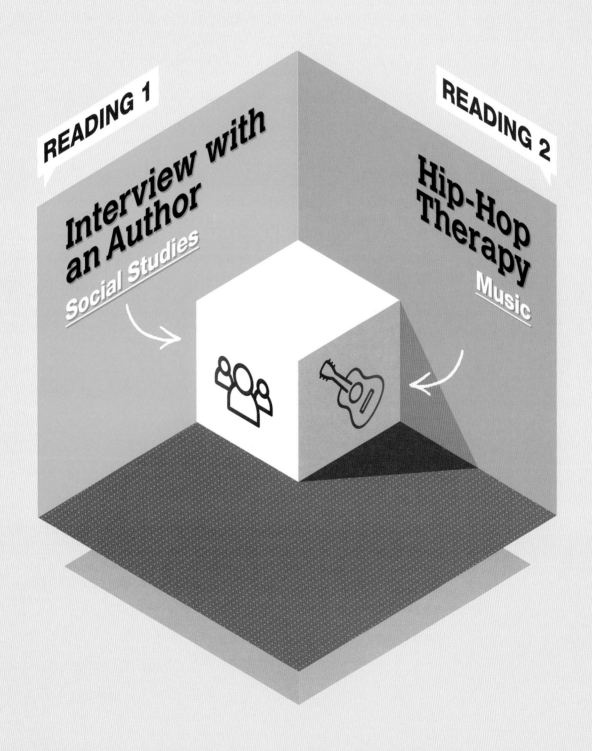

READING 1

Interview with an Author
Social Studies

READING 2

Hip-Hop Therapy
Music

Interview with an Author

Interviewer: Today, we are joined by Dr. Brown, who is the author of the best-selling book, *How Emotions Have Changed*. Dr. Brown, according to your book, the way we view emotions has changed over time. Can you tell us more, please?

Dr. Brown: Sure. Let's talk about homesickness, for example. It was 5 considered a serious illness and called "nostalgia" during the late 1700s. Sufferers became really exhausted and depressed when they longed to go home. They would also have bad sores and get fevers. Eventually, they stopped eating, **which** would lead to their deaths. But nowadays, we don't consider nostalgia deadly! 10

Interviewer: _____

Dr. Brown: Well, improvements in transportation, such as cars and planes, have made travel more convenient. Phones and the internet have also helped connect people living far away. But more than that, our culture and values have changed greatly. Rather 15 than staying in our comfortable homes, we now want to explore unknown things, **which** makes homesickness less serious.

Interviewer: What's another emotion that we think of differently now?

Dr. Brown: From the 1100s to the 1600s, looking at something 20 in wonder was a natural part of human experience. People thought our world was filled with magical animals and objects. For example, alligator teeth were considered treasure because people thought they came from dragons. And *bezoar stones were collected for medicine. Things changed in the 18th century, **when** 25 people began to consider science more important than magic. So the old days of wonder were left behind.

*bezoar (위 또는 장에 생기는) 결석

ⓥ Mini Quiz

Read and underline the answers in the passage.

Paragraph 1

1 What example does Dr. Brown use to explain how we view emotions differently now?

Paragraph 3

2 What do the examples of alligator teeth and bezoar stones imply? (Find two sentences.)

Reading Comprehension

1 What is the passage mainly about?

   a. an author's experiment on human emotions

   b. why people are less emotional than in the past

   c. how technology has led to new human emotions

   d. how human emotions have been viewed over time

2 What is the best question for the blank?

   a. What caused homesickness in the 1700s?

   b. What effects does homesickness have on people today?

   c. What has made people view homesickness so differently?

   d. What is the difference between homesickness and nostalgia?

3 What is mentioned in the passage?

   a. how many people died of homesickness

   b. how people cured homesickness during the 1700s

   c. where the word "wonder" came from

   d. why people collected bezoar stones

> **Writing Practice**

4 Fill in the blank with words from the passage.

   When 18th-century people began to _____,
   the feeling of wonder changed.

● ● ●   🔍 **GRAMMAR Inside** LEVEL 3   ☰

관계사의 계속적 용법

관계사의 계속적 용법은 선행사에 부가적인 설명을 덧붙일 때 사용하며, 관계사 앞에 콤마(,)를 붙인다.

• 관계대명사의 계속적 용법은 who와 which만 가능하며, 「접속사 + 대명사」로 바꿔 쓸 수 있다.
  계속적 용법의 관계대명사 which는 아래와 같이 앞 문장 전체를 선행사로 취할 수 있다.
  Eventually, they stopped eating, **which** would lead to their deaths. 〈관계대명사〉
  (= and it)

• 관계부사의 계속적 용법은 when과 where만 가능하며, 「접속사 + 부사(구)」로 바꿔 쓸 수 있다.
  I went to the swimming pool, **where** I saw someone diving. 〈관계부사〉
  (= and there)

Link to ...

📁 Chapter 09
📁 Unit 03

Hip-Hop Therapy

Therapists say that expressing emotions is the first step to dealing with them and healing. However, some teenagers struggle to talk about their feelings. Fourteen-year-old Ellis was one of them. **Whenever** he got angry, he would get into fights. But now he has found a new way to deal with his anger: he raps about it. In an interview, Ellis said, "Now 5 I make songs about my feelings instead of punching people. I write verses, and it cools me down."

Ellis was helped by a program that uses hip-hop. The program is used to reach teenagers who don't respond to traditional counseling. Hip-hop therapy is nothing new. _____(A)_____, it is becoming more 10 common with the increasing popularity of hip-hop music. It is now helping many troubled teenagers express their feelings and struggles. Hip-hop therapy programs offer students the chance to write and record songs and put them online. Through this process, they are encouraged to speak out about their personal troubles, such as fighting 15 with parents, losing a best friend, or being stressed about grades.

_____(B)_____ the therapy's direct benefits, teens also receive many learning opportunities. They often use dictionaries to improve their songwriting vocabulary. They also learn how to make music videos and use real recording and editing equipment. Clearly, this creative program 20 helps today's teens in many ways.

Mini Quiz

While you read, check *T* if it is true, or *F* if it is false.

1 Hip-hop therapy is becoming common because of the rising popularity of hip-hop music.

☐ T ☐ F

2 Hip-hop therapists teach teens how to overcome personal troubles.

☐ T ☐ F

Reading Comprehension

1   What is the best title for the passage?

a. How Hip-Hop Can Help Troubled Teenagers

b. Why Teens Refuse Traditional Counseling

c. Hip-Hop Music: More Popular Than Ever

d. Rap Music's Negative Impact on Teens

2   What is the best pair for blanks (A) and (B)?

(A)	(B)		(A)	(B)
a. However	– Unlike		b. Moreover	– Despite
c. However	– In addition to		d. Furthermore	– Thanks to

3   Which CANNOT be answered based on the passage?

a. How does Ellis deal with his negative emotions now?

b. How do teens benefit from traditional counseling?

c. How can hip-hop therapy help troubled children?

d. What kind of learning chances can hip-hop therapy give to teens?

Writing Practice

4   Fill in the blank with words from the passage.

Teens use dictionaries to _____. They also learn

how to make music videos and use specialized equipment.

🔍   **GRAMMAR Inside** LEVEL 3   ☰

복합관계부사

복합관계부사는 「관계부사＋-ever」의 형태로, whenever, wherever, however 등이 있다. 시간, 장소의 부사절이나 양보의 부사절을 이끈다. '~할 때마다, ~ 하는 곳은 어디든지' 또는, '언제[어디서/아무리] ~하더라도'로 해석한다.

Whenever he got angry, he would get into fights. (= **Any time** he got angry)
  그는 화가 날 때마다

Wherever you go, I'll be with you. (= **No matter where** you go)
  네가 어디를 가더라도

My mom always has the windows open, **however** cold it is outside.
                                       아무리 밖이 추워도

(= **no matter how** cold it is outside)

Link to ...
    Chapter 09
     Unit 04

VOCABULARY INSIDE

READING 1	READING 2
☐ **author** Ⓝ a person who writes books, articles, essays, etc. [syn] writer	☐ **express** Ⓥ to show your feelings or thoughts by speaking or writing about them Ⓝ expression Ⓐ expressive
☐ **emotion** Ⓝ a feeling such as love or hate Ⓐ emotional [syn] feeling	☐ **heal** Ⓥ to cure a physical or mental problem [syn] cure, recover [ant] injure
☐ **deadly** Ⓐ causing or likely to cause death ⒶⒹ deadly Ⓐ dead	☐ **common** Ⓐ happening often; existing in large numbers or in many places Ⓝ common ⒶⒹ commonly [syn] frequent [ant] uncommon
☐ **transportation** Ⓝ a system of moving something from one place to another Ⓥ transport	☐ **offer** Ⓥ to ask someone if they want something or would like you to do something [syn] provide
☐ **explore** Ⓥ to travel around to learn about or search for something Ⓝ explorer	☐ **opportunity** Ⓝ a chance to do something [syn] chance

Check Up   **Fill in the blanks with the words above. Change the form if necessary.**

1 The city has a very good _____ system.

2 She _____ me help with my homework last night.

3 Luckily, she had a(n) _____ to visit Iceland.

4 Your broken leg needs some time to _____.

5 The man showed no _____ when he heard the sad news.

6 Monument Valley is an amazing place to _____.

7 Smoking while pregnant is _____ to the baby.

8 He sent us a letter in which he _____ his sympathy for our loss.

UNIT
12 | Business

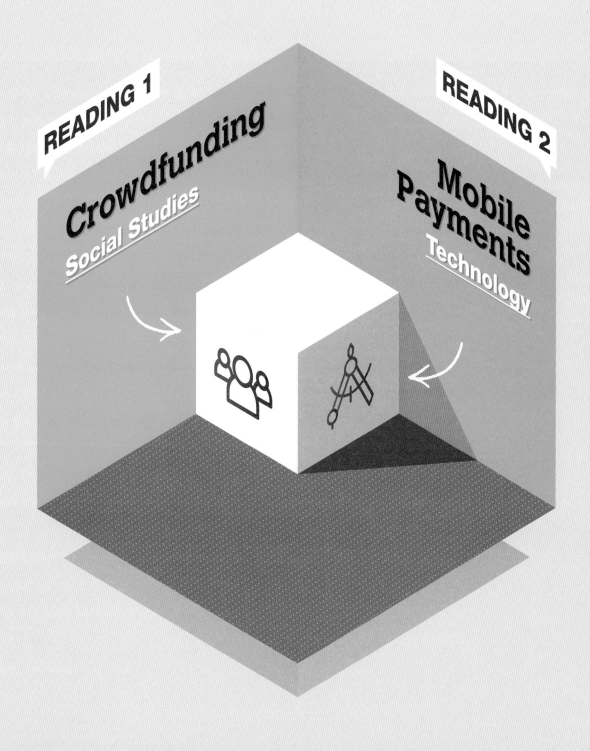

READING 1

Crowdfunding
Social Studies

READING 2

Mobile Payments
Technology

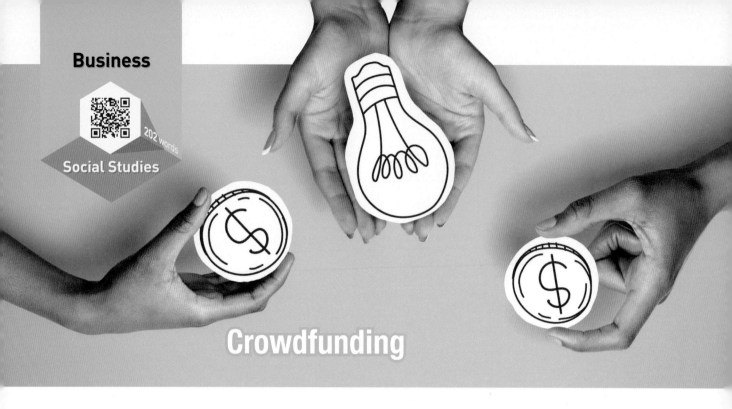

Crowdfunding

In the past, many business ideas and projects were usually funded by banks. This all changed with the introduction of crowdfunding. Crowdfunding is a way to raise money online. It allows businesses to gather small investments from ordinary people. Thanks to the internet, companies can instantly share information about projects with investors. This makes it easier to reach their funding goals. 5

Crowdfunding is typically done in three main ways. Donation-based crowdfunding involves donating money to a charity for a special *cause. When it comes to reward-based crowdfunding, investors contribute toward the total cost of a project. In return, they are 10 promised a product or service that **will be developed** with money from the campaign. Through equity crowdfunding, companies sell stocks to raise capital. Investors who buy the stocks become partial owners of the company and receive financial rewards.

Some of the biggest crowdfunding campaigns have been for 15 technologies such as smartwatches and electric vehicles. However, one recent crowdfunding success story was in publishing. (①) Brandon Sanderson started an online campaign to publish his latest novels. (②) His goal was to raise one million dollars in 30 days. (③) The campaign raised over 15 million dollars in just 24 hours. (④) 20 It was a new crowdfunding record.

*cause 대의, 명분

Reading Comprehension

1 What is the best title for the passage?

   a. How Social Networks Created Crowdfunding

   b. Crowdfunding: A New Way to Raise Funds

   c. The Three Most Common Types of Crowdfunding

   d. Technologies Made Possible by Online Crowdfunding

2 Where would the following sentence best fit?

Incredibly, he achieved this in about 35 minutes.

   a. ①   **b.** ②   **c.** ③   **d.** ④

3 Match each type of crowdfunding with its feature.

   (1) donation-based crowdfunding •   • **a.** works by selling company stocks to investors

   (2) reward-based crowdfunding •   • **b.** involves donating money to a charity

   (3) equity crowdfunding •   • **c.** promises a product or service that will be developed

Writing Practice

4 According to the passage, how does the internet help companies with crowdfunding?

The internet helps companies _____ with their

investors and makes it easier for them to _____.

GRAMMAR Inside LEVEL 3

수동태의 여러 형태

수동태는 「be v-ed」 형태로, 행위의 영향을 받는 대상에 초점을 둘 때 사용한다. 시제 혹은 함께 쓰는 조동사에 따라 형태가 달라진다.

Link to ...

📁 Chapter 03

📁 Unit 01

The printer **is being used** by someone. 〈진행형: be being v-ed〉
       사용되고 있다

The festival **has been canceled** because of the bad weather. 〈완료형: have been v-ed〉
      취소되었다

..., they are promised a product or service that **will be developed** with money ... . 〈미래형: will be v-ed〉
          개발될 것이다

More studies **should be done** to find a cure for this disease. 〈조동사가 있는 문장의 수동태: 조동사＋be v-ed〉
      되어야 한다

Check Up 우리말과 일치하도록 ( ) 안의 말을 이용하여 문장을 완성하시오.

   그때 그 트럭은 수리되는 중이었다. (repair)

   → The truck _____ _____ _____ at that time.

Mobile Payments

Q I saw a new commercial featuring a mobile wallet app for smartphones. It sounded amazing! It lets users buy stuff just by sliding their phone on a payment device. But when I considered getting the app, my friend told me that I shouldn't get it because of its security problems. Now I'm worried that my 5 financial information could be stolen while using the app. Is it really safe?

⊙ Mini Quiz

Read and underline the answers in the passage.

Paragraph 1

1 What security problem is the speaker worried about?

Paragraph 2

2 What kind of random number does a token contain?

A Yes, it is. You don't have to worry about security problems. Most mobile wallets use tokenization technology, and **it is** this technology **that** keeps your information 10 secure. To buy something with your app, you should save your financial information on the app. However, whenever you make a purchase, the app replaces your information with a random number, or digital *token. This token contains none of your real financial data. _____, it contains a one-time-use 15 security code. This is the key allowing the retailer to access your financial data.

Actually, this technology is more effective than the traditional payment system in preventing credit card crimes. In the past, hackers could steal financial data such as credit card numbers 20 from retailers. However, with tokenization, they will only find unusable digital tokens inside a retailer's system. Thanks to this technology, your real data stays safe inside the bank, so you can shop with your mobile device with confidence.

*token 암호

Reading Comprehension

1 **What is the passage mainly about?**
  a. protecting your financial information from hackers
  b. the weak security of mobile payment systems
  c. digital money replacing paper money
  d. the safety of mobile wallet apps

2 **What is NOT true about mobile wallets?**
  a. Customers don't have to save their information on the app.
  b. Tokenization replaces financial data with a digital token.
  c. Retailers can access your financial data through a digital token.
  d. Tokenization can prevent credit card crimes.

3 **What is the best choice for the blank?**
  a. Similarly   b. Instead   c. In addition   d. For example

Writing Practice

4 **According to the passage, what is the problem with the traditional payment system?**
  Hackers could _____ such as credit card numbers from _____.

Q GRAMMAR **Inside** LEVEL 3 ≡

「It is ~ that ...」을 이용한 강조 구문
강조하고자 하는 부분을 It is와 that 사이에 놓으며, '…한 것은 바로 ~이다'라고 해석한다.

... **it is** *this technology* **that** keeps your information secure. 〈주어 강조〉
　　　　　당신의 정보를 안전하게 보호해주는 것이 바로 이 기술이다.
It was *Jake* **that** I met on the subway. 〈목적어 강조〉
　　　내가 지하철에서 만난 사람은 바로 제이크였다.
It was *yesterday* **that** we had a big fight. 〈부사 강조〉
　　　우리가 크게 싸운 날은 바로 어제였다.

Link to ...
　Chapter 12
　Unit 01

Check Up 우리말과 일치하도록 ( ) 안에 주어진 단어를 바르게 배열하시오.
  1 폴이 나에게 전화한 것은 바로 어젯밤이었다. (that, was, it, last night)
    → _____ Paul called me.
  2 나에게 쿠키 굽는 법을 알려준 것은 바로 나의 언니였다. (my sister, was, that, it)
    → _____ taught me how to bake cookies.

◆ VOCABULARY INSIDE

READING 1	READING 2
☐ **raise** Ⓥ to collect something, especially money, for a certain purpose [syn] collect, gather	☐ **commercial** Ⓝ a television or radio advertisement [syn] advertisement
☐ **investment** Ⓝ the act of giving money to something that is expected to be profitable Ⓥ invest [syn] funding	☐ **security** Ⓝ the state of being safe from attack or damage ⓐ secure [syn] safety, protection [ant] danger, harm
☐ **reward** Ⓝ money or benefits that you receive as a result of what you have done Ⓥ reward [syn] return, compensation	☐ **steal** Ⓥ to take others' belongings secretly without permission
☐ **contribute** Ⓥ to participate in something and help it to become successful Ⓝ contribution [syn] play a part	☐ **random** ⓐ happening, done, or chosen by chance Ⓝ random ⓐⒹ randomly [ant] orderly, organized
☐ **achieve** Ⓥ to be successful in realizing a goal Ⓝ achievement [syn] accomplish, fulfill	☐ **prevent** Ⓥ to stop something from happening, or stop someone from doing something Ⓝ prevention

Check Up   Fill in the blanks with the words above. Change the form if necessary.

1 The new TV _____ for the product was very impressive.

2 The winning trophy was the _____ for her effort.

3 To _____ injuries, you should stretch before exercising.

4 It is important to set a goal that you can _____ .

5 The volunteers tasted the sodas in a(n) _____ order and then rated each of them.

6 She _____ to the success of the project and got promoted.

7 This city is dangerous, so _____ has to be improved.

8 We will hold a campaign to _____ money for orphans.

UNIT 13 | People

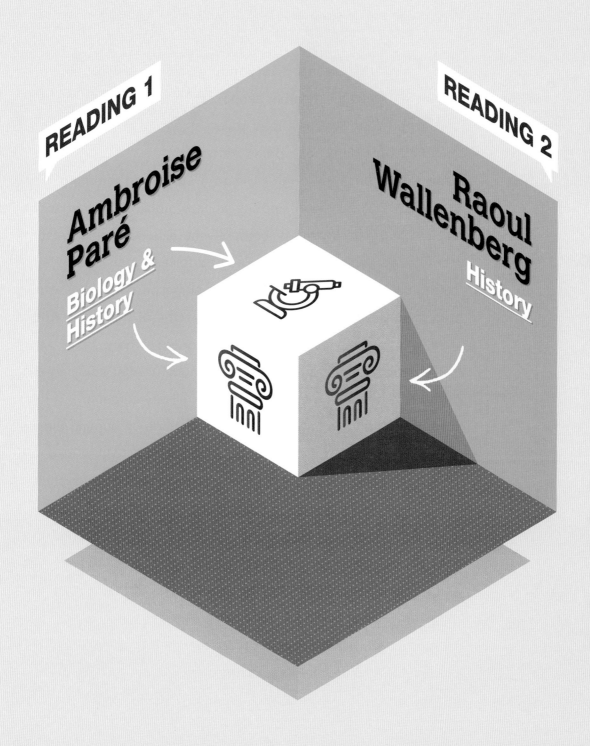

READING 1

Ambroise Paré

Biology & History

READING 2

Raoul Wallenberg

History

People

Biology & History

Ambroise Paré

In medieval Europe, **everyone** was able to recognize barber shops by the red- and white-striped pole they had outside. These poles are still used today, but they originally had a surprising meaning. The red 5 stripes symbolized blood, and the white symbolized bandages. This is because, in medieval times, barbers were also surgeons. In fact, they were called barber-surgeons. They performed many tasks, such as pulling out rotten teeth and performing surgery. Some barber-surgeons were also important to medical history. One of them was Ambroise 10 Paré, who took the first steps towards modern surgery.

Ambroise Paré was born in France in 1510. After studying under a barber-surgeon, he spent 30 years as a military surgeon. (①) At that time, military surgeons treated gunshot wounds by burning the wound with boiling oil. (②) Therefore, he treated wounds with a mild mixture 15 of egg yolk and rose oil. (③) His treatment was not only better for reducing the patient's suffering but was also less damaging. (④)

Paré carefully wrote down all his findings and published them in a series of books. Unlike other medical texts, which were written in Latin, Paré's were written in French. This allowed many more barber- 20 surgeons to read about his techniques. What's more, Paré's book was only based on his surgical experience, which laid the foundation for modern medical treatments in Europe.

Reading Comprehension

1 **What is the passage mainly about?**

a. how to treat gunshot wounds

b. a surgeon who cut people's hair

c. why barber shop poles are red and white

d. a barber-surgeon with an innovative treatment

2 **Where would the following sentence best fit?**

> Paré, however, observed that this dangerous approach caused patients great pain.

a. ①   b. ②   c. ③   d. ④

3 **What is NOT mentioned about Ambroise Paré?**

a. when he was born

b. where he served as a military surgeon

c. what he used to cure gunshot wounds

d. what the advantages of his treatments were

4 **According to the passage, what were the effects of Paré's books?**

His books were written in French, so many barber-surgeons could _____.

Also, his books laid the foundation for _____ in Europe.

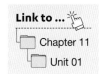

GRAMMAR Inside LEVEL 3

단수 취급하는 명사들

다음과 같은 표현이 주어 자리에 올 때 단수 취급하여 단수 동사를 쓴다.

- each, every와 같이 쓰인 명사 혹은 -thing, -one, -body로 끝나는 단어일 때

    …, **everyone** *was* able to recognize barber shops … .

    Something *is* wrong with my car. It makes a noise whenever I brake.

- (복수형의) 학과명, 국가명이 주어로 쓰일 때

    Mathematics *is* a subject that many students hate.

    The Philippines *consists* of about 7,100 islands.

- 〈시간, 거리, 금액, 무게〉를 나타내는 말이 주어로 쓰일 때

    Five kilometers *is* not a short distance to walk.

    Fifty dollars *is* a lot of money for students.

Link to …
Chapter 11
Unit 01

Raoul Wallenberg

During World War II, many people risked their lives to save Jewish people. However, perhaps **no other person** was **as brave as** Raoul Wallenberg. In 1944, the Nazis tried to transport around 700,000 Jewish people living in Hungary to German *concentration camps. In an attempt to help the Jewish people, Wallenberg was hired as a 5 Swedish diplomat and sent to Hungary. Despite having no experience in diplomacy, Wallenberg led the most successful rescue missions of the **Holocaust.

When Wallenberg arrived in Budapest, Hungary, he immediately opened a Swedish embassy near a Jewish ***ghetto and hired 400 10 Jewish people. Wallenberg and his team built safe houses, hospitals, and schools for thousands of Jewish people. Then Wallenberg made people raise the Swedish flag on the buildings. This meant that they were Swedish territories and the Nazis could not take any of the Jewish people inside. 15

In addition, Wallenberg personally rescued Jewish people from a train. Just as the train was about to take the Jewish people from Budapest to German concentration camps, Wallenberg appeared. He reached into the windows to hand out Swedish passports to every person he could reach. Then he argued that the people with the 20 passports had to be let off the train because they were legally Swedish. When the war finally ended in 1945, more than 100,000 Jewish people remained alive in Budapest, thanks to Wallenberg and his team.

*concentration camp 강제 수용소
**Holocaust 홀로코스트 (나치의 유대인 대학살)
***ghetto 유대인의 강제 거주 지역

Reading Comprehension

1 What is the best title for the passage?

a. A Hungarian Who Saved Jewish People from the Nazis

b. A Hero Who Rescued People in Concentration Camps

c. Raoul Wallenberg's Efforts during World War II

d. Raoul Wallenberg: the First Swedish Diplomat

2 What is NOT true about Wallenberg?

a. He was hired as a diplomat to help Jewish people.

b. He had a lot of diplomatic experience before going to Hungary.

c. He opened a Swedish embassy in Budapest.

d. He built schools and hospitals for Jewish people.

3 How did Wallenberg rescue Jewish people at the station?

a. by offering them jobs

b. by giving them Swedish passports

c. by letting them out through a window

d. by arguing that they should be treated equally

> **Writing Practice**

4 According to the passage, what did "the Swedish flag" represent?

It represented that the buildings were _____, so the Nazis

_____ inside.

GRAMMAR Inside LEVEL 3

원급과 비교급을 이용한 최상급 표현

최상급을 사용하지 않아도 원급과 비교급을 이용해 그에 준하는 의미를 나타낼 수 있다.

... Raoul Wallenberg was **the bravest** person. 〈the + 최상급〉

→ ... Raoul Wallenberg was **braver than any other person**.

〈비교급 + than any other + 단수 명사〉

→ ... **no other person** was **as brave as** Raoul Wallenberg. 〈부정 주어 ... as + 원급 + as〉

→ ... **no other person** was **braver than** Raoul Wallenberg. 〈부정 주어 ... 비교급 + than〉

Link to ...
Chapter 07
Unit 02

Check Up 두 문장의 의미가 비슷하도록 빈칸에 알맞은 말을 쓰시오.

She is the tallest girl in our class.

→ She is _____ _____ _____ _____ _____ in our class.

◆ VOCABULARY INSIDE

READING 1	READING 2
☐ **perform** ⓥ to do an action or complete something difficult ⓝ performance [syn] carry out	☐ **transport** ⓥ to move someone or something from one place to another ⓝ transportation [syn] move, carry
☐ **task** ⓝ an activity or piece of work that you need to complete [syn] job, duty	☐ **diplomat** ⓝ an official who represents his or her country in another country ⓐ diplomatic
☐ **surgery** ⓝ a medical treatment that involves cutting open a patient ⓐ surgical	☐ **immediately** [ad] now or without delay ⓐ immediate [syn] at once, now
☐ **treat** ⓥ to use medical methods to cure an illness ⓝ treatment	☐ **territory** ⓝ an area of land that belongs to a country [syn] area, land
☐ **foundation** ⓝ a fact, idea, or principle that something is based upon ⓥ found	☐ **appear** ⓥ to come into sight or start to be seen ⓝ appearance [syn] emerge, come out [ant] disappear

Check Up **Fill in the blanks with the words above. Change the form if necessary.**

1 He needed a truck to _____ the boxes.

2 Dokdo is Korean _____.

3 Galileo provided the _____ for modern physics.

4 Sam needed _____ on his shoulder.

5 She was _____ for cancer last year.

6 Scientists are _____ an experiment to test a new drug.

7 Subtitles didn't _____ on the screen.

8 Her career as a _____ helped her win the presidential election.

READING 1

Space Junk

Science

READING 2

A Beautiful View from HDEV

Technology

Space

Science

206 words

Space Junk

ⓥ Mini Quiz

Read and underline the answers in the passage.

Paragraph 2

1 What does "huge problems" refer to in the passage?
(Find two sentences.)

Paragraph 3

2 Find the word in the passage that has the given meaning.

> to take something away from a place

Humans **have launched** thousands of satellites and rockets into space. In the process, we **have** also **been creating** tons of junk in space. Space junk is called space *debris. Some is enormous, while other debris is as tiny as a potato chip.

About 23 thousand pieces of debris orbit around the Earth. Most of 5 them are larger than a softball and travel at up to 18 thousand meters per hour. Due to their _____, even a tiny piece of space junk can create huge problems. When a satellite crashes into a small piece of debris, it can break apart into thousands of new pieces. The resulting space debris can damage other satellites and spacecrafts. 10

In response to this problem, the United Nations **has been asking** companies to remove their satellites from orbit. If satellites complete their mission, they should be taken out of space within 25 years. To make this happen, several solutions **have been suggested**. For example, dead satellites could be pulled out of their orbit with magnets 15 or a huge net. Once they are pulled back into the Earth's atmosphere, they would burn up. Unfortunately, this method will only work for bigger satellites. More research is needed to find a solution in the long term.

*debris 잔해, 쓰레기

Reading Comprehension

1 **What is the purpose of this passage?**

   a. to describe what satellites do in space

   b. to explain the dangers of space pollution

   c. to emphasize the problem with space science

   d. to discuss the importance of space exploration

2 **What is the best choice for the blank?**

   a. speed   **b.** weight   **c.** size   **d.** location

3 **Which CANNOT be answered based on the passage?**

   a. How small can space junk be?

   b. Why is space debris dangerous?

   c. How fast do satellites orbit around the Earth?

   d. What methods are being discussed for removing space debris?

Writing Practice

4 **According to the passage, what would be the benefit of pulling satellites out of orbit and closer to the Earth?**

   The satellites would _____ when they entered _____ again.

GRAMMAR Inside LEVEL 3

현재완료와 현재완료 진행형

- **현재완료(have v-ed):** 과거의 한 시점에서 일어난 일이 현재에 영향을 미칠 때 쓰며, 〈완료, 경험, 계속, 결과〉 등의 의미를 나타낸다.

  Humans **have launched** thousands of satellites … . 〈완료〉

  I **have forgotten** the password. (So I can't unlock the door now.) 〈결과〉

- **현재완료 진행형(have been v-ing):** 과거에서 현재까지 계속 진행되고 있는 동작이나 상태(~해 오고 있다)를 나타낸다.

  In the process, we **have** also **been creating** tons of junk in space.

  (← We also started creating junk in space in the past. We are still creating it.)

  Danny **has been working** at the factory for 30 years.

  (← Danny started working at the factory 30 years ago. He still works there now.)

Link to …
> Chapter 01
>> Unit 01

A Beautiful View from HDEV

ⓥ Mini Quiz

While you read, check *T* if it is true, or *F* if it is false.

1 The cameras record videos of the Earth from their orbit around the ISS.

☐ T ☐ F

2 The cameras of the ISS are designed to study the climate of the Earth.

☐ T ☐ F

You **don't have to watch** a movie **if** you **want to view** the Earth from space. You can see this spectacular sight live on your smartphone! A NASA project called High Definition Earth Viewing (HDEV) has been running since April 2014. It broadcasts live images over the internet from four cameras in orbit around the Earth. 5

The project is led by the engineers at the Johnson Space Center in the US. The cameras are installed on the outside of the International Space Station (ISS), and each camera is set up to film the Earth from a different position. (①) They record videos from different angles while moving with the ISS in its orbit. (②) The recording process is 10 automatic and needs only the ISS's power to run. (③) Therefore, anyone can enjoy the images online at any time. (④)

So why does NASA show us these images of the Earth? Actually, the purpose of the HDEV project is to test the quality of the cameras and observe how they perform in space. The cameras are exposed to 15 the tough conditions of space such as harsh *radiation and extreme temperatures. **If** they **can endure** these challenges, they **will be used** in later space missions. Now pick up your smartphone and go to NASA's official website. It's time to enjoy the Earth!

*radiation 방사선

Reading Comprehension

1 **What is the best title for the passage?**

a. Recording the Earth from Space

b. Join the HDEV Space Mission

c. NASA's Efforts to Observe Space

d. Students Hope to Work on the ISS

2 **What is NOT true about the HDEV project?**

a. The HDEV project started in 2014.

b. Four cameras are installed outside of the ISS.

c. The cameras take images of the Earth at a fixed angle.

d. The cameras must withstand the tough conditions of space.

3 **Where would the following sentence best fit?**

> When the cameras send images to NASA, they are displayed on the internet in real time.

a. ① b. ② c. ③ d. ④

Writing Practice

4 **According to the passage, what is the purpose of the HDEV project?**

Its purpose is to test _____ and observe

_____.

GRAMMAR Inside LEVEL 3

단순 조건문과 가정법

단순 조건문은 실제로 발생 가능한 일을 나타낼 때 쓰지만, 가정법은 현재나 과거의 사실과 반대되거나 실현 불가능한 일을 가정할 때 쓴다. 단순 조건문에서는 if절의 주어와 시제에 따라 동사가 바뀌지만, 가정법에서는 if 절에 동사의 과거형이나 과거완료형을 쓴다.

Link to ...
Chapter 10
Unit 01

If they **can endure** these challenges, they **will be used** in later space missions. 〈단순 조건문〉
그것들(카메라)이 이러한 도전들을 견뎌낼 수 있는 것 (발생 가능한 일)

If I knew his phone number, I **would call** him. 〈가정법 과거〉
내가 그의 전화번호를 아는 것 (현재 사실과 반대되는 일: 전화번호를 모름)

VOCABULARY INSIDE

READING 1	READING 2
☐ **launch** (v) to put a ship in water or send a spacecraft into space for the first time	☐ **spectacular** (a) amazing to see and very impressive [syn] impressive
☐ **enormous** (a) extremely large [syn] huge, massive, vast	☐ **broadcast** (v) to send images or messages by radio or television (n) broadcasting
☐ **damage** (v) to cause harm to something (n) damage [syn] hurt, harm	☐ **automatic** (a) to operate or move independently of human control (ad) automatically
☐ **solution** (n) the answer to a problem (v) solve [syn] answer	☐ **quality** (n) how bad or good something is (v) qualify
☐ **unfortunately** (ad) used to say that something disappoints or saddens you (a) unfortunate [syn] unluckily [ant] fortunately	☐ **extreme** (a) very large in amount or degree (ad) extremely [syn] great

Check Up Fill in the blanks with the words above. Change the form if necessary.

1 South Korea's first satellite was _____ in 1999.

2 The _____ of this product is very high.

3 The travelers took shelter from the _____ heat under a palm tree.

4 The news was _____ for an hour.

5 The device with the _____ control function is more expensive.

6 _____, he failed to win a medal at the Olympics.

7 There is no _____ to the plastic garbage in the ocean.

8 The machines can be easily _____, so be careful with them.

UNIT
15 | Fiction

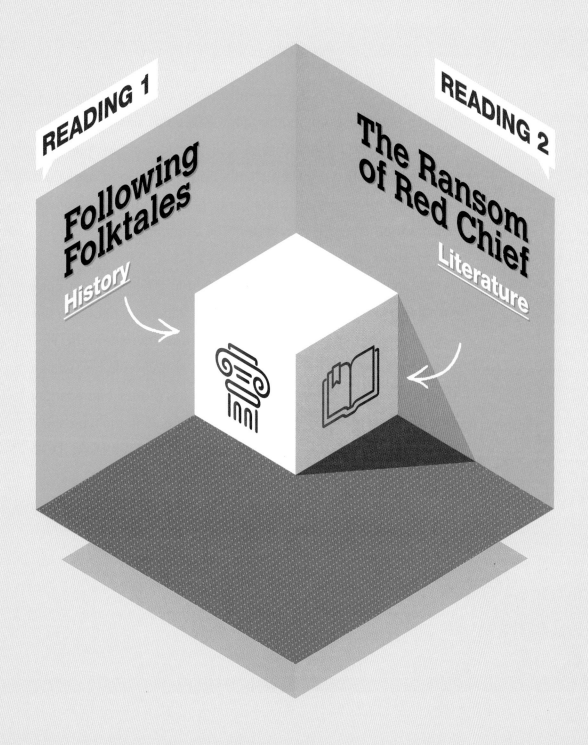

READING 1

Following Folktales

History

READING 2

The Ransom of Red Chief

Literature

Following Folktales

Mini Quiz

While you read, check *T* if it is true, or *F* if it is false.

1 Some countries have similar folktales.
□T □F

2 "Little Red Riding Hood" is the earliest version of the wolf story.
□T □F

In "The Wolf and the Seven Kids," a popular folktale in Europe and the Middle East, a mother goat leaves her kids at home while she searches for food. Meanwhile, a wolf tries to trick the kids into letting him into the house. Similarly, "Little Red Riding Hood" includes a wolf who tricks a little girl by pretending to be her grandmother. This tale 5 has many other versions, such as "The Grandmother Tiger" from China, Japan, and Korea.

Dr. Jamie Tehrani became interested in these different but similar folktales. He believed folktales change in different cultures in the same way biological species adapt to different environments. He found 10 that some parts of stories developed in certain cultures, while others disappeared. (A) He then looked at how the stories had changed over time. (B) They included the number of children and the type and trick of the bad character. (C) To find out how the stories evolved, Dr. Tehrani reviewed 58 stories and listed the differences. 15

The results were pretty interesting. From his research, he suggested that "Little Red Riding Hood" **not only** evolved from early versions of "The Wolf and the Seven Kids," **but also** inspired its later versions. Also, he suggested that the European version of "Little Red Riding Hood" inspired the Asian versions. In 20 the Asian stories, however, the wolf was changed into a tiger!

Reading Comprehension

1 **What is the passage mainly about?**
   a. the origin of "Little Red Riding Hood"
   b. how folktales change in different cultures
   c. the similarities among various kinds of folktales
   d. Dr. Tehrani's search for the most popular folktale

2 **What is the best order of the sentences (A)~(C)?**
   a. (A) – (C) – (B)   b. (B) – (C) – (A)
   c. (C) – (A) – (B)   d. (C) – (B) – (A)

3 **What can be answered based on the passage?**
   a. Who wrote "The Wolf and the Seven Kids?"
   b. How long has Dr. Tehrani studied folktales?
   c. How many different stories did Dr. Tehrani review?
   d. How do the children characters defend themselves from the wolf?

Writing Practice

4 **According to the passage, how is "Little Red Riding Hood" different in the Asian version?**
   Asian stories used a _____ instead of a _____.

Q **GRAMMAR Inside** LEVEL 3   ≡

병렬 구문과 부정 구문

Link to ...
Chapter 12
Unit 01

• 병렬 구문에서 등위접속사(and, but, or 등)나 상관접속사(both A and B, either A or B, neither A nor B, not only A but also B 등)에 의해 연결되는 말은 동일한 문법 형태와 구조를 가져야 한다.

   ... that "Little Red Riding Hood" **not only** evolved from early versions of "The
                                                    (동사의 과거형)
   Wolf and the Seven Kids," **but also** inspired its later versions.
                                          (동사의 과거형)

• 부정 구문에서 부분 부정은 「not + all[every/always]」의 형태로 '모두[항상] ~인 것은 아니다'의 의미이다.
   전체 부정을 나타내는 표현은 no, none, never, neither로 '아무도[결코, 둘 다] ~ 않다'의 의미이다.

   Not all of the jackets from the brand are popular. 〈부분 부정〉
               그 브랜드의 모든 재킷이 인기 있는 것은 아니다.

   Neither pair of shorts fits me. 〈전체 부정〉
               그 반바지들 중 어느 것도 내게 맞지 않는다.

Fiction

231 words

Literature

The Ransom of Red Chief

Written by O. Henry

V Mini Quiz

Find the answers from the passage and write them.

Paragraph 2

1 In the game of cowboys and Indians, which character does Johnny play?

→ _____

Paragraph 3

2 Who gets the ransom in the end?

→ _____

Two villains, Bill and Sam, plan to kidnap a child and demand a $2,000 *ransom. They select nine-year-old Johnny, the only child of Mr. Dorset, a rich man.

However, it's not easy to kidnap the boy, because he is very naughty. When Bill and Sam get close to the boy, Johnny throws a piece of 5 brick at Bill's eye. Bill and Sam grab Johnny and drive him out to a mountain cave. When Sam gets back from returning the car to the town, Bill has been forced to play a game of cowboys and Indians with the boy. Johnny is now "Red Chief," and Bill is covered with bruises. They soon realize that Johnny hates school and loves camping out in 10 the mountains. The next morning, little Red Chief leaps upon Bill like a horse and even puts a hot potato down his shirt.

Bill and Sam quickly write a letter, asking Mr. Dorset to pay only $1,500 for the return of his son. Surprisingly, Mr. Dorset replies that he will only take Johnny back if they pay him $250! **Considering** Johnny's 15 past behavior, they decide they'd rather lose some money. Bill and Sam return Johnny to his father and pay the money. However, Johnny doesn't want his adventure to end, and he clings to Bill's leg. Finally, Bill and Sam are able to escape while Mr. Dorset holds his son.

*ransom 몸값

Reading Comprehension

1 **What is the passage mainly about?**
   a. a cruel father and his poor son
   b. a ransom attempt that goes wrong
   c. Red Chief's adventure to the mountains
   d. a courageous boy who escapes from villains

2 **What is NOT true about Johnny?**
   a. He throws a piece of brick at Bill.
   b. He wants to be a chief in his school.
   c. He loves camping out in the mountains.
   d. He clings to the villain's leg.

3 **How did Bill and Sam's feelings change in the passage?**
   a. regretful → jealous   b. excited → ashamed
   c. determined → regretful   d. embarrassed → encouraged

Writing Practice

4 **According to the passage, what does Mr. Dorset say in his letter?**
   He says that he will only _____ if the villains _____.

GRAMMAR Inside LEVEL 3

숙어처럼 쓰이는 분사구문
분사구문의 의미상 주어가 주절의 주어와 다르더라도, we, you, one 등과 같은 막연한 일반인일 때는
분사구문의 주어를 생략하고 하나의 숙어처럼 쓸 수 있다.

Link to ...
Chapter 06
Unit 03

• frankly speaking: 솔직히 말해서   • considering: ~을 감안하면
• strictly speaking: 엄밀히 말해서   • judging from: ~으로 판단하건대
• generally speaking: 일반적으로 말해서   • speaking of: ~의 이야기가 나와서 말인데

Considering Johnny's past behavior, they decide they'd rather lose some money.
조니의 지난 행동을 감안하면

Judging from his haircut, he must be in the army.
그의 머리 모양으로 판단하자면

Check Up 우리말과 일치하도록 ( ) 안의 말을 이용하여 문장을 완성하시오.

그녀의 나이를 감안하면, 우리 할머니는 매우 건강하시다. (consider, age)
→ _____ _____ _____, my grandmother is very healthy.

VOCABULARY INSIDE

READING 1	READING 2
☐ **pretend** ⓥ to behave as if something is true when in fact it is not [syn] make believe	☐ **select** ⓥ to choose something from a group [syn] choose
☐ **environment** ⓝ the condition of a place that affects the species living there ⓐ environmental [syn] surroundings	☐ **naughty** ⓐ behaving badly; not willing to obey [syn] bad-mannered [ant] good
☐ **character** ⓝ a person in a movie, book, or play	☐ **force** ⓥ to make someone do something even though they don't want to [syn] make, compel
☐ **review** ⓥ to look carefully at something to judge or find meaningful information ⓝ review [syn] analyze, examine	☐ **adventure** ⓝ an exciting and unusual experience ⓐ adventurous
☐ **difference** ⓝ some qualities that make two things unlike each other ⓥ differ ⓐ different [syn] distinction, gap	☐ **escape** ⓥ to run away from an unpleasant or dangerous place ⓝ escape [syn] get away from

Check Up   **Fill in the blanks with the words above. Change the form if necessary.**

1 Please _____ the best restaurant from the list below.

2 Children are affected by the _____ in which they grow up.

3 His backpacking trip to India was a great _____.

4 The main _____ of many fairy tales is a princess.

5 I was punished for having been _____.

6 The police officer was _____ the report of the murder.

7 In some poor countries, young children are _____ to work.

8 I closed my eyes and _____ that I was sleeping.

UNIT
16 | Food

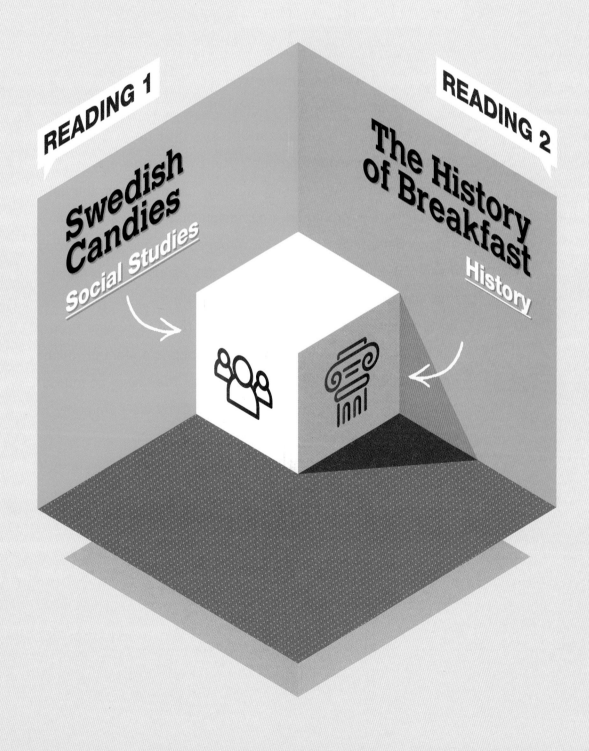

READING 1

Swedish Candies
Social Studies

READING 2

The History of Breakfast
History

Swedish Candies

Probably no country in the world eats as much candy as Sweden. In fact, most Swedes eat roughly 16 kilograms of candy every year. *The World Health Organization says **that** this is three times the average recommended amount. The Swedish government hoped to prevent children from getting so many cavities. So in the late 1950s, 5 the government promoted a campaign **that** encouraged eating candy only on Saturdays. This is how *lördagsgodis* was born. *Lördagsgodis* means "Saturday sweets" or "Saturday candy." It is a family activity **that** happens every weekend.

Swedish people love picking their favorite sweets from pick-n- 10 mix candy shops. A pick-n-mix candy shop is a store in which people can choose from many kinds of sweets. They have countless jellies, chocolates, and other colorful candies. They are commonly found in supermarkets, drug stores, and even gas stations.

Due to this national passion for sweets, the Swedish candy industry 15 has been evolving to be healthier. ① Companies are increasingly using organic ingredients and more natural flavors. ② Vegetarians can even find sweets just for them! ③ Candy is still regarded as an undesirable option for losing weight. ④ So, health-conscious Swedes should take a closer look at the ingredient labels. 20

*The World Health Organization 세계 보건 기구 (WHO)

Reading Comprehension

1 What is the best title for the passage?

a. Pick-N-Mix Shops: The Most Famous Candy Stores

b. What Kind of Sweets Swedes Like the Most

c. Candy Culture in Sweden and Its Popularity

d. Swedish Dessert Time for Vegetarians

Writing Practice

2 According to the passage, why did the Swedish government start lördagsgodis?

The government started lördagsgodis to _____.

3 Which sentence is NOT needed in the passage?

a. ①   b. ②   c. ③   d. ④

4 Which CANNOT be answered based on the passage?

a. What does *lördagsgodis* mean in English?

b. When do Swedish people enjoy lördagsgodis?

c. Where can we find pick-n-mix candy shops in Sweden?

d. How do food companies develop nutritious sweets?

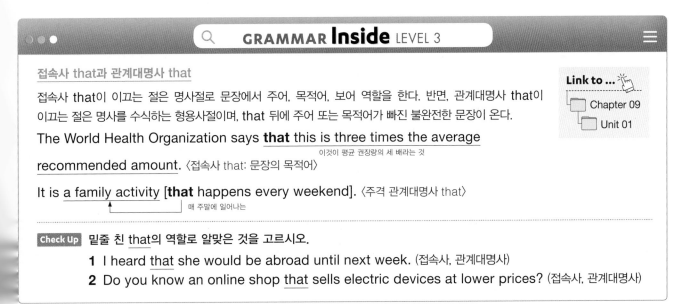

GRAMMAR **Inside** LEVEL 3

접속사 that과 관계대명사 that

접속사 that이 이끄는 절은 명사절로 문장에서 주어, 목적어, 보어 역할을 한다. 반면, 관계대명사 that이 이끄는 절은 명사를 수식하는 형용사절이며, that 뒤에 주어 또는 목적어가 빠진 불완전한 문장이 온다.

The World Health Organization says **that** this is three times the average
이것이 평균 권장량의 세 배라는 것
recommended amount. 〈접속사 that: 문장의 목적어〉

It is a family activity [**that** happens every weekend]. 〈주격 관계대명사 that〉
매 주말에 일어나는

Link to ...
Chapter 09
Unit 01

Check Up 밑줄 친 that의 역할로 알맞은 것을 고르시오.

1 I heard that she would be abroad until next week. (접속사, 관계대명사)

2 Do you know an online shop that sells electric devices at lower prices? (접속사, 관계대명사)

The History of Breakfast

Ⓥ Mini Quiz

Find the answers from the passage and write them.

Paragraph 2

1 What triggered changes in people's beliefs about breakfast?

→ _____

_____

Paragraph 3

2 What was popular for breakfast in the early 20th century?

→ _____

Having breakfast is the first thing many people do in the morning. However, it is a relatively recent tradition for Westerners. In medieval Europe, there were two daily meals—one at midday and one in the early evening. Surprisingly, some people considered it a sin to eat in the morning. Because of <u>this belief</u>, only people from the lower classes, 5 such as farmers or laborers, ate breakfast. These were people who needed the energy to work in the morning. Historians believe that the word "breakfast" originated around this time. They suggest the term refers to the breaking of the night's *fast.

This idea of breakfast changed with the Industrial Revolution in the 10 mid-19th century. At that time, all classes of people began to leave the house for work in the morning. Consequently, more and more people began the day by eating food such as cheese and bread before going to work.

Another shift happened around the early 20th century. (A) **Having** 15 **discovered** how tasty the cereal was, he advertised it as a healthy breakfast containing vitamins and minerals. (B) Ever since, eating a breakfast of cereal with milk has been popular with people around the world. (C) An American named John Harvey Kellogg accidentally created breakfast cereal by cooking wheat. 20

*fast 단식

Reading Comprehension

1 **What is the passage mainly about?**
   a. why we should eat breakfast before going to work
   b. how breakfast became a common morning meal
   c. why breakfast foods have changed
   d. how cereal became popular

Writing Practice
2 **What does the underlined part refer to?**
   Some people considered _____ in the morning to be a(n) _____.

3 **What is the best order of the sentences (A)~(C)?**
   a. (B) – (A) – (C)   b. (B) – (C) – (A)
   c. (C) – (A) – (B)   d. (C) – (B) – (A)

4 **What is NOT mentioned in the passage?**
   a. when people had two meals in Europe
   b. what the meaning of the word "breakfast" is
   c. when all classes of people began to have breakfast
   d. how Kellogg added vitamins and minerals to cereal

Q   GRAMMAR **Inside** LEVEL 3   ≡

여러 가지 분사구문
• 완료형 분사구문(having v-ed): 부사절의 시제가 주절의 시제보다 앞설 때 사용한다.
  Having discovered how tasty the cereal was, he advertised it … .
  (← After he *had discovered* how tasty the cereal was, he *advertised* it … .)
• 주어가 있는 분사구문: 부사절의 주어가 주절의 주어와 다를 경우, 보통 분사 앞에 주어를 쓴다.
  It being rainy, I took a taxi. (← As *it* was rainy, *I* took a taxi.)

Link to …
Chapter 06
Unit 03

Check Up   우리말과 일치하도록 (   ) 안의 말을 이용하여 문장을 완성하시오.
         우산을 놔두고 왔어서, 그녀는 다시 가게로 돌아갔다. (leave)
         → _____ _____ her umbrella, she went back to the shop.

VOCABULARY INSIDE

READING 1	READING 2
☐ **recommend** ⓥ to suggest something to someone ⓝ recommendation [syn] suggest, propose	☐ **relatively** [ad] when compared to other things [syn] comparatively
☐ **ingredient** ⓝ a food that is used with other foods to make a dish	☐ **belief** ⓝ a feeling of certainty that something exists or is true ⓥ believe [ant] disbelief
☐ **flavor** ⓝ the specific taste that something has when you eat or drink it ⓥ flavor [syn] taste	☐ **originate** ⓥ to begin to exist ⓝ origin ⓐ original [syn] arise
☐ **vegetarian** ⓝ someone who does not eat meat or fish by choice	☐ **advertise** ⓥ to inform the public of a product and persuade them to buy it ⓝ advertisement [syn] publicize, promote
☐ **option** ⓝ one thing that can be chosen from a set of possible choices ⓐ optional [syn] choice, selection	☐ **accidentally** [ad] happening without being planned ⓐ accidental [syn] by chance

Check Up | **Fill in the blanks with the words above. Change the form if necessary.**

1 Make sure you don't _____ lose the key again.

2 This energy bar is made of many healthy _____.

3 The midterm exam was _____ easy.

4 Could you _____ a good restaurant near here?

5 If you add some pepper, it will improve the _____ of the soup.

6 The company plans to _____ their new products on television.

7 My sister is a(n) _____, so she doesn't like going to steakhouses.

8 Yoga _____ in India thousands of years ago.

WORD LIST

UNIT 01 | Culture

O△X	adapt to	~에 적응하다
O△X	as well	또한[역시]
O△X	care about	~에 관심을 가지다
O△X	celebrate	동 기념하다, 축하하다
O△X	century	명 세기, 100년
O△X	conservation	명 보호
O△X	creativity	명 창의력
O△X	depth	명 깊이
O△X	discuss	동 상의하다; 논하다
O△X	environment	명 환경
O△X	ethnic	형 민족의[종족의]
O△X	float	동 떠가다[떠돌다]
O△X	generation	명 세대
O△X	harvest	명 수확
O△X	heritage	명 유산
O△X	honor	동 존경하다; 기리다
O△X	intend	동 의도하다
O△X	lifestyle	명 생활방식
O△X	marine	형 바다의[해양의]
O△X	narrow	형 좁은
O△X	nearly	부 거의
O△X	nomadic	형 유목의[방랑의]
O△X	ocean	명 대양, 바다
O△X	poem	명 시(詩)
O△X	prefer	동 선호하다
O△X	principle	명 원칙
O△X	probably	부 아마도
O△X	purpose	명 목적
O△X	relatively	부 비교적
O△X	research	동 조사하다[연구하다]
O△X	responsibility	명 책임(감)
O△X	species	명 종(種)
O△X	traditional	형 전통의, 전통적인
O△X	traditionally	부 전통적으로
O△X	vision	명 시력

UNIT 02 | Wealth

O△X	academy	명 학교
O△X	alchemist	명 연금술사
O△X	ancient	형 고대의
O△X	beginning	명 시작
O△X	chemistry	명 화학
O△X	construct	동 건설하다
O△X	cure	동 치료하다, 치유하다
O△X	development	명 발달, 성장
O△X	earn	동 (돈을) 벌다
O△X	essential	형 필수적인; 극히 중요한
O△X	establish	동 설립하다
O△X	eternal	형 영원한
O△X	focus on	~에 주력하다, 초점을 맞추다
O△X	illness	명 질병
O△X	influence	동 영향을 주다
O△X	interest	명 관심[흥미]
O△X	legend	명 전설
O△X	master	명 주인; 대가(大家)
O△X	medieval	형 중세의
O△X	modern	형 현대의
O△X	myth	명 신화, 근거 없는 믿음
O△X	ordinary	형 보통의
O△X	owner	명 주인, 소유주
O△X	philosopher	명 철학자
O△X	possible	형 가능한
O△X	practice	명 실행; 관행
O△X	proportion	명 비율
O△X	reach one's peak	절정에 이르다
O△X	rise	명 상승, 성장
O△X	sponsor	동 후원하다
O△X	support	동 후원하다 명 지지, 지원
O△X	supporter	명 후원자
O△X	text	명 글, 문서
O△X	transform	동 변형시키다
O△X	universe	명 우주

UNIT 03 Shapes

⃞ actually	🖣 사실상
⃞ agriculture	명 농업
⃞ algae	명 조류(藻類), 말
⃞ artwork	명 미술품
⃞ behavior	명 행동
⃞ block out	(빛·소리를) 차단하다
⃞ closely	🖣 긴밀하게; 자세히
⃞ combine	동 결합하다
⃞ compass	명 나침반; (제도용) 컴퍼스
⃞ complex	형 복잡한
⃞ decade	명 10년
⃞ degree	명 (각도의 단위인) 도
⃞ depict	동 묘사하다, 그리다
⃞ describe	동 말하다; 묘사하다
⃞ elegant	형 우아한
⃞ form	동 형성하다
⃞ freshwater	형 민물의[담수의]
⃞ geometric	형 기하학적인
⃞ give off	내뿜다, 발산하다
⃞ in particular	특히
⃞ infinite	형 무한한
⃞ mix	명 혼합체[섞인 것]
⃞ nature	명 자연; 본성, 본질
⃞ origin	명 기원[근원]
⃞ pattern	명 패턴; 무늬
⃞ pentagon	명 오각형
⃞ population	명 인구; 개체 수
⃞ produce	동 생산하다
⃞ repeat	동 반복하다
⃞ rival	형 경쟁하는
⃞ rotate	동 회전하다, 회전시키다
⃞ several	형 몇몇의
⃞ side by side	나란히
⃞ sink	동 가라앉다
⃞ tangled	형 헝클어진, 뒤얽힌

UNIT 04 Nature

⃞ active	형 활동적인, 활발한
⃞ attraction	명 끌림; 명소
⃞ battlefield	명 싸움터, 전쟁터
⃞ believe it or not	믿거나 말거나
⃞ bravely	🖣 용감하게
⃞ breathtaking	형 숨이 막히는
⃞ control	동 지배하다
⃞ draw	동 그리다; (마음을) 끌다
⃞ engine	명 엔진
⃞ erupt	동 분출하다
⃞ eruption	명 (화산의) 폭발, 분화
⃞ exotic	형 이국적인
⃞ glacier	명 빙하
⃞ grand	형 웅장한
⃞ heat	동 가열하다
⃞ homeland	명 고국[조국]
⃞ huge	형 거대한
⃞ ingredient	명 재료[성분]
⃞ landscape	명 풍경
⃞ local	형 지역의, 현지의
⃞ magma	명 마그마
⃞ match	명 성냥
⃞ melt	동 녹다
⃞ mineral	명 광물(질); 미네랄
⃞ overcome	동 극복하다
⃞ power station	발전소
⃞ product	명 제품; 산물
⃞ source	명 원천, 근원
⃞ steam	명 김, 증기
⃞ turn into	~으로 변하다
⃞ underground	형 지하의
⃞ valuable	형 귀중한, 소중한
⃞ volcanic	형 화산의
⃞ volcano	명 화산
⃞ wizard	명 마법사

UNIT 05 Buildings

O△X	appearance	몡 (겉)모습, 외모
O△X	architecture	몡 건축학, 건축술; 건축물
O△X	artificial	톙 인공의[인조의]
O△X	attention	몡 주목; 관심
O△X	brilliant	톙 훌륭한, 멋진
O△X	capture	통 포착하다, 담아내다
O△X	catastrophe	몡 참사, 재앙
O△X	chilly	톙 쌀쌀한, 추운
O△X	complete	통 완료하다
O△X	construction	몡 건설, 공사
O△X	crisis	몡 위기 ((pl.) crises)
O△X	curved	톙 곡선의, 약간 굽은
O△X	destroy	통 파괴하다
O△X	disaster	몡 참사, 재난, 재해
O△X	due to	~ 때문에
O△X	feature	몡 특색, 특징
O△X	floor	몡 (건물의) 층
O△X	government	몡 정부
O△X	importance	몡 중요성
O△X	in harmony with	~와 조화를 이루어
O△X	incident	몡 일[사건]
O△X	innovative	톙 획기적인
O△X	isolated	톙 외딴, 고립된
O△X	lessen	통 줄이다
O△X	Norwegian	톙 노르웨이의
O△X	over time	시간이 지나면서
O△X	place	통 놓다, 설치[배치]하다
O△X	pollution	몡 오염, 공해
O△X	practical	톙 현실적인; 실용적인
O△X	primary	톙 주된, 주요한
O△X	regional	톙 지방의, 지역의
O△X	shape	몡 모양, 형태
O△X	smoothly	뫼 부드럽게
O△X	store	통 저장[보관]하다
O△X	unusual	톙 특이한, 색다른

UNIT 06 Numbers

O△X	add	통 추가하다
O△X	calendar	몡 달력
O△X	come up with	(생각을) 떠올리다, 내놓다
O△X	cycle	몡 주기
O△X	demand	통 요구하다
O△X	disqualified	톙 자격을 잃은, 실격된
O△X	eventually	뫼 결국
O△X	exact	톙 정확한
O△X	exactly	뫼 정확히
O△X	exhaustion	몡 탈진, 기진맥진
O△X	extra	톙 추가의, 여분의
O△X	follow	통 따라가다
O△X	historian	몡 역사학자
O△X	initially	뫼 처음에
O△X	inspire	통 고무하다; 영감을 주다
O△X	international	톙 국제적인
O△X	last	통 지속되다
O△X	lawn	몡 잔디밭
O△X	lunar	톙 달의
O△X	permanent	톙 영구적인
O△X	political	톙 정치적인
O△X	process	몡 과정
O△X	receive	통 받다
O△X	referee	몡 심판
O△X	repeatedly	뫼 되풀이하여
O△X	request	통 요청하다 몡 요청, 요구
O△X	royal	톙 왕의, 왕실의
O△X	royalty	몡 왕족
O△X	slightly	뫼 약간
O△X	solar	톙 태양의
O△X	stadium	몡 경기장
O△X	track	통 추적하다
O△X	victory	몡 승리
O△X	whole	톙 전체의
O△X	will	몡 의지

WORD LIST

UNIT 07 | Sports

⃞ attacker	몡 공격자[공격수]
⃞ breathe	동 숨을 쉬다
⃞ breathless	혱 숨이 가쁜; 숨이 막히는
⃞ characteristic	몡 특징
⃞ compared to	~와 비교하여
⃞ competitive	혱 경쟁을 하는
⃞ continuously	뵘 계속해서, 연속적으로
⃞ creature	몡 생물, 생명체
⃞ defender	몡 수비수
⃞ defense	몡 방어, 수비
⃞ effective	혱 효과적인
⃞ equipment	몡 장비, 용품
⃞ escape	동 달아나다
⃞ global	혱 세계적인
⃞ half	몡 반[절반]
⃞ hollow	혱 속이 빈
⃞ hunting	몡 사냥
⃞ inhale	동 숨을 들이마시다
⃞ lung	몡 폐
⃞ occupy	동 차지하다
⃞ opponent	몡 상대
⃞ originate	동 비롯되다, 유래하다
⃞ participant	몡 참가자
⃞ reed	몡 갈대
⃞ southern	혱 남쪽의[남향의]
⃞ sponge	몡 수세미
⃞ succeed	동 성공하다
⃞ tag	동 ~을 달다; 터치하다
⃞ take a break	(잠시) 휴식을 취하다
⃞ take a breath	숨을 쉬다
⃞ take turns	교대로 ~하다
⃞ test	동 시험하다
⃞ tropical	혱 열대의
⃞ underwater	혱 물속의 뵘 물속에(서)
⃞ wildlife	몡 야생동물

UNIT 08 | Future

⃞ accessible	혱 접근할 수 있는
⃞ additionally	뵘 게다가
⃞ battery	몡 배터리, 전지
⃞ billion	몡 10억
⃞ broad	혱 폭넓은
⃞ charge	동 청구하다; 충전하다
⃞ comparison	몡 비교, 대조
⃞ compete	동 경쟁하다
⃞ competition	몡 경쟁; 경기
⃞ deserve	동 받을 만하다
⃞ firm	혱 단단한
⃞ fluid	혱 유동성의
⃞ frequently	뵘 자주
⃞ fully	뵘 완전히
⃞ gender	몡 성별
⃞ increasingly	뵘 점점 더
⃞ industry	몡 산업
⃞ install	동 설치하다
⃞ intense	혱 극심한; 치열한
⃞ involve	동 포함하다
⃞ limit	동 제한하다, 한정하다
⃞ liquid	몡 액체
⃞ manage	동 관리하다
⃞ organized	혱 조직적인
⃞ performance	몡 성능
⃞ phenomenon	몡 현상
⃞ physical	혱 신체의; 물리적인
⃞ promising	혱 전도유망한
⃞ rather than	~보다는
⃞ recharge	동 재충전하다
⃞ recognition	몡 인식; 인정
⃞ space	몡 공간
⃞ substitute	몡 대체품
⃞ varying	혱 변화하는[바뀌는]
⃞ virtual	혱 (컴퓨터를 이용한) 가상의

UNIT 09 Animals

O△X	a number of	얼마간의; 많은 ~
O△X	abandon	동 버리다
O△X	absorb	동 (액체·가스 등을) 흡수하다
O△X	affect	동 영향을 미치다
O△X	amount	명 양
O△X	barely	부 거의 ~ 아니게
O△X	biologist	명 생물학자
O△X	birth	명 탄생, 출생
O△X	breed	동 새끼를 낳다; 번식시키다
O△X	carbon dioxide	이산화탄소
O△X	chemical	명 화학 물질
O△X	concern	명 우려, 걱정
O△X	cozy	형 아늑한
O△X	ecological	형 생태계의
O△X	ecosystem	명 생태계
O△X	endangered	형 멸종 위기에 처한
O△X	face	동 ~에 직면하다
O△X	gene	명 유전자
O△X	generate	동 발생시키다, 만들어 내다
O△X	genetic	형 유전의
O△X	inform A of B	A에게 B를 알려주다
O△X	iron	명 철; 철분
O△X	lack	명 부족, 결핍
O△X	life span	수명
O△X	normal	형 보통의, 정상적인
O△X	nutrient	명 영양소
O△X	occur	동 발생하다
O△X	remove	동 제거하다
O△X	rescue	동 구하다[구조하다]
O△X	stay away	(~에게) 접근하지 않다
O△X	surface	명 표면[표층]
O△X	threat	명 위협
O△X	threaten	동 위태롭게 하다, 위협하다
O△X	tragedy	명 비극
O△X	wild	명 (야생 상태의) 자연

UNIT 10 Stories

O△X	admire	동 존경하다
O△X	analysis	명 분석
O△X	attack	동 공격하다
O△X	attractive	형 매력적인
O△X	be terrified of	~을 두려워하다
O△X	board	명 판자
O△X	body	명 몸; 시체
O△X	change A into B	A를 B로 바꾸다
O△X	commit	동 (범죄를) 저지르다
O△X	compose	동 구성하다; 작곡하다
O△X	confidently	부 자신 있게
O△X	continue to-v	계속하여 ~하다
O△X	convince	동 확신시키다
O△X	crime	명 범죄
O△X	detail	명 세부 사항
O△X	distinguish	동 구별하다
O△X	emotion	명 감정
O△X	evil	형 사악한
O△X	fear	명 공포
O△X	grab	동 붙잡다[움켜잡다]
O△X	heartbeat	명 심장 박동
O△X	imitate	동 흉내 내다
O△X	impressive	형 감명 깊은
O△X	legendary	형 전설적인
O△X	mad	형 화난; 미친
O△X	make a noise	소리를 내다
O△X	murderer	명 살인범
O△X	notice	동 알아채다
O△X	reader	명 독자
O△X	realize	동 깨닫다, 알아차리다
O△X	soften	동 부드러워지다, 은은해지다
O△X	sorrowful	형 슬픈
O△X	tragic	형 비극적인
O△X	tremble	동 (몸이) 떨다, 떨리다
O△X	unsolved	형 해결되지[풀리지] 않은

WORD LIST

UNIT 11 Psychology

⊙△✕ author	몡 작가, 저자
⊙△✕ common	휑 일반적인, 흔한
⊙△✕ consider	툉 여기다[생각하다]
⊙△✕ convenient	휑 편리한
⊙△✕ cool down	진정하게 하다
⊙△✕ counseling	몡 상담
⊙△✕ creative	휑 창의적인
⊙△✕ deadly	휑 치명적인
⊙△✕ deal with	~을 다루다, 처리하다
⊙△✕ depressed	휑 우울한
⊙△✕ dictionary	몡 사전
⊙△✕ direct	휑 직접적인
⊙△✕ emotional	휑 감정의; 감정적인
⊙△✕ exhausted	휑 기진맥진한, 탈진한
⊙△✕ grade	몡 등급; 성적
⊙△✕ heal	툉 치유하다[낫게 하다]
⊙△✕ homesickness	몡 향수병
⊙△✕ improvement	몡 향상, 발전
⊙△✕ long to-v	~하기를 애타게 바라다
⊙△✕ nostalgia	몡 향수(鄕愁)
⊙△✕ object	몡 물건, 물체
⊙△✕ opportunity	몡 기회
⊙△✕ personal	휑 개인의[개인적인]
⊙△✕ punch	툉 때리다
⊙△✕ respond to	~에게 대답하다[반응하다]
⊙△✕ songwriting	몡 작사, 작곡
⊙△✕ struggle	몡 싸움; 힘든 일
⊙△✕ sufferer	몡 고통받는 사람, 환자
⊙△✕ therapist	몡 치료사
⊙△✕ therapy	몡 치료, 요법
⊙△✕ transportation	몡 수송[운송], 교통수단
⊙△✕ troubled	휑 문제가 많은
⊙△✕ unknown	휑 알려지지 않은, 미지의
⊙△✕ vocabulary	몡 어휘
⊙△✕ wonder	몡 경탄, 경이

UNIT 12 Business

⊙△✕ access	툉 접근하다
⊙△✕ achieve	툉 성취하다, 해내다
⊙△✕ business	몡 사업; 사업체
⊙△✕ capital	몡 수도; 자금
⊙△✕ charity	몡 자선 단체
⊙△✕ commercial	몡 광고 (방송)
⊙△✕ confidence	몡 신뢰; 확신
⊙△✕ contribute	툉 기부하다, 기여하다
⊙△✕ cost	몡 비용
⊙△✕ device	몡 장치[기구]
⊙△✕ donate	툉 기부하다
⊙△✕ efficient	휑 능률적인, 유효한
⊙△✕ financial	휑 금융의, 재정의
⊙△✕ fund	툉 자금을 대다 몡 자금
⊙△✕ in return	대신에, 답례로
⊙△✕ incredibly	휜 놀랍게도
⊙△✕ instantly	휜 즉시
⊙△✕ introduction	몡 도입
⊙△✕ investment	몡 투자, 투자금
⊙△✕ latest	휑 최신의
⊙△✕ million	몡 100만
⊙△✕ partial	휑 부분적인
⊙△✕ payment	몡 지불
⊙△✕ prevent	툉 막다[방지하다]
⊙△✕ publish	툉 출판하다
⊙△✕ random	휑 무작위의
⊙△✕ record	몡 기록
⊙△✕ retailer	몡 소매업자, 소매상
⊙△✕ reward	몡 보상
⊙△✕ secure	휑 안전한
⊙△✕ security	몡 보안
⊙△✕ stock	몡 (상품 등의) 재고; 주식
⊙△✕ stuff	몡 물건
⊙△✕ technology	몡 기술
⊙△✕ unusable	휑 사용할 수 없는

UNIT 13 People

O△X	a series of	일련의
O△X	alive	형 살아 있는
O△X	approach	명 접근법, 처리 방법
O△X	argue	동 주장하다
O△X	bandage	명 붕대
O△X	boil	동 끓이다
O△X	diplomat	명 외교관
O△X	diplomatic	형 외교의
O△X	embassy	명 대사관
O△X	equally	부 동등하게
O△X	flag	명 깃발
O△X	foundation	명 토대[기초]
O△X	hire	동 고용하다
O△X	legally	부 법률[합법]적으로
O△X	mild	형 가벼운[순한]
O△X	military	형 군사의
O△X	mixture	명 혼합물
O△X	pain	명 통증, 고통
O△X	passport	명 여권
O△X	patient	명 환자
O△X	personally	부 직접, 개인적으로
O△X	pole	명 막대기, 기둥
O△X	recognize	동 알아보다
O△X	risk	동 위태롭게 하다
O△X	rotten	형 썩은, 부패한
O△X	suffering	명 고통
O△X	surgeon	명 외과 의사
O△X	surgery	명 수술
O△X	surgical	형 수술의
O△X	symbolize	동 상징하다
O△X	task	명 일, 과업
O△X	territory	명 지역, 영토
O△X	transport	동 수송하다
O△X	treatment	명 치료
O△X	wound	명 상처

UNIT 14 Space

O△X	angle	명 각도, 각
O△X	atmosphere	명 (지구의) 대기
O△X	automatic	형 자동의
O△X	broadcast	동 방송하다
O△X	challenge	명 도전
O△X	crash	동 충돌하다
O△X	damage	동 손상을 입히다
O△X	emphasize	동 강조하다
O△X	engineer	명 기술자, 공학자
O△X	exploration	명 탐험, 탐사
O△X	expose	동 노출시키다
O△X	extreme	형 극심한
O△X	film	동 촬영하다
O△X	fixed	형 고정된
O△X	harsh	형 가혹한; 너무 강한
O△X	in response to	~에 대응하여
O△X	in the long term	장기적으로
O△X	junk	명 쓰레기
O△X	launch	동 발사하다
O△X	method	명 방법
O△X	mission	명 임무
O△X	observe	동 관찰하다
O△X	orbit	동 (다른 천체의) 궤도를 돌다 명 궤도
O△X	position	명 위치
O△X	pull back	후퇴하다, 물러나다
O△X	quality	명 품질
O△X	resulting	형 그 결과로 초래된
O△X	satellite	명 (인공)위성
O△X	sight	명 시야; 광경[모습]
O△X	solution	명 해결책
O△X	spacecraft	명 우주선
O△X	spectacular	형 장관을 이루는
O△X	tiny	형 아주 작은[적은]
O△X	tough	형 힘든, 어려운
O△X	withstand	동 견뎌 내다

WORD LIST

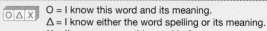
UNIT 15 Fiction

O△X	ashamed	형 부끄러워하는
O△X	biological	형 생물학의
O△X	brick	명 벽돌
O△X	bruise	명 멍
O△X	cave	명 동굴
O△X	chief	명 최고위자; 추장, 족장
O△X	cling to	~에 매달리다
O△X	courageous	형 용감한
O△X	cruel	형 잔혹한, 잔인한
O△X	decide	동 결정하다
O△X	defend	동 방어하다
O△X	determined	형 단호한, 완강한
O△X	difference	명 차이(점)
O△X	embarrassed	형 당혹스러운
O△X	folktale	명 민간 설화, 전래 동화
O△X	force	동 강요하다
O△X	goat	명 염소
O△X	kidnap	동 납치하다
O△X	leap	동 뛰다, 뛰어오르다
O△X	list	동 (목록을) 작성하다
O△X	meanwhile	부 그동안에
O△X	naughty	형 버릇없는, 말을 안 듣는
O△X	past	형 지난
O△X	pretend	동 ~인 척하다
O△X	pretty	부 아주[매우]
O△X	regretful	형 유감스러워하는
O△X	reply	동 대답하다, 답장하다
O△X	result	명 결과
O△X	review	동 재검토하다
O△X	similarity	명 유사성
O△X	similarly	부 비슷하게, 유사하게
O△X	suggest	동 제안하다; 시사하다
O△X	surprisingly	부 놀랍게도
O△X	tale	명 (허구의) 이야기
O△X	villain	명 악당

UNIT 16 Food

O△X	accidentally	부 우연히, 뜻하지 않게
O△X	activity	명 활동
O△X	advertise	동 광고하다
O△X	average	형 평균의
O△X	be regarded as	~으로 여겨지다
O△X	belief	명 신념, 믿음
O△X	breaking	명 파괴, 절단
O△X	campaign	명 캠페인, (조직적인) 운동
O△X	cavity	명 충치
O△X	commonly	부 흔히
O△X	conscious	형 의식하는
O△X	consequently	부 그 결과, 따라서
O△X	contain	동 ~이 들어 있다, 함유하다
O△X	countless	형 셀 수 없이 많은
O△X	daily	형 매일 일어나는, 나날의
O△X	encourage	동 격려하다; 장려하다
O△X	evolve	동 발전하다
O△X	flavor	명 맛; 향료
O△X	healthy	형 건강한; 건강에 좋은
O△X	label	명 라벨, 상표
O△X	laborer	명 노동자
O△X	lower class	하층 계급
O△X	national	형 국가의, 전국민의
O△X	nutritious	형 영양분이 많은
O△X	option	명 선택 (사항)
O△X	passion	명 열정
O△X	recommend	동 추천하다; 권장하다
O△X	refer to	~을 지칭하다
O△X	roughly	부 대략
O△X	shift	명 변화
O△X	tasty	형 맛있는
O△X	undesirable	형 바람직하지 않은
O△X	vegetarian	명 채식주의자
O△X	weight	명 체중, 무게
O△X	Westerner	명 서양인

Photo Credits

PAGE	PHOTO	SOURCE
p. 34	It's No Game. *The Gherkin and the Lloyd's Building.* Photograph. *flickr*, December 2012.	https://commons.wikimedia.org/wiki/File:The_Gherkin_and_the_Lloyd%27s_Building_(8299994107).jpg
others		www.shutterstock.com

지은이

NE능률 영어교육연구소

NE능률 영어교육연구소는 혁신적이며 효율적인 영어 교재를 개발하고
영어 학습의 질을 한 단계 높이고자 노력하는 NE능률의 연구조직입니다.

Reading Inside 〈Level 3〉

펴 낸 이	주민홍
펴 낸 곳	서울특별시 마포구 월드컵북로 396(상암동) 누리꿈스퀘어 비즈니스타워 10층 ㈜NE능률 (우편번호 03925)
펴 낸 날	2022년 9월 15일 개정판 제1쇄 발행 2023년 9월 15일 제4쇄
전 화	02 2014 7114
팩 스	02 3142 0356
홈 페 이 지	www.neungyule.com
등 록 번 호	제1-68호
I S B N	979-11-253-4033-1 53740
정 가	15,500원

NE 능률

고객센터

교재 내용 문의 : contact.nebooks.co.kr (별도의 가입 절차 없이 작성 가능)
제품 구매, 교환, 불량, 반품 문의 : 02-2014-7114
☎ 전화문의는 본사 업무시간 중에만 가능합니다.

NE능률 교재 MAP

독해

초1-2	초3	초3-4	초4-5	초5-6
초등영어 리딩이 된다 Start 1	리딩버디 1	리딩버디 2	리딩버디 3	초등영어 리딩이 된다 Jump 1
초등영어 리딩이 된다 Start 2		초등영어 리딩이 된다 Basic 1	주니어 리딩튜터 스타터 1	초등영어 리딩이 된다 Jump 2
초등영어 리딩이 된다 Start 3		초등영어 리딩이 된다 Basic 2		초등영어 리딩이 된다 Jump 3
초등영어 리딩이 된다 Start 4		초등영어 리딩이 된다 Basic 3		초등영어 리딩이 된다 Jump 4
		초등영어 리딩이 된다 Basic 4		주니어 리딩튜터 스타터 2

초6-예비중	중1	중1-2	중2-3	중3
주니어 리딩튜터 1	1316 Reading 1	1316 Reading 2	1316 Reading 3	리딩튜터 입문
Junior Reading Expert 1	주니어 리딩튜터 2	주니어 리딩튜터 3	주니어 리딩튜터 4	정말 기특한 구문독해 완성
Reading Forward Basic 1	Junior Reading Expert 2	정말 기특한 구문독해 입문	정말 기특한 구문독해 기본	Reading Forward Advanced 1
	Reading Forward Basic 2	Junior Reading Expert 3	Junior Reading Expert 4	열중 16강 독해+문법 3
	열중 16강 독해+문법 1	Reading Forward Intermediate 1	Reading Forward Intermediate 2	Reading Inside 3
	Reading Inside Starter	열중 16강 독해+문법 2	Reading Inside 2	
		Reading Inside 1		

중3-예비고	고1	고1-2	고2-3, 수능 실전	고3 이상, 수능 고난도
Reading Expert 1	빠바 기초세우기	빠바 구문독해	빠바 유형독해	Reading Expert 5
리딩튜터 기본	리딩튜터 실력	리딩튜터 수능 PLUS	빠바 종합실전편	능률 고급영문독해
Reading Forward Advanced 2	Reading Expert 2	Reading Expert 3	Reading Expert 4	
	TEPS BY STEP G+R Basic		TEPS BY STEP G+R 1	

수능 이상/ 토플 80-89· 텝스 600-699점	수능 이상/ 토플 90-99· 텝스 700-799점	수능 이상/ 토플 100· 텝스 800점 이상		
ADVANCED Reading Expert 1	ADVANCED Reading Expert 2	RADIX TOEFL Black Label Reading 2		
TEPS BY STEP G+R 2	RADIX TOEFL Black Label Reading 1	TEPS BY STEP G+R 3		
RADIX TOEFL Blue Label Reading 1, 2				

READING Inside

workbook

LEVEL 3

A 4-level curriculum
integration reading course

NE_ Neungyule

Workbook

READING
Inside

LEVEL 3

VOCABULARY TEST 1

반 / 이름:

[01-30] 다음 단어의 뜻을 쓰시오.

01 adaptation _____

02 century _____

03 community _____

04 coral reef _____

05 creativity _____

06 poem _____

07 depth _____

08 develop _____

09 drift _____

10 environment _____

11 heritage _____

12 honor _____

13 intend _____

14 light _____

15 conservation _____

16 narrow _____

17 nearly _____

18 nomad _____

19 peacefully _____

20 physical _____

21 prepare _____

22 relatively _____

23 represent _____

24 responsibility _____

25 species _____

26 traditionally _____

27 trust _____

28 unite _____

29 unity _____

30 vision _____

[31-40] 다음 뜻을 지닌 단어를 쓰시오.

31 상의하다; 논하다 _____

32 기념하다, 축하하다 _____

33 바다의[해양의] _____

34 민족의[종족의] _____

35 학자 _____

36 원칙 _____

37 선호하다 _____

38 세대 _____

39 묘사하다 _____

40 가치 _____

[41-44] 다음 숙어의 뜻을 쓰시오.

41 care about _____

42 adapt to _____

43 be proud of _____

44 as well _____

A 다음 단어의 영영풀이를 바르게 연결하시오.

1 celebrate •   • ⓐ to do something on a special day

2 float   •   • ⓑ a basic law or rule that is followed by people

3 ethnic   •   • ⓒ to talk about something

4 discuss •   • ⓓ related to a certain race or people

5 principle •   • ⓔ to stay or move on the surface of a liquid

B 다음 밑줄 친 단어와 의미가 유사한 단어를 고르시오.

1 I don't intend to stay here very long.

　　ⓐ resist　　　　ⓑ order　　　　ⓒ refuse　　　　ⓓ adapt　　　　ⓔ plan

2 She prefers traveling by train.

　　ⓐ depends　　　ⓑ favors　　　ⓒ prepares　　　ⓓ demands　　　ⓔ hates

3 We should unite in order to win this game.

　　ⓐ give up　　　ⓑ share　　　ⓒ honor　　　ⓓ cooperate　　　ⓔ separate

C 우리말과 같은 뜻이 되도록 빈칸에 들어갈 말을 보기 에서 찾아 알맞은 형태로 쓰시오.

보기　　care about　　　adapt to　　　be proud of　　　as well

1 네 부모님은 너의 시험 결과를 자랑스러워하실 것이다.

　▶ Your parents will _____ your exam results.

2 우리는 이 새로운 환경에 적응해야 했다.

　▶ We had to _____ this new environment.

3 나는 그들이 나에 대해서 말했던 것에 신경 쓰지 않는다.

　▶ I don't _____ what they said about me.

4 그녀의 조언은 아이들에게뿐만 아니라 어른들에게도 역시 도움이 된다.

　▶ Her advice is helpful to children and to adults _____.

A 다음 두 문장이 같은 뜻이 되도록 빈칸에 알맞은 말을 쓰시오.

1 To plan your trip in advance is important.

▶ _____ is important _____ _____ your trip in advance.

2 To go shopping with Emily is always fun.

▶ _____ is always fun _____ _____ shopping with Emily.

3 To read novels in English is difficult.

▶ _____ is difficult _____ _____ novels in English.

4 To swim right after eating could be dangerous.

▶ _____ could be dangerous _____ _____ right after eating.

B 다음 문장에서 진목적어에 밑줄을 친 후, 문장 전체를 해석하시오.

1 She thinks it impossible to build a boat in a week.

▶ _____

2 Roy believes it worthwhile to help the poor.

▶ _____

3 The man made it a rule to exercise every day.

▶ _____

4 I consider it my duty to take care of my family.

▶ _____

C 밑줄 친 부분을 어법에 맞게 고쳐 쓰시오.

1 It is always fun <u>listen</u> to his jokes.

2 I think <u>that</u> impossible to talk to him without yelling.

3 She found it interesting <u>play</u> chess with him.

4 It might be strange <u>to giving</u> him a toy as a gift.

A 우리말과 일치하도록 (   ) 안에 주어진 말을 알맞게 배열하시오.

1 그들은 콴자라고 불리는 휴일을 기념한다. (called, celebrate, a holiday)

▶ They _____ Kwanzaa.

2 그는 사람들이 자신들의 유산에 관심을 갖길 원했다.

(to, people, wanted, care about)

▶ He _____ their heritage.

3 그는 '수확'을 뜻하는 스와힐리어로 그 휴일의 이름을 지었다.

(named, a Swahili word, with, the holiday)

▶ He _____ that means "harvest."

4 그들은 바다를 자신들의 집이라 부른다. (call, their home, the ocean)

▶ They _____.

5 물고기를 사냥할 때, 그들은 수심이 깊은 곳에 맨몸으로 다이빙할 수 있다.

(for, hunting, fish, when)

▶ _____, they can free dive to great depths.

B 우리말과 일치하도록 (   ) 안의 말을 이용하여 문장을 완성하시오.

1 당신은 산호초 사이에서 떠다니는 배를 찾을 수 있다. (float)

▶ You can find the boats _____ among the coral reefs.

2 그들은 심지어 해양 환경에 맞는 신체적 적응들을 발달시켜 왔다. (develop)

▶ They _____ even _____ physical adaptations to marine environments.

3 그들은 바다에서 사는 것을 매우 힘들다고 생각한다. (find, live)

▶ They _____ _____ too difficult _____ _____ at sea.

4 아프리카의 기념일들을 조사한 후에, 그는 이 휴일을 만들었다. (research)

▶ _____ _____ African celebrations, he created the holiday.

5 이 휴일은 그들이 유산을 기리도록 돕는 좋은 방법이 되어 오고 있다. (become, help)

▶ This holiday _____ _____ a great way _____ _____ them honor

their heritage.

VOCABULARY TEST 1

반 / 이름:

[01-30] 다음 단어의 뜻을 쓰시오.

01 alchemist _____

02 attract _____

03 chemistry _____

04 construct _____

05 cure _____

06 development _____

07 element _____

08 essential _____

09 establish _____

10 eternal _____

11 financial _____

12 illness _____

13 influence _____

14 interest _____

15 iron _____

16 legend _____

17 medieval _____

18 modern _____

19 myth _____

20 ordinary _____

21 owner _____

22 period _____

23 philosopher _____

24 possible _____

25 practice _____

26 proportion _____

27 rise _____

28 sponsor _____

29 supporter _____

30 transform _____

[31-40] 다음 뜻을 지닌 단어를 쓰시오.

31 글, 문서 _____

32 고대의 _____

33 금속 _____

34 시작 _____

35 주인; 대가(大家) _____

36 우주 _____

37 줄다[감소하다] _____

38 부유한 _____

39 초기의 _____

40 (돈을) 벌다 _____

[41-44] 다음 숙어의 뜻을 쓰시오.

41 be composed of _____

42 focus on _____

43 reach one's peak _____

44 turn A into B _____

VOCABULARY TEST 2

A 다음 단어의 영영풀이를 바르게 연결하시오.

1 eternal •   • ⓐ something that is routinely done as a habit or custom

2 practice •   • ⓑ to receive money as payment for work that you do

3 support •   • ⓒ to set up a business or organization

4 earn •   • ⓓ to help someone succeed

5 establish •   • ⓔ continuing or existing forever

B 다음 빈칸에 들어갈 말을 보기에서 찾아 쓰시오.

> 보기   sponsored   attract   constructed   financial

1 The little girl likes to _____ a lot of attention from people.

2 I lent some money to Janet, who was having _____ problems.

3 My father has _____ students in need for years.

4 The gallery will be _____ in a modern design.

C 우리말과 같은 뜻이 되도록 빈칸에 들어갈 말을 보기에서 찾아 알맞은 형태로 쓰시오.

> 보기   turn A into B   reach one's peak   be composed of   focus on

1 너는 네 장기적인 목표에 집중할 필요가 있다.
  ▶ You need to _____ your long-term goal.

2 마술사는 그 돼지를 토끼로 바꾸었다.
  ▶ The magician _____ the pig _____ a rabbit.

3 테니스 선수로서, 그녀는 아직 그녀의 정점에 이르지 못했다.
  ▶ As a tennis player, she hasn't _____ yet.

4 아기의 몸은 75퍼센트의 물로 구성되어 있다.
  ▶ A baby's body _____ 75% water.

A 다음 문장에서 주어에 밑줄을 친 후, 문장 전체를 해석하시오.

1 What I want to do is shop in that shopping mall.

▶ _____

2 Drinking coffee is what I do first in the morning.

▶ _____

3 The girl on the bench is my older sister.

▶ _____

4 Reading books to kids is one of my favorite things.

▶ _____

5 The woman wearing a yellow dress is my mother.

▶ _____

6 Playing soccer with my friends is exciting.

▶ _____

7 The boy that talked to me was Mike's son.

▶ _____

B 다음 문장에서 목적어에 밑줄을 친 후, 문장 전체를 해석하시오.

1 Does she know that we will go camping without her?

▶ _____

2 I wonder whether Sam is interested in movies.

▶ _____

3 The woman liked the cake that was made by her husband.

▶ _____

4 Do you remember where you put your keys?

▶ _____

5 I like collecting foreign coins.

▶ _____

6 My mom thought that I was at the beach.

▶ _____

WRITING TEST

A 우리말과 일치하도록 (   ) 안에 주어진 말을 알맞게 배열하시오.

1 세계의 초창기 과학자들 중 많은 사람들은 그것이 가능하다고 믿었다.

(believed, early scientists, was, it, possible)

▶ Many of the world's _____.

2 그 돌은 질병을 치료하는 힘을 가졌다고 여겨졌다.

(had, it, the power, believed, the stone, was, that)

▶ _____ to cure illnesses.

3 예술가들은 재정적 후원자의 도움을 필요로 했다.

(needed, artists, the help, of)

▶ _____ financial supporters.

4 그들은 학자들이 고전 문헌들을 연구하도록 도왔다.

(helped, study, ancient texts, scholars)

▶ They _____.

B 우리말과 일치하도록 (   ) 안의 말을 이용하여 문장을 완성하시오.

1 이런 일이 일어나게 하기 위해서, 특별한 어떤 것이 필요했다. (make, happen)

▶ _____ _____ it _____, something special was needed.

2 그 돌은 평범한 금속을 값비싼 것들로 바꿀 수 있었다. (able, change)

▶ The stone _____ _____ _____ _____ ordinary metals into expensive ones.

3 그들은 돈에 관한 걱정 없이 자신들의 작업에 집중할 수 있었다. (worry about)

▶ They could focus on their work _____ _____ _____ money.

4 그들의 예술에 대한 사랑이 없었다면, 오늘날 예술의 역사는 달라져 있을 것이다. (would)

▶ _____ their love for arts, the history of the arts _____ _____ different today.

5 고대 이집트와 중국에서 비롯된 후, 이 독특한 관행은 중세 유럽에서 절정에 달했다. (come from)

▶ _____ _____ ancient Egypt and China, this unique practice reached its peak in Medieval Europe.

VOCABULARY TEST 1

반 / 이름:

[01-30] 다음 단어의 뜻을 쓰시오.

01 mosque _____

02 elegant _____

03 mix _____

04 depict _____

05 artwork _____

06 pentagon _____

07 combine _____

08 aquarium _____

09 rival _____

10 agriculture _____

11 fertilizer _____

12 elegant _____

13 population _____

14 decade _____

15 rotate _____

16 complex _____

17 lay _____

18 geometric _____

19 describe _____

20 infinite _____

21 represent _____

22 several _____

23 fade _____

24 disappear _____

25 oxygen _____

26 behavior _____

27 produce _____

28 algae _____

29 unusual _____

30 moss _____

[31-40] 다음 뜻을 지닌 단어를 쓰시오.

31 천장 _____

32 궁전 _____

33 패턴; 무늬 _____

34 반복하다 _____

35 자연; 본성, 본질 _____

36 민물의[담수의] _____

37 사실상 _____

38 헝클어진, 뒤얽힌 _____

39 형성하다 _____

40 가라앉다 _____

[41-44] 다음 숙어의 뜻을 쓰시오.

41 in particular _____

42 side by side _____

43 give off _____

44 block out _____

VOCABULARY TEST 2

A 다음 단어의 영영풀이를 바르게 연결하시오.

1 complex •

• ⓐ to move or turn something in a circle

2 rotate •

• ⓑ to become less in number or amount

3 sink •

• ⓒ having a lot of details and small parts

4 decrease •

• ⓓ to move down below the surface of water

B 다음 빈칸에 들어갈 말을 보기에서 찾아 쓰시오.

| 보기 | depicts | fade | infinite | repeat | rival |

1 Our memories of childhood _____ as we grow older.

2 Mothers' love for their children is _____.

3 The boy promised not to _____ his bad behavior.

4 This movie _____ two women suffering from their past.

5 We beat the _____ team two to one.

C 우리말과 같은 뜻이 되도록 빈칸에 들어갈 말을 보기에서 찾아 알맞은 형태로 쓰시오.

| 보기 | block out | in particular | side by side | give off |

1 그는 특별히 누군가를 비난하지 않았다.
   ▶ He didn't blame anyone _____.

2 두 절친한 친구는 나란히 앉기를 원했다.
   ▶ The two best friends wanted to sit _____.

3 창문 앞의 나무가 태양을 차단한다.
   ▶ The tree in front of the window _____ the sun.

4 그 쓰레기가 불쾌한 냄새를 내뿜었다.
   ▶ The trash _____ an unpleasant smell.

GRAMMAR TEST

A 다음 ( ) 안의 단어를 빈칸에 알맞은 형태로 쓰시오.

1 Patrick will continue _____ students. (teach)

2 I'll never forget _____ the president last year. (meet)

3 Mike tries hard _____ close to his son. (be)

4 You should remember _____ off the light before going to bed. (turn)

5 Karen began _____ to lose some weight. (exercise)

B 우리말과 같은 뜻이 되도록 할 때, <u>틀린</u> 부분을 찾아 바르게 고쳐 쓰시오.

1 내 생각에 너는 좀 더 신중했어야 했다.

▶ I think you might have been more careful.

2 크리스가 그녀에게 사과했을 리가 없다.

▶ Chris should have apologized to her.

3 밤에 비가 왔음에 틀림없다.

▶ It can't have rained during the night.

4 그는 이미 집에 갔을지도 모른다.

▶ He must have gone home already.

5 너는 그들이 한 말을 믿지 말았어야 했다.

▶ You can't have believed what they said.

C 어법상 <u>어색한</u> 곳을 찾아 바르게 고쳐 쓰시오.

1 I won't forget to dance with you last night.

2 I remember to write a letter to you when I was a kid.

3 Zoey was late again. She should have get up earlier.

4 She isn't answering my call. She might has went to bed already.

A 우리말과 일치하도록 ( ) 안에 주어진 말을 알맞게 배열하시오.

1 당신은 고급스러운 무늬로 뒤덮인 천장을 발견할 것이다.

(ceilings, elegant, covered, find, in, patterns)

▶ You'll _____ .

2 이슬람 미술에서 반복되는 기하학적 모형은 깊은 뜻이 있다.

(repeating, shapes, geometric)

▶ _____ in Islamic art have a deep meaning.

3 이슬람 예술가들은 삼각형, 사각형, 오각형과 같은 모형을 사용하여 아름다움을 보여주려고 한다.

(to, beauty, by, show, try)

▶ Islamic artists _____ using shapes such as triangles, squares, and pentagons.

4 당신은 녹색 벨벳 같은 공들이 물에 떠다니는 것을 봤을지도 모른다.

(may, velvety balls, some, green, have, seen)

▶ You _____ floating in the water.

5 이 작은 특이한 공들은 마리모 모스볼로 알려져 있는데, (이것들은) 사실 이끼가 아니다.

(as, Marimo, moss balls, known)

▶ _____ , these small unusual balls are not actually moss.

B 우리말과 일치하도록 ( ) 안의 말을 이용하여 문장을 완성하시오.

1 그 예술가들은 멋진 무늬를 개발하는 것을 자랑스러워한다. (proud, develop)

▶ The artists _____ _____ _____ _____ wonderful patterns.

2 미술은 사람들이 어떻게 세상을 보는지를 나타내는 방법이다. (see)

▶ Art is a way to represent _____ _____ _____ the world.

3 당신은 그것들이 낮에는 떠 있고 밤에는 가라앉는다는 것을 알아챘을지도 모른다. (might, notice)

▶ You _____ _____ _____ _____ they float during the day and sink at night.

4 마리모 볼은 수십 년 전에는 찾아보기 쉬웠다. (easy, find)

▶ Marimo balls _____ _____ _____ _____ several decades ago.

VOCABULARY TEST 1

반 / 이름:

[01-30] 다음 단어의 뜻을 쓰시오.

01 volcano _____

02 breathtaking _____

03 landscape _____

04 local _____

05 legend _____

06 wizard _____

07 spread _____

08 control _____

09 mineral _____

10 spirit _____

11 bravely _____

12 grand _____

13 material _____

14 lava _____

15 ingredient _____

16 battlefield _____

17 match _____

18 resident _____

19 form _____

20 erupt _____

21 drive _____

22 engine _____

23 electricity _____

24 factory _____

25 draw _____

26 attraction _____

27 shape _____

28 overcome _____

29 melt _____

30 cover _____

[31-40] 다음 뜻을 지닌 단어를 쓰시오.

31 화산의 _____

32 영양분 _____

33 제품; 산물 _____

34 마그마 _____

35 귀중한[소중한] _____

36 빙하 _____

37 (화산의) 폭발, 분화 _____

38 지하의 _____

39 활동적인, 활발한 _____

40 이국적인 _____

[41-45] 다음 숙어의 뜻을 쓰시오.

41 bubble up _____

42 turn into _____

43 provide A with B _____

44 fall in love with _____

45 according to _____

A 단어의 첫 철자를 참조하여 다음 정의에 해당하는 단어를 쓰시오.

1 to cover a large area   s_____

2 located beneath the earth's surface   u_____

3 to explode and send smoke and fire into the sky e_____

4 a type of energy used to produce heat, light, or power e_____

5 to change from a solid substance into a liquid   m_____

B 다음 밑줄 친 단어와 의미가 유사한 단어를 고르시오.

1 I drove slowly down the road to enjoy the landscape.
ⓐ weather   ⓑ status   ⓒ scenery   ⓓ country   ⓔ screen

2 Look at the huge statue in the center of the town.
ⓐ gigantic   ⓑ stylish   ⓒ costly   ⓓ modern   ⓔ tiny

3 The benefits of this system include faster production and better efficiency.
ⓐ harms   ⓑ problems   ⓒ advantages   ⓓ operations   ⓔ disadvantages

C 우리말과 같은 뜻이 되도록 빈칸에 들어갈 말을 보기에서 찾아 알맞은 형태로 쓰시오.

| 보기 | turn into | provide A with B | according to | bubble up |

1 한 기자에 의하면, 그 정치인은 선거에 출마할 것이라고 한다.
▶ _____ a reporter, the politician will run in the election.

2 콜라를 흔들지 마! 네가 그것을 열 때 거품이 솟을 거야.
▶ Don't shake the cola! It will _____ when you open it.

3 저희 매장은 고객들에게 최상의 서비스를 제공하기 위해 노력합니다.
▶ Our shop tries to _____ customers _____ the best service.

4 늑대 인간은 늑대로 변할 수 있는 인간이다.
▶ A werewolf is a human that can _____ a wolf.

A 다음 ( ) 안의 단어를 알맞은 형태로 쓰시오.

1 He is one of the _____ boys on his soccer team. (healthy)

2 The more I exercise, the _____ I feel. (good)

3 Can you make this soup as _____ as possible? (hot)

4 As days passed, his room got _____ and _____. (dirty)

5 Chris is the _____ man I've ever met. (funny)

6 The _____ I wake up, the faster I can get to school. (early)

B 다음 문장의 밑줄 친 부분이 다음 중 어떤 의미로 쓰였는지 보기 에서 골라 쓰시오.

보기 완료   경험   계속   결과

1 The library <u>had</u> already <u>closed</u> when I got there. _____

2 Mike <u>had broken</u> his leg, so he couldn't play baseball. _____

3 Sarah <u>had worked</u> as a reporter for 35 years by the time she retired. _____

4 I <u>had never met</u> Ben until I saw him at the school festival. _____

5 Brian <u>had lost</u> his tennis racket, so he couldn't play tennis yesterday. _____

C 밑줄 친 부분을 어법에 맞게 고쳐 쓰시오.

1 Jess <u>has never baked</u> a cake until she took a cooking class with me.

2 Yesterday, I lost the wallet that Lucy <u>has given</u> to me.

3 The <u>most</u> you laugh, the healthier you will get.

4 This is one of <u>the expensive dessert</u> in the restaurant.

5 Cathy <u>has done</u> her homework before she went out.

6 Try to walk as carefully <u>than</u> possible.

A 우리말과 일치하도록 ( ) 안에 주어진 말을 알맞게 배열하시오.

1 얼음은 아이슬란드를 형성하고 있는 또 다른 자연의 힘이다.

(is, Iceland, shaping, that)

▶ Ice is another natural force _____.

2 그것은 당신이 마법을 믿도록 할 것이다.

(make, believe, in, will, you)

▶ It _____ magic.

3 그는 그 섬의 요정들에 의해 저지되었다.

(stopped, he, by, was)

▶ _____ the island's spirits.

4 메라피 산은 세계적으로 가장 활발한 화산들 중 하나이다.

(of, the world's, is, active, most, volcanoes, one)

▶ Mount Merapi _____.

5 왜 그렇게 많은 사람이 그토록 위험한 곳 근처에 거주하는 것일까?

(dangerous, near, so, something, live)

▶ Why would so many people _____?

B 우리말과 일치하도록 ( ) 안의 말을 이용하여 문장을 완성하시오.

1 거주민들은 자신들이 고대의 땅을 발견했다고 믿었다. (find)

▶ The residents thought they _____ _____ an ancient land.

2 모든 화산들 중 그림스뵈튼 화산이 가장 활발하다. (active)

▶ Of all the volcanoes, Grímsvötn is _____ _____ _____.

3 사람들은 지하 마그마로 데워진 증기를 사용한다. (heat)

▶ People use steam _____ _____ underground magma.

4 관광객들은 검은 모래가 화산암으로 만들어진 해변을 방문할 수 있다. (make, from, volcanic rocks)

▶ Tourists can visit beaches whose black sand _____ _____ _____

_____ _____.

VOCABULARY TEST 1

반 / 이름:

[01-30] 다음 단어의 뜻을 쓰시오.

01 architecture _____

02 artificial _____

03 attention _____

04 brilliant _____

05 capture _____

06 complete _____

07 construction _____

08 crisis _____

09 curved _____

10 incident _____

11 essential _____

12 feature _____

13 smoothly _____

14 innovative _____

15 lessen _____

16 nickname _____

17 ordinary _____

18 pedestrian _____

19 pollution _____

20 practical _____

21 pressure _____

22 primary _____

23 disaster _____

24 appearance _____

25 chilly _____

26 shade _____

27 importance _____

28 unusual _____

29 government _____

30 flooding _____

[31-40] 다음 뜻을 지닌 단어를 쓰시오.

31 저장[보관]하다 _____

32 (건물의) 층 _____

33 파괴하다 _____

34 전기, 전력 _____

35 지방의, 지역의 _____

36 위협하다 _____

37 외딴, 고립된 _____

38 모양, 형태 _____

39 농업의 _____

40 보호하다 _____

[41-44] 다음 숙어의 뜻을 쓰시오.

41 add A to B _____

42 due to _____

43 in harmony with _____

44 over time _____

A 다음 단어의 영영풀이를 바르게 연결하시오.

1 incident •

2 pedestrian •

3 artificial •

4 pressure •

5 government •

• ⓐ an event that is either unpleasant or unusual

• ⓑ the group of people who officially control a country

• ⓒ the force created by pressing on or against something

• ⓓ unnatural; produced by humans

• ⓔ a person walking on the street

B 다음 밑줄 친 단어와 의미가 유사한 단어를 고르시오.

1 People were sad to see the <u>destroyed</u> houses.

ⓐ protected   ⓑ unique   ⓒ weak   ⓓ damaged   ⓔ clean

2 Providing free education is their <u>primary</u> goal.

ⓐ useful   ⓑ usual   ⓒ main   ⓓ illegal   ⓔ hopeless

3 The police are investigating the <u>incident</u> that happened last week.

ⓐ occurrence   ⓑ issue   ⓒ crime   ⓓ accident   ⓔ competition

C 우리말과 같은 뜻이 되도록 빈칸에 들어갈 말을 보기에서 찾아 알맞은 형태로 쓰시오.

| 보기 | due to | in harmony with | over time | add A to B |

1 우리 가족은 이웃과 사이좋게 산다.

▶ My family lives _____ our neighbors.

2 시간이 지나면서, 당신의 부러진 발목이 나을 것이다.

▶ _____, your broken ankle will get better.

3 왜 당신의 사진을 이력서에 추가하지 않았나요?

▶ Why didn't you _____ your picture _____ your résumé?

4 그 화재 때문에, 그들은 집을 잃었다.

▶ _____ the fire, they lost their house.

A 다음 ( ) 안에서 알맞은 것을 고르시오.

1 He was seen (singing, to singing) by his classmates.

2 I was made (cook, to cook) by my brother.

3 The traffic is expected (to be, being) heavy this weekend.

4 David was heard (yell, yelling) at his friends by his mom.

5 We were not allowed (to pick, picking) those flowers.

6 The children were asked (stopped, to stop) talking.

B ( ) 안의 말을 이용하여 문장을 완성하시오.

1 Dad lets me _____ games for 30 minutes a day. (play)

2 My brother asked me _____ him a spoon. (give)

3 I heard Kate _____ my name upstairs. (call)

4 Her parents wanted her _____ a pilot. (become)

5 The detective was secretly watching me _____. (work)

6 The website advises people _____ certain books. (pick)

C 밑줄 친 부분을 어법에 맞게 고쳐 쓰시오.

1 Did you see Sean to score a goal?

2 I had my wisdom teeth pull out.

3 I let my cat lied on my belly.

4 The owner had the store remodeling.

5 We were allowed for using the tent here.

6 Sandra will be made clean her room by her mother.

A 우리말과 일치하도록 ( ) 안에 주어진 말을 알맞게 배열하시오.

1 그 저장고는 홍수로부터 보호된다. (is, from, protected, flooding)

▶ The vault _____.

2 그 저장고는 2015년에 최초로 개방되었다. (opened, for, was, time, the first)

▶ The vault _____ in 2015.

3 그것은 대기 오염을 줄이면서 건물에 그늘을 제공할 것이다.

(reducing, while, air pollution)

▶ It will provide shade for the building _____.

4 그 건물은 런던 사람들에 의해 별칭이 붙었다.

(the nickname, was, by, given, Londoners)

▶ The building _____.

5 과학자들은 그 저장고 측에서 그들이 필요로 했던 주요 종자들을 그들에게 보내주기를 원했다.

(send, them, to, the vault, wanted)

▶ The scientists _____ the essential seeds

they needed.

B 우리말과 일치하도록 ( ) 안의 말을 이용하여 문장을 완성하시오.

1 가장 특이한 건물들 중 하나가 2004년에 완공되었다. (unusual, building)

▶ _____ _____ _____ _____ _____ _____ was completed in

2004.

2 그것들은 저장고가 종자들을 얼린 상태로 유지하기에 충분히 차갑도록 만들어준다. (cold, keep)

▶ They make the vault _____ _____ _____ _____ the seeds frozen.

3 그것은 최대 50퍼센트까지의 에너지를 절감할 것으로 예상된다. (expect)

▶ _____ _____ _____ _____ use up to 50% less energy.

4 건축된 이후로, 그 건물은 많은 관심을 받아 오고 있다. (receive)

▶ Since its construction, the building _____ _____ a lot of attention.

5 그 건물은 멋진 디자인적인 특징을 가진 것이 분명하다. (clear)

▶ _____ _____ _____ the building also has brilliant design features.

VOCABULARY TEST 1

[01-30] 다음 단어의 뜻을 쓰시오.

01 messenger _____

02 international _____

03 exhaustion _____

04 inspire _____

05 initially _____

06 increase _____

07 demand _____

08 solar _____

09 track _____

10 movement _____

11 follow _____

12 similarly _____

13 define _____

14 complete _____

15 stadium _____

16 royal _____

17 request _____

18 fall _____

19 impress _____

20 referee _____

21 disqualified _____

22 media _____

23 official _____

24 share _____

25 whole _____

26 process _____

27 period _____

28 exactly _____

29 slightly _____

30 extra _____

[31-40] 다음 뜻을 지닌 단어를 쓰시오.

31 거리 _____

32 역사학자 _____

33 승리 _____

34 길이 _____

35 영구적인 _____

36 달력 _____

37 달의 _____

38 주기 _____

39 용어 _____

40 균형을 맞추다 _____

[41-44] 다음 숙어의 뜻을 쓰시오.

41 struggle to-v _____

42 give up _____

43 be known as _____

44 in order to-v _____

VOCABULARY TEST 2

A 단어의 첫 철자를 참조하여 다음 정의에 해당하는 단어를 쓰시오.

1 in an accurate or precise way   e_____

2 lasting or intending to last forever or for a long time   p_____

3 related to or involving two or more countries   i_____

4 a set of actions or events that repeat in the same order   c_____

B 다음 밑줄 친 단어와 의미가 유사한 단어를 고르시오.

1 <u>Initially</u>, he refused to come to my party.

  ⓐ later   ⓑ soon   ⓒ at first   ⓓ depth   ⓔ at last

2 You can <u>request</u> special music or different dance music.

  ⓐ inspire   ⓑ share   ⓒ occupy   ⓓ invite   ⓔ ask for

3 Researchers <u>tracked</u> the progress of each student.

  ⓐ showed   ⓑ reviewed   ⓒ discussed   ⓓ traced   ⓔ described

C 우리말과 같은 뜻이 되도록 빈칸에 들어갈 말을 **보기**에서 찾아 알맞은 형태로 쓰시오.

보기 give up   in order to-v   struggle to-v   be known as

1 나는 그 책을 찾는 데 30분을 썼지만, 결국 포기했다.

  ▶ I spent thirty minutes looking for the book, but eventually I _____.

2 그것은 세계에서 가장 높은 건물로 알려져 있다.

  ▶ It _____ the tallest building in the world.

3 그 부부는 돈을 절약하기 위해 고군분투했다.

  ▶ The couple _____ save money.

4 그는 가족과 저녁 식사를 하기 위해 집에 일찍 왔다.

  ▶ He came home early _____ have dinner with his family.

A 다음 밑줄 친 부분을 생략할 수 있으면 O, 생략할 수 없으면 X 표시하시오.

1 The dinner <u>that</u> we had was great.　　　　　　　(　　)

2 Karen was wearing a dress <u>that was</u> made by her mom.　　(　　)

3 Mr. Donald, <u>who</u> was my neighbor, moved to Chicago.　　(　　)

4 The musician <u>who is</u> singing on the stage is my friend.　　(　　)

5 Bring me the laptop <u>that</u> is on the table.　　　　　(　　)

6 This is an image <u>that is</u> borrowed from the company logo.　(　　)

B 다음 (　) 안에서 알맞은 것을 고르시오.

1 Can you remember (that, what) he said to you?

2 The book (that, what) you gave me was so useful.

3 (That, What) they ate was a little bit salty.

4 No one agreed with (that, what) I said during the discussion.

5 The new device helps blind people see (that, what) others see.

6 Let's think about the problems (that, what) pollution can cause.

C 다음 문장을 우리말로 해석하시오.

1 She couldn't believe what her friends said.

2 Eddie ordered what he needed for the science project.

3 The book I bought yesterday was a gift for Brian.

4 What you said that day gave me hope.

5 She showed me some pictures painted by Jason.

6 It doesn't represent the values that we stand for.

WRITING TEST

A 우리말과 일치하도록 (   ) 안에 주어진 말을 알맞게 배열하시오.

1 그녀는 왕실 자녀들이 집에서 경주를 보길 원했다.

(the royal kids, to, wanted, watch, the race)

▶ She _____ from home.

2 그녀는 관람석 앞에서 경주가 끝나도록 요청했다.

(end, in front of, requested, that, the race)

▶ She _____ the viewing box.

3 그 거리가 어떻게 영구적인 것이 되었는지에 관한 또 다른 이야기가 있다.

(how, became, the distance, about, permanent)

▶ There's another story _____.

4 지구가 태양 주위를 도는 데 걸리는 시간은 태양년으로 알려져 있다.

(to, it, move around, takes, the Earth)

▶ The time _____ the Sun is known as a solar year.

5 각 태음월은 달의 상이 한 주기를 완료하는 데 걸리는 시간으로 정의된다.

(the moon, takes, the time, to complete)

▶ Each lunar month is defined as _____ one cycle of
its phases.

B 우리말과 일치하도록 (   ) 안의 말을 이용하여 문장을 완성하시오.

1 또 다른 주자가 우승자로 지명되었다. (name)

▶ Another runner _____ _____ the winner.

2 1908년 런던 올림픽에서, 그 길이가 오늘날의 것인 42.195킬로미터로 늘어났다. (increase, to)

▶ At the 1908 London Olympics, the length _____ _____ _____ _____
it is today: 42.195 kilometers.

3 'epact'라는 용어는 이 11일간의 차이를 설명하기 위해 사용되었다. (use, describe)

▶ The term "epact" _____ _____ _____ _____ this 11-day difference.

4 양력에는 4년마다 2월에 추가된 '윤일(閏日)'이 있다. (add, to)

▶ On the solar calendar, there is a "leap day" _____ _____ the month of
February every four years.

VOCABULARY TEST 1

반 / 이름:

[01-30] 다음 단어의 뜻을 쓰시오.

01 breathless _____

02 originate _____

03 hunting _____

04 evolve _____

05 occupy _____

06 attacker _____

07 opponent _____

08 snorkeling _____

09 underwater _____

10 discover _____

11 especially _____

12 popular _____

13 area _____

14 creature _____

15 escape _____

16 tag _____

17 chant _____

18 continuously _____

19 equipment _____

20 surface _____

21 breathe _____

22 effective _____

23 championship _____

24 competitive _____

25 participant _____

26 length _____

27 global _____

28 side _____

29 hollow _____

30 characteristic _____

[31-40] 다음 뜻을 지닌 단어를 쓰시오.

31 방어, 수비 _____

32 폐 _____

33 반[절반] _____

34 숨을 들이마시다 _____

35 경험하다 _____

36 야생 동물 _____

37 열대의 _____

38 탐험하다 _____

39 산소 _____

40 현대의 _____

[41-45] 다음 숙어의 뜻을 쓰시오.

41 take turns _____

42 take a breath _____

43 take a break _____

44 a wide variety of _____

45 compared to _____

A 다음 단어의 영영풀이를 바르게 연결하시오.

1 succeed •

2 opponent •

3 equipment •

4 length •

5 escape •

• ⓐ someone you are competing against

• ⓑ to achieve a desired result

• ⓒ a measurement of something from one end to the other

• ⓓ to run away from a place or situation

• ⓔ a set of tools or devices needed for a particular purpose

B 다음 빈칸에 들어갈 말을 보기 에서 찾아 쓰시오.

보기	surface	evolve	effective	occupied	inhaled

1 Drawing _____ most of my free time during the summer.

2 To be a good writer, you must _____ your own writing style.

3 The _____ of the pond was covered with yellow leaves.

4 He lay back on the grass and _____ the fresh air.

5 The training was much more _____ than expected.

C 우리말과 같은 뜻이 되도록 빈칸에 들어갈 말을 보기 에서 찾아 알맞은 형태로 쓰시오.

보기	compared to	take turns	take a breath	take a break

1 떨린다면, 숨을 쉬고 다른 것을 생각하도록 해라.
▶ If you feel nervous, try to _____ and think of something else.

2 우리는 교대로 저녁을 만들고 설거지한다.
▶ We _____ making dinner and doing the dishes.

3 휴식을 취할 시간이야! 간식을 좀 먹자.
▶ It's time to _____! Let's have some snacks.

4 지난번 것과 비교하면 오늘의 시험은 아무것도 아니었다.
▶ Today's quiz was nothing _____ the last one.

A 다음 (   ) 안에서 알맞은 것을 고르시오.

1 Far away (flew the birds, the birds flew).

2 Rarely (we do, do we) go to the amusement park.

3 Little (did I, I did) know that he loved me.

4 Never (has she, she has) had this kind of expensive jewelry.

5 Here (the bus comes, comes the bus) that goes downtown.

6 Right around the corner (the store is, is the store) that my dad owns.

B 우리말과 일치하도록 (   ) 안의 말을 이용하여 문장을 완성하시오.

1 그 콘서트는 두 시간을 기다릴 가치가 있었다. (worth, wait)

▶ The concert _____ two hours for.

2 그는 너와 저녁을 먹는 것을 고대하고 있다. (look, have)

▶ He is _____ dinner with you.

3 나는 다른 나라를 혼자 여행하는 것에 익숙하다. (use, travel)

▶ I _____ alone in other countries.

4 우리는 그 사고가 일어나는 것을 막도록 노력했다. (prevent, the accident, occur)

▶ We tried to _____.

C 밑줄 친 부분을 어법에 맞게 고쳐 쓰시오.

1 He didn't see me because he was busy to read.

2 We couldn't help to laugh at his funny jokes.

3 He kept me from talk with his parents.

4 Never I have heard such a funny story.

5 On the top of the hill my friend stood.

A 우리말과 일치하도록 (　) 안에 주어진 말을 알맞게 배열하시오.

1 공격수는 자기 팀으로 돌아오기 전에 숨을 쉬어서는 안 된다.

(a breath, to, getting, before, take, back)

▶ The attacker cannot _____ his or her team's side.

2 만약 공격수가 되풀이하기를 멈추거나 잠깐 쉬면, 그 사람은 경기에서 나가야 한다.

(chanting, or, stops, takes, if, the attacker, a break)

▶ _____, he or she must leave the game.

3 스노클링은 수중 세계를 경험하는 좋은 방법이다.

(experience, is, a, to, great, way)

▶ Snorkeling _____ the underwater world.

4 그것은 사람들이 산호초를 탐험하고 매우 다양한 바다 생물들을 볼 수 있게 해준다.

(explore, allows, it, to, people)

▶ _____ coral reefs and see a wide variety of

sea creatures.

5 그들은 바다 수세미를 채집하는 동안 물속에서 숨을 쉬기 위해 속이 빈 갈대를 사용했다.

(to, while, breathe, underwater, collecting)

▶ They used hollow reeds _____ sea sponges.

B 우리말과 일치하도록 (　) 안의 말을 이용하여 문장을 완성하시오.

1 그들은 교대로 공격수를 상대편 쪽으로 보낸다. (turns, send)

▶ They _____ _____ _____ an attacker into their opponents' half.

2 카바디는 1990년 이래로 아시안 게임에 있어 왔다. (be)

▶ Kabaddi _____ _____ in the Asian Games since 1990.

3 수비수들은 공격수가 그들 쪽에서 달아나는 것을 막으려고 한다. (escape)

▶ The defenders try to prevent the attacker _____ _____ their side.

4 그것은 세계에서 가장 큰 스노클링 행사일 뿐만 아니라, 경쟁을 하는 유일한 행사이기도 하다. (be)

▶ Not only _____ _____ the largest snorkeling event in the world, but

_____ _____ also the only competitive one.

VOCABULARY TEST 1

반 / 이름:

[01-30] 다음 단어의 뜻을 쓰시오.

01 material _____

02 install _____

03 extra _____

04 fully _____

05 frequently _____

06 fluid _____

07 substitute _____

08 billion _____

09 value _____

10 deserve _____

11 recognition _____

12 industry _____

13 accessible _____

14 gender _____

15 promising _____

16 explosion _____

17 aspect _____

18 temperature _____

19 performance _____

20 include _____

21 manage _____

22 electric _____

23 participation _____

24 broad _____

25 environment _____

26 intense _____

27 typically _____

28 major _____

29 competition _____

30 consider _____

[31-40] 다음 뜻을 지닌 단어를 쓰시오.

31 액체 _____

32 흐름 _____

33 이득 _____

34 부정적인 _____

35 공간 _____

36 연습하다 _____

37 인기 _____

38 현상 _____

39 전자의; 전자 장비와 관련된 _____

40 연결하다; 접속하다 _____

[41-44] 다음 숙어의 뜻을 쓰시오.

41 first of all _____

42 be likely to-v _____

43 rather than _____

44 take place _____

VOCABULARY TEST 2

A 다음 단어의 영영풀이를 바르게 연결하시오.

1 limit   •   • ⓐ likely to be successful or have good results

2 physical   •   • ⓑ better than before

3 promising •   • ⓒ having a material existence in the world

4 improved •   • ⓓ to keep something within a particular range

B 다음 빈칸에 들어갈 말을 보기에서 찾아 쓰시오.

보기	accessible	deserves	extra	electric	include

1 They let the kids play a(n) _____ hour.

2 Do you prefer _____ or gas heaters?

3 My hobbies _____ swimming and painting.

4 She _____ praise for all of her hard work.

5 Make sure your service is _____ to everyone who needs it.

C 우리말과 같은 뜻이 되도록 빈칸에 들어갈 말을 보기에서 찾아 알맞은 형태로 쓰시오.

보기	be likely to-v	rather than	first of all	take place

1 표가 곧 매진될 것 같다.
  ▶ The tickets _____ be sold out soon.

2 나는 외식하는 것보다는 요리하는 것을 더 좋아한다.
  ▶ I prefer cooking _____ eating out.

3 우선, 물어보고 싶은 것이 있다.
  ▶ _____, I'd like to ask you something.

4 다음 회의는 다음 달에 열릴 것이다.
  ▶ The next meeting will _____ next month.

A 다음 ( ) 안에서 알맞은 것을 고르시오.

1 She has never left the island (when, where) she was born.

2 I don't know the reason (why, how) Max is angry at me.

3 I am afraid of (scolding, being scolded) by my teacher.

4 Ella feels bad about not (having invited, having been invited) to the party.

B 다음 빈칸에 들어갈 말을 보기에서 찾아 쓰시오. (한 번씩만 쓸 것)

보기	when	how	why	where

1 Let's meet at the restaurant _____ we used to have lunch together.

2 He didn't tell me the reason _____ he left the team.

3 I remember the day _____ you moved in next door.

4 She explained _____ she solved the puzzle so fast.

C 두 문장이 같은 뜻이 되도록 동명사를 이용하여 빈칸에 알맞은 말을 쓰시오.

1 He doesn't mind that he is called a liar by his friends.
  ▶ He doesn't mind _____ a liar by his friends.

2 Mark is proud that he was educated by his parents.
  ▶ Mark is proud of _____ by his parents.

3 She is angry that she was treated rudely.
  ▶ She is angry about _____ rudely.

4 I don't like when I am laughed at.
  ▶ I don't like _____ at.

5 The customers complain that they were served poorly.
  ▶ The customers complain about _____ poorly.

A 우리말과 일치하도록 ( ) 안에 주어진 말을 알맞게 배열하시오.

1 이것은 첫 주요 e스포츠 토너먼트가 열린 해였다.

(the year, this, when, was)

▶ _____ the first major e-sports tournament was held.

2 스트리밍은 e스포츠가 매우 접근하기 쉬운 세 번째 이유이다.

(why, third, reason, is, a, e-sports)

▶ Streaming _____ is so accessible.

3 더 많은 리튬 이온 전지가 기계를 작동시키기 위해 기업들에 의해 사용되고 있다.

(used, being, companies, by, are)

▶ More lithium-ion batteries _____ for powering our machines.

4 그 안의 액체는 그것들을 상당히 무겁게 만드는 경향이 있다.

(to, make, tends, heavy, them, quite)

▶ The liquid inside of them _____.

5 전고체 전지는 배터리 수명을 늘릴 물질을 위한 공간이 더 많다.

(that, materials, battery life, increase)

▶ Solid-state batteries have more space for _____.

B 우리말과 일치하도록 ( ) 안의 말을 이용하여 문장을 완성하시오.

1 전고체 전지는 자주 충전될 필요가 없다. (have to, recharge)

▶ Solid-state batteries _____ _____ _____ _____ _____ frequently.

2 그것들은 손상 없이 오랫동안 사용될 수 있다. (without, damage)

▶ They can be used for a long time _____ _____ _____.

3 비디오 게임은 다른 스포츠보다 더 연습하기 쉽다. (easy)

▶ Video games _____ _____ to practice _____ other sports.

4 당신은 게임 시스템과 인터넷에 연결할 수 있는 장소만 있으면 된다. (a place, can)

▶ All you need is a gaming system and _____ _____ _____ _____ _____ connect to the internet.

[01-30] 다음 단어의 뜻을 쓰시오.

01 ecological _____

02 threat _____

03 biologist _____

04 chemical _____

05 surface _____

06 abandon _____

07 affect _____

08 rescue _____

09 barely _____

10 gene _____

11 occur _____

12 wild _____

13 breed _____

14 rest _____

15 absorb _____

16 amount _____

17 increase _____

18 concern _____

19 decrease _____

20 reduce _____

21 available _____

22 relationship _____

23 endangered _____

24 protect _____

25 clear _____

26 trick _____

27 marketing _____

28 purpose _____

29 coat _____

30 birth _____

[31-40] 다음 뜻을 지닌 단어를 쓰시오.

31 ~에 직면하다 _____

32 부족, 결핍 _____

33 철; 철분 _____

34 바다의[해양의] _____

35 생태계 _____

36 사유의[개인 소유의] _____

37 유전의 _____

38 보통의, 정상적인 _____

39 (동물원) 사육사 _____

40 제거하다 _____

[41-45] 다음 숙어의 뜻을 쓰시오.

41 suffer from _____

42 a number of _____

43 stay away _____

44 be essential to _____

45 over and over (again) _____

A 다음 단어의 영영풀이를 바르게 연결하시오.

1 threat •   • ⓐ the people or things that remain; the others

2 absorb •   • ⓑ something that can cause danger or harm

3 surface •   • ⓒ to happen or be found to exist

4 rest •   • ⓓ to take in something

5 occur •   • ⓔ the outer layer of something

B 다음 빈칸에 들어갈 말을 보기에서 찾아 쓰시오.

| 보기 | trick | reduce | private | lack | endangered |

1 We need to protect _____ animals.

2 The new law will help _____ the number of traffic accidents.

3 He tried to _____ me into buying the watch.

4 The family owned a(n) _____ farm near the city.

5 His only problem is a(n) _____ of experience.

C 우리말과 같은 뜻이 되도록 빈칸에 들어갈 말을 보기에서 찾아 알맞은 형태로 쓰시오.

| 보기 | stay away | a number of | suffer from | over and over |

1 비가 많이 오는 해에는, 그 나라의 농장들이 홍수로 고통받는다.

  ▶ During rainy years, the farms in the countries often _____ floods.

2 너는 물가에서 떨어져 있을 필요가 있다.

  ▶ You need to _____ from the water.

3 아이들은 계속해서 같은 질문을 반복하여 묻는다.

  ▶ Children keep asking the same questions _____.

4 우리는 그 회의에서 많은 문제를 논의했다.

  ▶ We discussed _____ issues at the meeting.

A 다음 문장을 분사구문으로 바꾸어 쓰시오.

1 While I was walking to school, I saw a beautiful rainbow.

▶ _____ _____ _____, I saw a beautiful rainbow.

2 Because he was angry, he didn't say a word to me.

▶ _____ _____, he didn't say a word to me.

3 After she finished her homework, she watched TV.

▶ After _____ _____ _____, she watched TV.

B 다음 우리말과 일치하도록 주어진 단어를 빈칸에 알맞은 형태로 바꿔 쓰시오.

1 그는 마치 그가 우리 아버지인 것처럼 말한다. (be)

▶ He talks as if he _____ my father.

2 그녀는 마치 그녀가 그 대회에 나갔던 것처럼 행동한다. (enter)

▶ She acts as if she _____ the contest.

3 그들은 마치 그들이 그 사고를 봤던 것처럼 말한다. (see)

▶ They speak as if they _____ the accident.

4 샘은 마치 그가 파티에 있는 모든 사람을 아는 것처럼 행동했다. (know)

▶ Sam acted as if he _____ everyone at the party.

C 다음 문장을 우리말로 해석하시오.

1 She talks as if she had been to New York.

▶ _____

2 He acted as if he hadn't heard the news.

▶ _____

3 Sitting on her seat, she gave me a smile.

▶ _____

4 Turning off his computer, he went out for dinner.

▶ _____

A 우리말과 일치하도록 ( ) 안에 주어진 말을 알맞게 배열하시오.

1 그것들 중의 하나가 고래 배설물의 부족임을 아는 사람은 거의 없다.

(them, a lack of, one, of, is)

▶ Few people know that _____ whale poop.

2 고래는 배설하기 위해 수면 위로 헤엄쳐 오른다.

(to the surface, swim, to, up, poop)

▶ Whales _____.

3 호랑이는 그 유전자를 만들어내기 위해 교배되고 있다.

(bred, being, produce, to, the gene)

▶ Tigers are _____.

4 케니는 동족 교배로 인한 유전적 문제들로 고통받았다.

(genetic, suffered, caused, problems, from, by)

▶ Kenny _____ inbreeding.

5 나는 사람들이 이런 동물원을 멀리해야 한다고 강력히 제안한다.

(these zoos, people, from, suggest, stay away)

▶ I strongly _____.

B 우리말과 일치하도록 ( ) 안의 말을 이용하여 문장을 완성하시오.

1 고래의 배설물은 기후 변화에 맞서 싸우는 데 필수적이다. (essential, fight)

▶ Whale poop _____ _____ _____ _____ climate change.

2 광합성을 하는 동안, 식물성 플랑크톤은 공기 중에서 엄청난 양의 이산화탄소를 흡수한다.

(while, photosynthesize)

▶ _____ _____, phytoplankton absorb huge amounts of CO_2 from the air.

3 백호는 1951년 이후 야생에서 보이지 않고 있다. (see)

▶ White tigers _____ _____ _____ in the wild since 1951.

4 일부 사육사들은 마치 백호가 멸종 위기에 있는 것처럼 말한다. (talk, be)

▶ Some zookeepers _____ _____ _____ white tigers _____ endangered.

VOCABULARY TEST 1

반 / 이름:

[01-30] 다음 단어의 뜻을 쓰시오.

01 panic _____

02 heartbeat _____

03 fool _____

04 notice _____

05 beginning _____

06 reader _____

07 confidently _____

08 piece _____

09 poem _____

10 admire _____

11 narrator _____

12 smooth _____

13 attractive _____

14 imitate _____

15 board _____

16 scream _____

17 necessary _____

18 convince _____

19 mad _____

20 sweetly _____

21 murderer _____

22 body _____

23 tremble _____

24 fear _____

25 soften _____

26 gentle _____

27 lure _____

28 intense _____

29 sorrowful _____

30 realize _____

[31-40] 다음 뜻을 지닌 단어를 쓰시오.

31 경찰관 _____

32 사악한 _____

33 비밀히, 몰래 _____

34 공격하다 _____

35 세부 사항 _____

36 전설적인 _____

37 구성하다; 작곡하다 _____

38 성격; 등장인물 _____

39 붙잡다[움켜잡다] _____

40 비극적인 _____

[41-44] 다음 숙어의 뜻을 쓰시오.

41 make a noise _____

42 confess to _____

43 continue to-v _____

44 be terrified of _____

A 단어의 첫 철자를 참조하여 다음 정의에 해당하는 단어를 쓰시오.

1 a piece of writing in verse   p_____

2 to respect someone very much   a_____

3 to say or write what someone or something is like   d_____

4 someone who intentionally kills a person   m_____

B 다음 빈칸에 들어갈 말을 보기 에서 찾아 쓰시오.

> 보기   convince   tremble   necessary   emotions   legendary

1 I started to _____ when I thought of the accident.

2 He was a(n) _____ singer in the 1970s.

3 Jessica barely expresses her _____.

4 I had to _____ myself that I could do it.

5 Is it really _____ for me to attend the meeting?

C 우리말과 같은 뜻이 되도록 빈칸에 들어갈 말을 보기 에서 찾아 알맞은 형태로 쓰시오.

> 보기   confess to   make a noise   continue to-v   be terrified of

1 그 아이들은 계속해서 자란다.
   ▶ The children _____ grow.

2 우리는 어두운 곳에 있는 것을 두려워했다.
   ▶ We _____ being in the dark.

3 나는 그 범죄에 관해 아무것도 모른다고 시인해야 한다.
   ▶ I must _____ knowing nothing about the crime.

4 우리는 담요 아래 숨으면서 소리를 내지 않으려 노력했다.
   ▶ We tried not to _____ as we hid under the blankets.

A 다음 밑줄 친 부분이 동명사인지 현재분사인지 쓰시오.

1 They kept me <u>waiting</u> for half an hour.

2 One of my hobbies is <u>taking</u> pictures of flowers.

3 We watched the <u>sleeping</u> puppies for a while.

4 <u>Drinking</u> too much soda can have negative effects on your body.

5 This area is famous for <u>producing</u> some of the best cheeses in the world.

B 다음 문장을 간접 화법으로 바꿀 때 빈칸에 알맞은 말을 쓰시오.

1 Peter asked me, "What are you looking for?"
▶ Peter asked me _____ _____ _____ looking for.

2 Jackie told him, "You are the best drummer."
▶ Jackie told him that _____ _____ the best drummer.

3 Erin asked me, "Did you go to the movies with Mark?"
▶ Erin asked me _____ _____ _____ _____ to the movies with Mark.

4 She told me, "I heard a strange sound at night."
▶ She told me _____ _____ _____ _____ a strange sound at night.

C 다음 문장을 우리말로 해석하시오.

1 Jake finished writing his first novel last night.
▶ _____

2 The boy playing the violin is only six years old.
▶ _____

3 I asked him how he got home that early.
▶ _____

4 He told me that he would help me with my homework.
▶ _____

A 우리말과 일치하도록 ( ) 안에 주어진 말을 알맞게 배열하시오.

1 그는 한 노인을 죽인 것을 자백한다.

(to, killing, an, old, confesses, man)

▶ He _____.

2 그는 경찰이 문을 두드리는 것을 들었다.

(the police, knocking, heard, on)

▶ He _____ his door.

3 그것은 그 노인의 심장 박동 소리처럼 들렸고, 점점 더 커졌다.

(getting, and, louder, kept, louder)

▶ It sounded like the old man's heartbeat, and it _____.

4 그는 각각의 등장인물에게 다른 목소리를 사용했다.

(a, he, different, used, voice)

▶ _____ for each character.

5 아들은 그의 아버지에게 마왕이 두렵다고 이야기한다.

(that, is, he, tells, of, terrified, his father)

▶ The son _____ the Elf-King.

B 우리말과 일치하도록 ( ) 안의 말을 이용하여 문장을 완성하시오.

1 살인자는 자신이 미치지 않았다는 것을 독자에게 확신시키려고 한다. (convince, the reader)

▶ The murderer tries to _____ _____ _____ _____ he is not mad.

2 살인범은 그들을 속이는 것을 즐겼다. (enjoy, fool)

▶ The murderer _____ _____ _____.

3 그는 소년에게 왜 두려워하는지 묻는다. (afraid)

▶ The father asks the boy _____ _____ _____ _____.

4 그는 소년을 꾀어내려 하면서, 상냥하게 말을 건넨다. (try, lure)

▶ He speaks sweetly to the boy, _____ _____ _____ him away.

UNIT 11 | Psychology

[01-30] 다음 단어의 뜻을 쓰시오.

01 common _____

02 author _____

03 benefit _____

04 connect _____

05 convenient _____

06 counseling _____

07 deadly _____

08 depressed _____

09 emotion _____

10 exhausted _____

11 explore _____

12 fever _____

13 heal _____

14 homesickness _____

15 improvement _____

16 nostalgia _____

17 personal _____

18 popularity _____

19 eventually _____

20 punch _____

21 troubled _____

22 sore _____

23 struggle _____

24 sufferer _____

25 therapy _____

26 transportation _____

27 unknown _____

28 vocabulary _____

29 direct _____

30 offer _____

[31-40] 다음 뜻을 지닌 단어를 쓰시오.

31 기회 _____

32 향상시키다[개선하다] _____

33 편집 _____

34 장비, 장치 _____

35 사전 _____

36 분명히 _____

37 나타내다, 표현하다 _____

38 편안한 _____

39 과정 _____

40 등급; 성적 _____

[41-44] 다음 숙어의 뜻을 쓰시오.

41 deal with _____

42 long to-v _____

43 cool down _____

44 die of _____

VOCABULARY TEST 2

A 다음 단어의 영영풀이를 바르게 연결하시오.

1 explore •   • ⓐ causing or likely to cause death

2 offer •   • ⓑ to travel around to learn about or search for something

3 opportunity •   • ⓒ to ask someone if they want something

4 emotion •   • ⓓ a chance to do something

5 deadly •   • ⓔ a feeling such as love or hate

B 다음 밑줄 친 단어와 의미가 유사한 단어를 고르시오.

1 I hope that your broken arm will <u>heal</u> soon.

  ⓐ suffer   ⓑ prevent   ⓒ recover   ⓓ dull   ⓔ supply

2 My grandfather <u>provided</u> some food to the people in need.

  ⓐ accepted   ⓑ offered   ⓒ improved   ⓓ asked   ⓔ developed

3 I need to <u>connect</u> the printer to my computer.

  ⓐ link   ⓑ control   ⓒ create   ⓓ asked   ⓔ communicate

C 우리말과 같은 뜻이 되도록 빈칸에 들어갈 말을 보기 에서 찾아 알맞은 형태로 쓰시오.

보기   long to-v   deal with   die of   cool down

1 찬물 한 잔이 너를 진정시켜 줄 것이다.

▶ A glass of cold water will _____ you _____.

2 그는 화가 났을 때 자신의 감정을 처리하려고 애썼다.

▶ He struggled to _____ his emotions when he was angry.

3 삼 년 전 그가 떠난 이후로, 우리는 그를 다시 볼 수 있기를 애타게 바라고 있다.

▶ We've _____ see him again since he left three years ago.

4 매시간 두 명이 넘는 미국인들이 피부암으로 죽는다.

▶ More than two people _____ skin cancer in the US every hour.

GRAMMAR TEST

A 다음 ( ) 안에서 알맞은 것을 고르시오.

1 (Whenever, However) I visited her, she seemed busy.

2 (However, Whenever) hard you try, you cannot win this game.

3 He called Julie at night, (when, which) she was not in.

4 They went to the zoo, (which, where) they saw a lion eating meat.

5 My brother made a mess in the kitchen, (which, that) made my mom angry.

B 두 문장이 같은 뜻이 되도록 빈칸에 알맞은 말을 쓰시오.

1 I went for a walk last night, and it was raining then.
  ▶ I went for a walk last night, _____ it was raining.

2 She really liked to read the cartoon, and it surprised me.
  ▶ She really liked to read the cartoon, _____ surprised me.

3 I will go to the gallery, and there I will work as a volunteer.
  ▶ I will go to the gallery, _____ I will work as a volunteer.

4 No matter how spicy this soup is, I will finish eating it.
  ▶ _____ spicy this soup is, I will finish eating it.

5 Every time I went to the bakery, all the bread was sold out.
  ▶ _____ I went to the bakery, all the bread was sold out.

C 밑줄 친 부분을 어법에 맞게 고쳐 쓰시오.

1 Martha, <u>that</u> works as a waitress, is very diligent.

2 I lost my cell phone, <u>what</u> made me very sad.

3 Grace finished cooking at two o'clock, <u>which</u> all the guests arrived.

4 Henry exercises at this gym, <u>that</u> he also works as a trainer.

5 <u>Whenever</u> crowded the pool is, I like to swim there.

WRITING TEST

A 우리말과 일치하도록 ( ) 안에 주어진 말을 알맞게 배열하시오.

1 우리가 감정을 보는 방식은 시간이 지남에 따라 변해 왔다.

(we, the way, emotions, view)

▶ _____ has changed over time.

2 그들은 먹기를 중단했고, 이것은 그들을 죽음에 이르게 하곤 했다.

(their deaths, would, lead, which, to)

▶ They stopped eating, _____.

3 그는 화가 날 때마다, 싸움에 빠져들곤 했다. (got, angry, he, whenever)

▶ _____, he would get into fights.

4 그 프로그램은 학생들에게 곡을 쓸 기회를 제공한다.

(to, the chance, offer, write songs, students)

▶ The programs _____.

5 이는 기업의 자금 조달 목표에 더 쉽게 도달할 수 있도록 해준다.

(it, to, makes, easier, reach)

▶ This _____ their funding goals.

B 우리말과 일치하도록 ( ) 안의 말을 이용하여 문장을 완성하시오.

1 그것은 심각한 병으로 여겨졌고, '향수(鄕愁)'라고 불렸다. (consider, call)

▶ It _____ _____ a serious illness and _____ "nostalgia."

2 전화기와 인터넷은 멀리 떨어져 사는 사람들이 연결되도록 도왔다. (connect, live)

▶ Phones and the internet have helped _____ people _____ far away.

3 감정을 표현하는 것이 치료하는 첫 번째 단계이다. (express, heal)

▶ _____ emotions is the first step to _____.

4 그들은 뮤직비디오를 제작하는 법을 배운다. (how, make)

▶ They learn _____ _____ _____ music videos.

5 일부 십 대들은 그들의 감정에 관해 이야기하는 것을 힘겨워한다. (struggle, talk)

▶ Some teenagers _____ _____ _____ _____ their feelings.

UNIT 12 | Business

반 / 이름:

[01-30] 다음 단어의 뜻을 쓰시오.

01 raise _____

02 ordinary _____

03 instantly _____

04 investor _____

05 typically _____

06 donate _____

07 charity _____

08 commercial _____

09 feature _____

10 stuff _____

11 payment _____

12 device _____

13 financial _____

14 secure _____

15 contribute _____

16 incredibly _____

17 stock _____

18 capital _____

19 campaign _____

20 technology _____

21 electric _____

22 publishing _____

23 record _____

24 retailer _____

25 effective _____

26 prevent _____

27 unusable _____

28 confidence _____

29 latest _____

30 million _____

[31-40] 다음 뜻을 지닌 단어를 쓰시오.

31 사업; 사업체 _____

32 자금을 대다; 자금 _____

33 도입 _____

34 투자, 투자금 _____

35 기부 _____

36 보안 _____

37 훔치다 _____

38 무작위의 _____

39 접근하다 _____

40 범죄 _____

[41-43] 다음 숙어의 뜻을 쓰시오.

41 when it comes to _____

42 make a purchase _____

43 replace A with B _____

A 단어의 첫 철자를 참조하여 다음 정의에 해당하는 단어를 쓰시오.

1 to be successful in realizing a goal   a_____

2 happening, done, or chosen by chance   r_____

3 a television or radio advertisement   c_____

4 the state of being safe from attack or damage   s_____

5 money or benefits that you receive as a result of what you have done   r_____

B 다음 빈칸에 들어갈 말을 보기 에서 찾아 쓰시오.

보기	steal	capital	incredibly	publishing	effective

1 The war has left the country _____ poor.

2 He found a(n) _____ way to educate his children.

3 Do you have the _____ to start your own business?

4 I had an interview for a job with a well-known _____ company.

5 Jack approached an elderly woman to _____ some money from her.

C 우리말과 같은 뜻이 되도록 빈칸에 들어갈 말을 보기 에서 찾아 알맞은 형태로 쓰시오.

보기	make a purchase	when it comes to	replace A with B

1 그는 오래된 비밀번호를 새것으로 교체했다.

▶ He _____ his old password _____ a new one.

2 구매하기 전에 가격을 주의 깊게 확인해라.

▶ Check the price carefully before you _____.

3 요리에 관한 한, 우리 엄마가 최고이다.

▶ _____ cooking, my mom is the best.

GRAMMAR TEST

A 다음 문장을 수동태 문장으로 고쳐 쓰시오.

1 Some students are playing soccer in the field.

▶ _____

2 Fred has just finished the science homework.

▶ _____

3 Any of our customers can use our shopping carts.

▶ _____

4 He will buy a new jacket.

▶ _____

B 다음 밑줄 친 부분을 「It is ~ that」 구문을 사용하여 강조할 때 빈칸에 알맞은 말을 쓰시오.

1 Lucy found a ball under the table yesterday.

▶ It _____ Lucy found under the table yesterday.

2 Emma finally joined the school soccer team.

▶ It _____ finally joined the school soccer team.

3 I left my wallet on the bus this morning.

▶ It _____ I left my wallet on the bus.

4 I met David in front of the shopping mall.

▶ It _____ I met David.

C 어법상 어색한 곳을 찾아 바르게 고쳐 쓰시오.

1 The cups are be washed in the dishwasher. We can't use them now.

2 Your pants will deliver within seven days.

3 Her achievement has recently been recognizing by the media.

4 She is Megan that is talented in swimming.

5 It was on the hill what we were supposed to meet that night.

WRITING TEST

A 우리말과 일치하도록 (   ) 안에 주어진 말을 알맞게 배열하시오.

1 많은 사업 아이디어와 프로젝트들이 보통 은행에서 자금을 지원받았다.

(by, usually, funded, were, banks)

▶ Many business ideas and projects _____.

2 이는 그들의 자금 조달 목표에 더 쉽게 도달할 수 있도록 해준다.

(it, easier, reach, makes, to)

▶ This _____ their funding goals.

3 당신은 보안 문제에 관해 걱정할 필요가 없다.

(have, worry, don't, about, to)

▶ You _____ security problems.

4 이것은 소매업자가 당신의 금융 정보에 접근하도록 하는 열쇠이다.

(to, the retailer, allowing, access)

▶ This is the key _____ your financial data.

5 당신은 모바일 기기를 이용해서 안심하고 쇼핑할 수 있다.

(your mobile device, shop, with)

▶ You can _____ with confidence.

B 우리말과 일치하도록 (   ) 안의 말을 이용하여 문장을 완성하시오.

1 그것은 전통적인 결제 방식보다 더 효과적이다. (effective)

▶ It _____ _____ _____ _____ the traditional payment system.

2 그의 목표는 30일 안에 백만 달러를 모으는 것이었다. (be, raise)

▶ His goal _____ _____ _____ one million dollars in 30 days.

3 당신의 정보를 안전하게 보호해주는 것은 바로 이 기술이다. (it, that)

▶ _____ _____ this technology _____ keeps your information secure.

4 그들은 그 활동으로부터 온 자금으로 개발될 제품이나 서비스를 약속 받는다. (will, develop)

▶ They are promised a product or service that _____ _____ _____ with money from the campaign.

UNIT 13 | People

반 / 이름:

[01-30] 다음 단어의 뜻을 쓰시오.

01 alive _____

02 appear _____

03 argue _____

04 bandage _____

05 boil _____

06 symbolize _____

07 damaging _____

08 equally _____

09 diplomat _____

10 embassy _____

11 hire _____

12 immediately _____

13 legally _____

14 mixture _____

15 observe _____

16 pain _____

17 passport _____

18 patient _____

19 personally _____

20 recognize _____

21 rescue _____

22 risk _____

23 striped _____

24 surgery _____

25 territory _____

26 transport _____

27 mild _____

28 pole _____

29 suffering _____

30 innovative _____

[31-40] 다음 뜻을 지닌 단어를 쓰시오.

31 썩은, 부패한 _____

32 중세의 _____

33 외과 의사 _____

34 (일·과제 등을) 수행하다 _____

35 일, 과업 _____

36 깃발 _____

37 군사의 _____

38 상처 _____

39 접근법, 처리 방법 _____

40 기법, 기술 _____

[41-45] 다음 숙어의 뜻을 쓰시오.

41 a series of _____

42 hand out _____

43 be about to-v _____

44 write down _____

45 in an attempt to-v _____

VOCABULARY TEST 2

A 다음 단어의 영영풀이를 바르게 연결하시오.

1 appear •   • ⓐ to do an action or complete something difficult

2 transport •   • ⓑ to come into sight or start to be seen

3 territory •   • ⓒ to use medical methods to cure an illness

4 perform •   • ⓓ an area of land that belongs to a country

5 treat •   • ⓔ to move someone or something from one place to another

B 다음 밑줄 친 단어와 의미가 유사한 단어를 고르시오.

1 The cause of the bad smell is <u>rotten</u> food.

ⓐ alive   ⓑ fresh   ⓒ sweet   ⓓ soft   ⓔ decaying

2 The <u>wound</u> to my shoulder really hurts.

ⓐ mole   ⓑ harm   ⓒ pain   ⓓ injury   ⓔ spot

3 The surgeons <u>performed</u> an emergency surgery.

ⓐ played   ⓑ ran   ⓒ carried out   ⓓ worked   ⓔ entertained

4 When people start smoking, they <u>risk</u> their health.

ⓐ kill   ⓑ endanger   ⓒ prevent   ⓓ decrease   ⓔ dismiss

C 우리말과 같은 뜻이 되도록 빈칸에 들어갈 말을 보기에서 찾아 알맞은 형태로 쓰시오.

보기	in an attempt to-v	hand out	write down	a series of

1 그 종이를 참가자들에게 건네줄 수 있겠니?

▶ Can you _____ the papers to the participants?

2 그녀는 아동용 독서물 시리즈를 구입했다.

▶ She bought _____ reading books for children.

3 함께 사는 가족 구성원의 이름을 적으십시오.

▶ _____ the names of the family members who live with you.

4 출퇴근 교통 체증을 줄이려는 시도로 여분의 도로가 건설될 것이다.

▶ Extra roads will be constructed _____ reduce rush-hour traffic.

A 다음 ( ) 안에서 알맞은 것을 고르시오.

1 Physics (is, are) a branch of science.

2 (Is, Are) there anyone here who saw the game last night?

3 Every student in our school (has, have) to wear a school uniform.

4 Ten dollars (seem, seems) to be a good price for this bag.

B 다음 주어진 문장과 같은 뜻이 되도록 할 때, 빈칸에 알맞은 말을 쓰시오.

> Kate is the kindest student in the class.

1 No student in the class is as _____ _____ Kate.

2 No student in the class is _____ _____ Kate.

3 Kate is _____ _____ _____ _____ _____ in the class.

> The Nile River is the longest river in the world.

4 No river in the world is _____ _____ _____ the Nile River.

5 No river in the world is _____ _____ the Nile River.

6 The Nile River is _____ _____ _____ _____ _____ in the world.

C 밑줄 친 부분을 어법에 맞게 고쳐 쓰시오.

1 Economics <u>have</u> been a popular major in most universities.

2 Someone <u>were</u> sitting in my seat, so I told him to move.

3 Austin is stronger than any other <u>boys</u> in his class.

4 No other ring in this shop is as <u>nicer</u> as this one.

5 No player on the soccer team runs <u>fastest</u> than John.

A 우리말과 일치하도록 (   ) 안에 주어진 말을 알맞게 배열하시오.

1 많은 사람들이 유대인들을 구하기 위해 자신들의 목숨을 걸었다.

(their lives, save, risked, Jewish people, to)

▶ Many people _____.

2 스웨덴 여권을 가진 사람들은 기차에서 내려져야만 했다.

(the train, be, off, let, had to)

▶ The people with Swedish passports _____.

3 이 위험한 방법이 환자에게 큰 고통을 가했다.

(approach, caused, great, dangerous, pain, patients)

▶ This _____.

4 그의 책은 자신의 수술 경험을 바탕으로 하였다.

(based, was, his book, on)

▶ _____ his surgical experience.

5 군의관들은 끓는 기름으로 상처를 달구어 총상을 치료했다.

(the wound, boiling, burning, with, by, oil)

▶ Military surgeons treated gunshot wounds _____.

B 우리말과 일치하도록 (   ) 안의 말을 이용하여 문장을 완성하시오.

1 아무도 발렌베리만큼 용감하지 않다. (brave)

▶ No other person is _____ _____ _____ Wallenberg.

2 그는 스웨덴 외교관으로 고용되었다. (hire)

▶ He _____ _____ _____ a Swedish diplomat.

3 그는 사람들이 건물 위로 스웨덴 깃발을 올리도록 했다. (make, raise)

▶ He _____ _____ _____ the Swedish flag on the buildings.

4 그것은 고통을 줄이는 데 더 나았을 뿐만 아니라, 몸에 덜 해로웠다. (not, but)

▶ It was _____ _____ better for reducing pain _____ was _____ less damaging.

5 라틴어로 쓰인 다른 의학 서적과는 달리, 파레의 것들은 불어로 쓰였다. (write)

▶ Unlike other medical texts, _____ _____ _____ in Latin, Paré's were written in French.

VOCABULARY TEST 1

반 / 이름:

[01-30] 다음 단어의 뜻을 쓰시오.

01 human _____

02 satellite _____

03 enormous _____

04 orbit _____

05 huge _____

06 crash _____

07 spacecraft _____

08 spectacular _____

09 challenge _____

10 within _____

11 film _____

12 position _____

13 purpose _____

14 observe _____

15 remove _____

16 complete _____

17 endure _____

18 unfortunately _____

19 method _____

20 research _____

21 solution _____

22 perform _____

23 expose _____

24 tough _____

25 condition _____

26 harsh _____

27 engineer _____

28 extreme _____

29 temperature _____

30 official _____

[31-40] 다음 뜻을 지닌 단어를 쓰시오.

31 발사하다 _____

32 우주 _____

33 그 결과로 초래된 _____

34 손상을 입히다 _____

35 임무 _____

36 방송하다 _____

37 생방송의 _____

38 각도, 각 _____

39 자동의 _____

40 품질 _____

[41-45] 다음 숙어의 뜻을 쓰시오.

41 break apart _____

42 in response to _____

43 thousands of _____

44 at any time _____

45 up to _____

A 다음 단어의 영영풀이를 바르게 연결하시오.

1 damage • • ⓐ amazing to see and very impressive

2 unfortunately • • ⓑ to cause harm to something

3 spectacular • • ⓒ used to say that something disappoints or saddens you

4 automatic • • ⓓ how bad or good something is

5 quality • • ⓔ to operate or move independently of human control

B 다음 빈칸에 들어갈 말을 보기에서 찾아 쓰시오.

| 보기 | extreme | install | solutions | orbit | endured |

1 I've _____ these harsh conditions for a long time.

2 He will _____ this computer program onto my laptop.

3 A new satellite was launched into _____.

4 He suggested some practical _____ to the problem.

5 Climate change has led to an increase in _____ weather conditions like hurricanes and floods.

C 우리말과 같은 뜻이 되도록 빈칸에 들어갈 말을 보기에서 찾아 알맞은 형태로 쓰시오.

| 보기 | in response to | thousands of | break apart | at any time |

1 당신이 원한다면, 언제든지 저에게 전화하세요.

▶ If you want, you can call me _____.

2 그 초콜릿 바는 쉽게 쪼개진다.

▶ The chocolate bar _____ easily.

3 그 부자는 매년 수천 달러를 자선 단체에 기부한다.

▶ The rich man donates _____ dollars to the charity every year.

4 고객의 요구에 응하여, 저희는 영업시간을 연장할 것입니다.

▶ _____ customer demand, we will be extending our opening hours.

A 다음 ( ) 안에서 알맞은 것을 고르시오.

1 She (lives, has lived) in Paris since she was young.

2 I (am eating, have been eating) vegan food since last year.

3 I have never (see, seen) such a beautiful view before.

4 Have you ever (traveling, traveled) abroad by yourself?

5 I (just receive, have just received) the letter that Sue sent.

B 다음 문장이 조건문인지, 가정법인지 고른 후, 문장을 해석하시오.

1 If I had a car, I would drive you home. (조건문, 가정법)

▶ _____

2 If it weren't raining, we could play soccer outside. (조건문, 가정법)

▶ _____

3 If you go to the mall now, you can buy the shirt at 50% off. (조건문, 가정법)

▶ _____

4 If I knew how to speak Japanese, I could help the Japanese tourists. (조건문, 가정법)

▶ _____

C 밑줄 친 부분을 어법에 맞게 고쳐 쓰시오.

1 We have moved to this city in 2015.

2 I know the teacher for about 10 years.

3 They have be talking about baseball for hours.

4 If she isn't so angry now, I would talk to her.

5 If he were friendlier, he can make more friends.

A 우리말과 일치하도록 ( ) 안에 주어진 말을 알맞게 배열하시오.

1 인간은 수천 개의 위성과 로켓을 우주로 쏘아 올렸다.

(have, launched, humans)

▶ _____ thousands of satellites and rockets into space.

2 국제 연합은 기업들에게 그들의 위성을 궤도에서 제거할 것을 요청해 오고 있다.

(to, been, asking, has, companies, remove)

▶ The United Nations _____ their satellites from orbit.

3 각각의 카메라는 다른 위치에서 지구를 촬영하도록 설치되어 있다.

(set up, film, camera, to, each, is)

▶ _____ the Earth from a different position.

4 왜 NASA는 우리에게 이러한 지구의 영상을 보여주는가?

(NASA, us, why, show, does, these images)

▶ _____ of the Earth?

5 카메라가 이 어려움들을 견딜 수 있다면, 그것들은 나중에 우주 탐사 임무에 사용될 것이다.

(they, used, be, will)

▶ If the cameras can endure these challenges, _____
in later space missions.

B 우리말과 일치하도록 ( ) 안의 말을 이용하여 문장을 완성하시오.

1 우리는 우주에 엄청난 양의 쓰레기를 만들어 오고 있다. (have, create)

▶ We _____ _____ _____ tons of junk in space.

2 이를 실현하기 위해 몇 가지 해결책이 제시되었다. (have, suggest)

▶ To make this happen, several solutions _____ _____ _____.

3 한 NASA 프로젝트가 2014년 4월부터 운영되어 오고 있다. (run)

▶ A NASA project _____ _____ _____ since April 2014.

4 그 프로젝트는 우주 기지에서 공학자들에 의해 주도된다. (lead)

▶ The project _____ _____ _____ the engineers at the Space Center.

VOCABULARY TEST 1

반 / 이름:

[01-30] 다음 단어의 뜻을 쓰시오.

01 biological _____

02 brick _____

03 cave _____

04 character _____

05 pretty _____

06 similarity _____

07 difference _____

08 disappear _____

09 follow _____

10 evolve _____

11 folktale _____

12 force _____

13 goat _____

14 inspire _____

15 kidnap _____

16 leap _____

17 list _____

18 meanwhile _____

19 naughty _____

20 past _____

21 pretend _____

22 reply _____

23 result _____

24 return _____

25 review _____

26 courageous _____

27 surprisingly _____

28 select _____

29 trick _____

30 demand _____

[31-40] 다음 뜻을 지닌 단어를 쓰시오.

31 악당 _____

32 최고위자; 추장, 족장 _____

33 붙잡다[움켜잡다] _____

34 멍 _____

35 깨닫다 _____

36 행동 _____

37 모험 _____

38 탈출하다 _____

39 비슷하게, 유사하게 _____

40 포함하다 _____

[41-44] 다음 숙어의 뜻을 쓰시오.

41 be covered with _____

42 cling to _____

43 find out _____

44 trick A into B _____

A 다음 단어의 영영풀이를 바르게 연결하시오.

1 difference •   • ⓐ an exciting and unusual experience

2 select   •   • ⓑ to choose something from a group

3 character •   • ⓒ a person in a movie, book, or play

4 pretend   •   • ⓓ to behave as if something is true when in fact it is not

5 adventure •   • ⓔ some qualities that make two things unlike each other

B 다음 빈칸에 들어갈 말을 보기에서 찾아 쓰시오.

| 보기 | select | review | kidnap | grab | include |

1 The lunch special doesn't _____ drinks or dessert.

2 Can you _____ her hand and help her stand up?

3 People who _____ children should be punished severely.

4 You have to _____ the best dress among these options.

5 I will _____ the report with the project manager.

C 우리말과 같은 뜻이 되도록 빈칸에 들어갈 말을 보기에서 찾아 알맞은 형태로 쓰시오.

| 보기 | trick A into B | cling to | be covered with | find out |

1 이 언덕들은 야생화로 덮여 있다.

▶ These hills _____ wildflowers.

2 지난밤에 무슨 일이 일어났는지 알아내야 한다.

▶ I have to _____ what happened last night.

3 두 마리의 고양이가 발톱으로 모서리에 매달려 있다.

▶ Two cats are _____ the edge by their claws.

4 그 악당은 사람들을 속여 거짓말을 하게 한다.

▶ The villain _____ people _____ telling lies.

A 다음 ( ) 안에서 알맞은 것을 고르시오.

1 You can either take a bus or (walk, to walk).

2 The movie was neither sad nor (funny, was funny).

3 I ran really hard to catch the thief but (lost, to lose) him.

4 I decided to buy some snacks and (baking, to bake) cookies for the party.

5 He not only introduced me to the restaurant but also (recommend, recommended) a dish.

B 다음 문장이 부분 부정인지 전체 부정인지 고른 후, 문장을 해석하시오.

1 None of the students agree with his idea. (부분 부정, 전체 부정)

▶ _____

2 Not all of my friends came to my birthday party. (부분 부정, 전체 부정)

▶ _____

3 Neither of us is good at drawing pictures. (부분 부정, 전체 부정)

▶ _____

4 My mom is not always at home in the afternoon. (부분 부정, 전체 부정)

▶ _____

C 어법상 어색한 곳을 찾아 바르게 고쳐 쓰시오.

1 Generally to speak, she looks better without glasses.

2 To consider his ability, he can be a team leader.

3 Judged from her accent, she's from India.

4 Strictly to say, he is not an expert.

5 Frankly speak, I forgot his daughter's name.

A 우리말과 일치하도록 ( ) 안에 주어진 말을 알맞게 배열하시오.

1 그는 그 이야기들이 시간이 지나면서 어떻게 변하는지 살펴보았다.

(had, the stories, how, changed)

▶ He looked at _____ over time.

2 그 소년을 납치하기는 쉽지 않다. (to, it's, easy, not, kidnap)

▶ _____ the boy.

3 그들은 한 아이를 납치하고 2천 달러의 몸값을 요구할 계획이다.

(kidnap, to, a child, plan, and, demand)

▶ They _____ a $2,000 ransom.

4 엄마 염소는 자신이 먹이를 찾는 동안 아이들을 집에 남겨둔다.

(searches for, at home, while, her kids, she)

▶ A mother goat leaves _____ food.

5 그들은 차라리 돈을 잃는 것이 더 낫다고 판단한다. (would, some, rather, money, lose)

▶ They decide they _____.

B 우리말과 일치하도록 ( ) 안의 말을 이용하여 문장을 완성하시오.

1 그는 게임을 하도록 강요받아 왔다. (be, force, play)

▶ He has _____ _____ _____ _____ a game.

2 늑대는 아이들을 속여서 집 안으로 들어오려고 한다. (let)

▶ A wolf tries to trick the kids _____ _____ him into the house.

3 그들은 도셋 씨에게 1,500달러를 내라고 요청하며 편지를 쓴다. (ask, play)

▶ They write a letter, _____ Mr. Dorset _____ _____ $1,500.

4 늑대는 그녀의 할머니인 척하여 소녀를 속인다. (pretend, be)

▶ A wolf tricks a girl by _____ _____ _____ her grandmother.

5 그 이야기들이 어떻게 진화했는지 알아내기 위해, 그는 많은 이야기를 검토하고 차이점을 열거하였다.

(the story, evolve)

▶ To find out _____ _____ _____ _____, he reviewed many stories
   and listed their differences.

VOCABULARY TEST 1

반 / 이름:

[01-30] 다음 단어의 뜻을 쓰시오.

01 label _____

02 option _____

03 undesirable _____

04 vegetarian _____

05 flavor _____

06 natural _____

07 ingredient _____

08 relatively _____

09 Westerner _____

10 medieval _____

11 midday _____

12 sin _____

13 laborer _____

14 consequently _____

15 evolve _____

16 national _____

17 commonly _____

18 countless _____

19 happen _____

20 activity _____

21 amount _____

22 roughly _____

23 Swedish _____

24 historian _____

25 shift _____

26 tasty _____

27 advertise _____

28 healthy _____

29 contain _____

30 accidentally _____

[31-40] 다음 뜻을 지닌 단어를 쓰시오.

31 평균의 _____

32 추천하다; 권장하다 _____

33 충치 _____

34 홍보하다 _____

35 산업 _____

36 신념, 믿음 _____

37 스웨덴 _____

38 비롯되다, 유래하다 _____

39 용어, 말 _____

40 발견하다; 알아내다 _____

[41-44] 다음 숙어의 뜻을 쓰시오.

41 in fact _____

42 refer to _____

43 be regarded as _____

44 take a closer look at _____

A 다음 단어의 영영풀이를 바르게 연결하시오.

1 recommend •   • ⓐ a food that is used with other foods to make a dish

2 relatively •   • ⓑ to begin to exist

3 originate •   • ⓒ happening without being planned

4 accidentally •   • ⓓ when compared to other things

5 ingredient •   • ⓔ to suggest something to someone

B 다음 밑줄 친 단어와 의미가 유사한 단어를 고르시오.

1 There were roughly 200 people in the hall.

ⓐ over   ⓑ only   ⓒ about   ⓓ exactly   ⓔ less than

2 We called more people to work; consequently, we finished early.

ⓐ because   ⓑ nevertheless   ⓒ otherwise   ⓓ as a result   ⓔ instead

3 The shift to using wireless systems brought a lot of convenience to our lives.

ⓐ feature   ⓑ change   ⓒ danger   ⓓ warning   ⓔ benefit

C 우리말과 같은 뜻이 되도록 빈칸에 들어갈 말을 보기에서 찾아 알맞은 형태로 쓰시오.

| 보기 | be regarded as | refer to | in fact | take a closer look at |

1 그 영화는 그의 최고작으로 여겨진다.

▶ The film _____ his best.

2 그 사진들을 자세히 살펴봐도 될까요?

▶ May I _____ those pictures?

3 사실, 요즘 점점 더 많은 아이들이 나쁜 시력을 가지고 있다.

▶ _____, more and more children have bad eyesight nowadays.

4 그 수치들은 시험에 통과한 학생 수를 나타낸다.

▶ The figures _____ the number of students that passed the test.

A 다음 문장을 분사구문으로 바꾸어 쓰시오.

1 As I had walked home in the rain, I got wet.

▶ _____ _____ home in the rain, I got wet.

2 Because it was sunny, we had lunch at the park.

▶ _____ _____ _____, we had lunch at the park.

3 Since she left her cell phone at home, she can't call him.

▶ _____ _____ her cell phone at home, she can't call him.

B 다음 밑줄 친 부분이 문장에서 어떤 역할을 하는지 **보기** 에서 골라 빈칸에 쓰시오.

보기 주어	목적어	보어	형용사

1 I believe <u>that he will come back to us soon.</u> _____

2 This is the girl <u>that I saw at the music festival.</u> _____

3 The problem is <u>that we have no more food to eat.</u> _____

4 She knew <u>that the ending of the movie was sad.</u> _____

5 <u>That he failed the test</u> was not a secret. _____

C 다음을 우리말로 해석하시오.

1 The fact is that he is older than you.

▶ _____

2 Jennifer bought the car that was on sale.

▶ _____

3 The bus being too crowded, we took the train.

▶ _____

4 Having lost the watch she gave me, I became depressed.

▶ _____

A 우리말과 일치하도록 ( ) 안에 주어진 말을 알맞게 배열하시오.

1 정부는 토요일에만 사탕을 먹도록 장려하는 운동을 홍보했다.

(a campaign, promoted, encouraged, that)

▶ The government _____ eating candy only on Saturdays.

2 그것은 주말마다 일어나는 가족 활동이다.

(that, it, a family activity, is, happens)

▶ _____ every weekend.

3 그것은 서양 사람들에게는 비교적 최근의 관습이다.

(recent, for, tradition, relatively, Westerners)

▶ It is a _____ .

4 어떤 사람들은 아침에 먹는 것을 죄라고 여겼다.

(it, a sin, considered, to eat)

▶ Some people _____ in the morning.

5 시리얼이 얼마나 맛있는지 알아낸 후, 그는 그것을 건강에 좋은 아침 식사라고 광고했다.

(how, discovered, the cereal, tasty, having, was)

▶ _____ , he advertised it as a healthy breakfast.

B 우리말과 일치하도록 ( ) 안의 말을 이용하여 문장을 완성하시오.

1 세계 보건 기구는 이것이 평균 권장량의 세 배라고 한다. (say)

▶ The World Health Organization _____ _____ this is three times the average recommended amount.

2 아마도 세계에서 스웨덴만큼 사탕을 많이 먹는 나라는 없을 것이다. (eat, much)

▶ Probably no country in the world _____ _____ _____ candy _____ Sweden.

3 아침을 먹는 것은 많은 사람들이 아침에 하는 첫 번째 일이다. (have)

▶ _____ _____ is the first thing many people do in the morning.

4 점점 더 많은 사람들이 음식을 먹는 것으로 하루를 시작했다. (more)

▶ _____ _____ _____ people began the day by eating food.

 MEMO

MEMO

MEMO

MEMO

MEMO

MEMO

READING Inside

workbook

A 4-level curriculum
integration reading course

- **A thematic reading program that integrates with school curriculum**
  중등 교육과정이 지향하는 문이과 통합 및 타교과 연계 반영한 독해서

- **Informative content with well-designed comprehension questions**
  정보성 있는 지문과 질 높은 다양한 유형의 문항 그리고 서술형 평가도 대비

- **Grammar points directly related to the *Grammar Inside* series**
  베스트셀러 Grammar Inside와 직접적으로 연계된 문법 항목 및 문항 제공

- **Exercises with useful, essential, and academic vocabulary**
  중등 필수 어휘 학습 코너 제공

- **A workbook for more vocabulary, grammar, and reading exercises**
  풍부한 양의 어휘, 문법, 그리고 쓰기 추가 문제 등을 수록한 워크북

Level	Grade	Words Limit
Reading Inside Starter	Low-Intermediate	140-160
Reading Inside Level 1	Intermediate	160-180
Reading Inside Level 2	Intermediate	180-200
Reading Inside Level 3	**Low-Advanced**	**200-220**

READING Inside

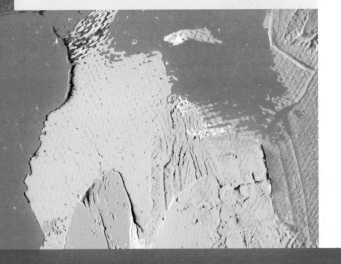

LEVEL 3

A 4-level curriculum
integration reading course

NE_ Neungyule

READING
Inside

LEVEL 3

UNIT 01 | Culture

pp. 7-12

READING 1 Kwanzaa

[V] **Mini Quiz**
1 T 2 T

▶ **Reading Comprehension**
1 d 2 a 3 d 4 improve the African-American community

▶ **Grammar Inside LEVEL 3**
[Check Up] It, to complete

해석 매년 아프리카계 미국인들은 12월 26일부터 1월 1일까지 콴자라고 불리는 휴일을 기념한다. 아프리카계 미국인 학자인 Maulana Karenga 박사는 아프리카계 미국인들을 결속시키기 위해 1966년에 이 휴일을 시작했다. Maulana 박사는 그들이 자신들의 유산에 관심을 갖길 원했다. 아프리카의 기념일들을 조사한 후에, 그는 이 휴일을 만들었고 '수확'을 뜻하는 스와힐리어로 이름을 지었다.

콴자는 7가지 원칙을 포함하는데, 이는 통합, 선택, 책임, 협동, 목적성, 창의력, 그리고 신뢰이다. Maulana 박사는 그것들이 아프리카계 미국인 공동체가 발전하는 데 이바지할 거라고 믿기 때문에 이 가치들을 선택했다. 콴자 기간에 사람들은 Mishumaa Saba라는 일곱 개의 촛불을 준비한다. 빨간색 세 개, 초록색 세 개, 그리고 검은색 한 개이다. 각각의 촛불은 일곱 개의 원칙 중 하나를 나타낸다.

콴자 기간 동안 매일 밤에, 촛불 중 하나에 불을 붙이고 일곱 개의 원칙 중 한 가지에 관하여 논의하는 것이 전통이다. 예를 들어, 첫 번째 밤에는 중앙에 있는 검은 촛불이 켜지고, 통합의 원칙이 논의된다. 콴자를 기념하는 다른 방법들도 많이 있다. 사람들은 아프리카 드럼으로 음악을 만들고, 시와 이야기를 읽는다. 또한, 모든 가족이 함께 식사를 즐기러 모인다. Maulana 박사가 의도한 대로, 이 비교적 새로운 휴일은 아프리카계 미국인들이 자신의 유산을 기리도록 하는 좋은 방법이 되어 오고 있다.

어휘 celebrate [동] 기념하다, 축하하다 (celebration [명] 기념[축하]행사) scholar [명] 학자 unite [동] 연합하다; *통합하다[결속하다] (unity [명] 통합) care about ~에 관심을 가지다 heritage [명] 유산 research [동] 조사하다[연구하다] harvest [명] 수확 include [동] 포함하다 principle [명] 원칙 responsibility [명] 책임(감) purpose [명] 목적 creativity [명] 창의력 trust [명] 신뢰 value [명] 가치 improve [동] 개선하다 community [명] 주민, 지역 사회; *공동체 prepare [동] 준비하다 represent [동] 대표하다; *나타내다, 상징하다 light [동] 불을 붙이다 discuss [동] 상의하다; *논하다 as well 또한[역시] poem [명] 시(詩) intend [동] 의도하다 relatively [부] 비교적 honor [동] 존경하다; *기리다 [문제] promote [동] 홍보하다

구문 [1행] Every year, African Americans celebrate **a holiday** [called Kwanzaa] from December 26 to January 1.
→ [ ]는 a holiday를 수식하는 과거분사구이다.

[2행] **Dr. Maulana Karenga, an African-American scholar**, began this holiday in 1966 *to unite* African Americans.
→ Dr. Maulana Karenga와 an African-American scholar는 동격 관계이다.
→ to unite는 '결속시키기 위해'의 의미로, 〈목적〉을 나타내는 to부정사의 부사적 용법이다.

[4행] **After researching** African celebrations, he created the holiday and named it with *a Swahili word* [that means "harvest."]

→ After researching은 〈때〉를 나타내는 분사구문으로, 의미를 명확히 하기 위해 접속사를 생략하지 않았다.

→ [ ]는 선행사 a Swahili word를 수식하는 주격 관계대명사절이다.

19행 ..., this relatively new holiday **has become** *a great way* [to help African Americans honor their heritage].

→ has become은 〈계속〉을 나타내는 현재완료이다.

→ [ ]는 a great way를 수식하는 형용사적 용법의 to부정사구이다.

READING 2   Sea Nomads

◎ Mini Quiz

1 Indonesia, Malaysia, and the Philippines

2 Traditionally, they live on long, narrow boats called lepa-lepa and drift with the currents.

▶ Reading Comprehension

1 b   2 a, d   3 c   4 spend so much time at sea

▶ Grammar Inside LEVEL 3

Check Up 나는 우리 부모님을 설득하는 것을 불가능하다고 생각했다.

해석 지구상의 모든 종의 거의 절반 정도가 바다에 살지만, 대부분의 사람들은 아마도 육지에서 사는 것을 선호할 것이다. 그러나 동남아시아의 사마 바자우족 사람들은 다르다. 그들은 바다를 자신들의 집이라 부른다.

사마 바자우족은 수 세기 동안 바다에서 살아온 민족이다. 인도네시아, 말레이시아, 그리고 필리핀의 영해 위를 이동하면서, 그들은 바다와 깊은 관계를 갖고 있다. 사마 바자우족은 자신들의 유목 생활 방식을 자랑스러워한다. 전통적으로, 그들은 lepa-lepa라고 하는 길고 좁은 배에서 살면서 해류를 따라 떠돈다. 이로 인해 몇몇 사람들은 사마 바자우족을 '바다 유목민'이라고 묘사한다.

여러 세대에 걸쳐, 사마 바자우족은 심지어 해양 환경에 맞는 신체적 적응을 발달시켜 왔다. 물고기를 사냥할 때, 그들은 수심이 엄청나게 깊은 곳에 맨몸으로 다이빙할 수 있다. 또한 그들은 한 번의 호흡으로 수중에 오래 있을 수 있다. 사마 바자우족 아이들의 눈은 염분이 있는 물에 적응되었기 때문에 물속에서 아주 잘 볼 수 있다. 게다가, 사마 바자우족은 바다에서 아주 오랜 시간을 보내기 때문에, 땅에 발을 디딜 때 때로는 '육지 멀미'를 느낀다.

최근에, 일부 사마 바자우 사람들은 바다에서 사는 것을 매우 힘들다고 여겨 육지로 이동하기 시작했다. 그러나, 당신은 오늘날 여전히 산호초 사이에서 평화롭게 떠다니는 전통 사마 바자우족의 배를 찾을 수 있다.

어휘 nomad 몡 유목민 (nomadic 톙 유목의[방랑의])   nearly 閉 거의   species 몡 종(種)   ocean 몡 대양, 바다   probably 閉 아마도   prefer 동 선호하다   ethnic 톙 민족의[종족의]   century 몡 세기, 100년   link 몡 관련(성), 관계   be proud of ~을 자랑스러워하다   lifestyle 몡 생활방식   traditionally 閉 전통적으로 (traditional 톙 전통의, 전통적인)   narrow 톙 좁은   drift 동 (물·공기에) 떠가다, 표류하다   describe 동 묘사하다   generation 몡 세대   develop 동 발달시키다   physical 톙 육체의[신체의]   adaptation 몡 적응 (adapt to ~에 적응하다)   marine 톙 바다의[해양의]   environment 몡 환경   depth 몡 깊이   period 몡 시간, 기간   breath 몡 숨, 호흡   underwater 톙 물속의[수중의] 閉 물속에서   vision 몡 시력   recently 閉 최근에   peacefully 閉 평화롭게   float 동 떠가다[떠돌다]   coral reef 산호초   [문제] conservation 몡 보호

구문 3행 They **call** the ocean **their home**.

→ 「call A B」는 'A를 B라고 부르다'라는 의미이며, 이때 their home은 동사 call의 목적격 보어이다.

4행 The Sama-Bajau are **an ethnic group** [who *has lived* at sea *for* centuries].

→ [ ]는 선행사 an ethnic group을 수식하는 주격 관계대명사절이다.

→ has lived는 〈계속〉을 나타내는 현재완료로, 전치사 for 또는 since와 함께 많이 쓰인다.

5행 [Traveling the waters of Indonesia, Malaysia, and the Philippines], they have deep links to the ocean.

→ [ ]는 〈동시동작〉을 나타내는 분사구문이며, '~하면서'로 해석한다.

8행 This has **led some people to describe** the Sama-Bajau as "sea nomads."

→ 「lead+목적어+to-v」는 '~가 …하게 하다'의 의미이며, 이때 to describe는 led의 목적격 보어이다.

11행 [**When** hunting for fish], they can free dive to great depths.

→ [ ]는 〈때〉를 나타내는 분사구문으로, 의미를 명확하게 하기 위해 접속사(when)를 생략하지 않았다.

18행 However, you can still find **the traditional Sama-Bajau boats** [peacefully floating among the coral reefs] today.

→ [ ]는 앞의 the traditional Sama-Bajau boats를 수식하는 현재분사구이다.

● **VOCABULARY INSIDE**

Check Up 1 ethnic 2 celebrate 3 united 4 discussed
5 adaptations 6 floating 7 generation 8 principle

UNIT 02 | Wealth

READING 1 Alchemy

Ⅴ Mini Quiz
1 F 2 T

▶ **Reading Comprehension**
1 b 2 c 3 a 4 Changing the proportions

▶ **Grammar Inside LEVEL 3**
Check Up 1 Eating too many sweets ⌒gives⌒ you cavities.
2 It ⌒is⌒ very surprising that Luke is at the party.
3 The wedding of the two young movie stars ⌒was held⌒ on the island.

해석 오늘날, 철을 금으로 바꾼다는 생각은 마치 「해리포터」 시리즈에서 나오는 말 같다. 그러나, 세계의 초창기 과학자들 중 많은 사람들은 그것이 가능하다고 믿었다. 연금술이라고 하는 이 관행은 과학 역사의 일부이다.

고대 이집트와 중국에서 비롯된 후, 이 독특한 관행은 중세 유럽에서 절정에 달했다. (C) 연금술사들은 금속이 불, 공기, 물, 그리고 흙의 네 가지 성분으로 구성된다고 생각했다. (A) 그들은 또한 이 성분들의 비율을 바꾸는 것이 금과 같은

4 | Answer Key

다른 금속을 만들 것이라고 생각했다. (B) 하지만, 이런 일이 일어나게 하기 위해서는 특별한 어떤 것이 필요했는데, 바로 현자의 돌이었다.

전설에 따르면, 현자의 돌은 철과 같은 평범한 금속을 금과 은을 포함한 값비싼 것들로 바꿀 수 있었다. 또한 그 돌은 질병을 치료하는 힘을 가지며 심지어 소유자에게 영생을 줄 수 있을 거라고 여겨졌다.

그러나, 현대 과학의 성장으로 연금술에 관한 관심은 줄어들었다. 현자의 돌은 비록 근거 없는 믿음이었지만, 연금술사들의 업적은 현대 과학에 영향을 미쳤다. 그들은 많은 금속을 연구했고, 이것은 화학의 시작으로 이어졌다.

어휘 turn A into B A를 B로 바꾸다 iron [명] 철 early [형] 초기의 possible [형] 가능한 practice [명] 실행; *관행 ancient [형] 고대의 reach one's peak 절정에 이르다 medieval [형] 중세의 proportion [명] 비율 element [명] 요소, 성분 metal [명] 금속 philosopher [명] 철학자 alchemist [명] 연금술사 legend [명] 전설 ordinary [형] 보통의 cure [동] 치료하다, 치유하다 illness [명] 질병 eternal [형] 영원한 owner [명] 주인, 소유주 interest [명] 관심[흥미] decrease [동] 줄다[감소하다] rise [명] 상승, 성장 modern [형] 현대의 myth [명] 신화, 근거 없는 믿음 influence [동] 영향을 주다 beginning [명] 시작 chemistry [명] 화학 [문제] transform [동] 변형시키다

구문

[2행] But **many of the world's early scientists** *believed* [(*that*) it was possible].

→ of the world's early scientists는 전치사구로 주어 many를 수식한다. 이때 many는 대명사로 '많은 사람들'의 의미이다.

→ [ ]는 동사 believed의 목적어 역할을 하는 명사절로, 접속사 that이 생략되었다.

[5행] **Coming** from ancient Egypt and China, this unique practice reached its peak in medieval Europe.

→ Coming은 〈때〉를 나타내는 분사구문으로, After it came으로 바꿀 수 있다.

[9행] Alchemists **thought** [**that** metals *were composed of* four elements: ... earth].

→ that은 명사절을 이끄는 접속사로, [ ]는 동사 thought의 목적어 역할을 한다.

→ 「be composed of」는 '~으로 구성되다'라는 의미이다.

[11행] ... was able to change ordinary **metals** such as iron into expensive **ones**, including gold and silver.

→ ones는 앞서 나온 명사의 반복을 피하기 위해 쓰는 대명사로, metals를 가리킨다.

[17행] **They studied a lot of metals**, and **this** led to the beginnings of chemistry.

→ this는 앞 절의 내용 전체(They studied a lot of metals)를 가리킨다.

READING 2 The Medici Family

Mini Quiz

1 the Milan Cathedral 2 Galileo was able to study the universe with the money he earned from teaching the Medici children.

▶ **Reading Comprehension**

1 b 2 c 3 c 4 focus on their work, worrying about money

▶ **Grammar Inside LEVEL 3**

[Check Up] 1 that Amy had her hair cut, 너는 에이미가 머리를 자른 것을 눈치 챘니?

2 the action movie you recommended yesterday, 나는 어제 네가 추천했던 액션 영화를 보았다.

르네상스 시대는 이탈리아 피렌체에서 1300년대에 시작되었다. 부유한 가문들의 권력은 그 시대의 발달에 극히 중요했는데, 메디치는 이러한 가문들 중 하나였다.

그 당시에, 예술가들은 돈에 관한 걱정 없이 자신들의 작업에 집중할 수 있도록 재정적 후원자의 도움을 필요로 했다. 메디치 가문은 미켈란젤로, 레오나르도 다빈치, 보티첼리와 같은 르네상스 대가을 후원했다. 그 가문의 지원으로, 미켈란젤로는 시스티나 성당에 그림을 그릴 수 있었다. 이는 또한 밀라노 대성당을 포함하여 유명 건축물들이 건설되도록 했다.

예술뿐 아니라, 과학도 메디치 가문의 큰 관심거리였다. 그들은 다빈치와 갈릴레오 같은 많은 과학자들을 후원했다. 갈릴레오는 메디치 가문의 자녀들을 가르쳐서 번 돈으로 우주를 연구할 수 있었다. 그는 심지어 자신이 발견한 별들 중 일부를 그 가문 아이들의 이름을 따서 지었다. 게다가, 그 가문은 많은 과학자를 피렌체로 끌어들인 과학 아카데미를 설립했다. 그들은 또한 학자들이 고전 문헌들을 연구하도록 돕고 학교와 도서관을 후원했다. 그 가문의 예술, 과학, 그리고 문화에 대한 사랑이 없었다면, 예술의 역사는 오늘날 많이 달라져 있을 것이다.

어휘 period 영 기간; *시대   wealthy 형 부유한   essential 형 필수적인; 극히 중요한   development 영 발달, 성장   financial 형 재정의, 금전적인   supporter 영 후원자 (support 동 후원하다 영 지지, 지원)   focus on ~에 주력하다, 초점을 맞추다   master 영 주인; *대가(大家)   construct 동 건설하다   in addition to ~에 더하여   of interest to ~에 흥미 있는   universe 영 우주   earn 동 (돈을) 벌다   establish 동 설립하다   academy 영 학교   attract 동 마음을 끌다; *(사람을) 끌어들이다   scholar 영 학자   text 영 글, 문서   sponsor 동 후원하다

구문 4행 ..., artists needed the help [of financial supporters] **so that they could** focus on their work without worrying about money.
→ [ ]는 the help를 수식하는 전치사구이다.
→ 「so that+주어+could」는 '~가 …할 수 있도록'의 의미이며, so that은 in order that으로 바꿀 수 있다.

11행 It also **allowed famous buildings to be constructed**, including the Milan Cathedral.
→ 「allow+목적어+to-v」는 '~가 …하게 하다'라는 의미이다. 유명한 건물이 '지어지는' 것이므로, 목적격 보어인 to부정사가 수동형(to be constructed)으로 쓰였다.

16행 He even **named** some of *the stars* [(that) he found] **after** the children of the family.
→ 「name A after B」는 'B(의 이름)를 따서 A(의 이름)를 짓다'의 의미이다.
→ [ ]는 선행사 the stars를 수식하는 목적격 관계대명사절로, 관계대명사 that이 생략되었다.

16행 Moreover, the family established **a science academy** [that attracted many scientists to Florence].
→ [ ]는 선행사 a science academy를 수식하는 주격 관계대명사절이다.

19행 **Without** the family's love for arts, ..., the history of the arts **would be** a lot different today.
→ without은 '~가 없었다면'의 의미로 가정법의 if를 대신할 수 있다. 이 문장은 '만일 ~였다면 …할 텐데'의 의미로 과거에 실현되지 못한 일이 현재까지 영향을 미칠 때 사용하는 혼합가정법이며, 'If it had not been for the family's love for arts, ..., the history of the arts would be a lot different today.'로 바꿀 수 있다.

Check Up 　1 elements　　2 cure　　3 eternal　　4 financial
　　　　　　　5 support　　6 interest　　7 practice　　8 earn

UNIT 03 | Shapes

pp. 19-24

READING 1 　Islamic Art

♥ Mini Quiz
1 T　　2 F

▶ **Reading Comprehension**
1 b　　2 only Allah can create life　　3 c　　4 c

해석　　튀르키예와 같은 이슬람 국가에서 당신은 고급스러운 무늬로 뒤덮인 사원과 궁전들의 천장과 바닥을 발견할 것이다. 이슬람 미술은 수학, 예술, 이슬람 문화의 혼합이라는 점에서 독특하다. 특히 이슬람 예술가들은 멋진 무늬를 개발하는 것을 자랑스러워한다.

　　무슬림들은 오직 그들의 신, 알라만이 생명을 창조해낼 수 있다고 여기기 때문에, 그들은 자신들의 작품에서 사람이나 동물의 이미지를 묘사하지 않는다. 그 대신에 이슬람 예술가들은 삼각형, 사각형, 오각형과 같은 모형을 사용하여 아름다움을 보여주려고 한다. (B) 게다가, 그들은 더 복잡한 모형을 만들어내기 위해 그것들을 결합하고 회전시킨다. (C) 예를 들어, 여덟 개의 꼭짓점을 가진 별은 그들의 작품에서 종종 사용된다. (A) 그것은 두 개의 사각형에서 하나를 45도 회전해서 만들어진다. 그리고 나서, 이슬람 예술가들은 수천 개의 모형들을 나란히 놓아서 그 별들의 반복되는 무늬를 만들어낸다. 놀랍게도, 예술가들은 오직 한 개의 자와 컴퍼스로 복잡한 무늬를 만들어낼 수 있다.

　　이슬람 미술에서 반복되는 기하학적 모형은 깊은 뜻이 있다. 무슬림들에게 반복되는 수학적 무늬는 알라의 무한한 본질을 묘사한다. 이슬람 미술은 미술이 어떻게 사람들이 세상을 보는지를 나타내는 아주 좋은 방법이라는 것을 보여준다.

어휘　　Islamic ⓗ 이슬람교의, 회교도의 (Islam ⓜ 이슬람교, 회교)　Türkiye ⓜ 튀르키예(터키)　ceiling ⓜ 천장　mosque ⓜ 모스크, 회교 사원　palace ⓜ 궁전　elegant ⓗ 우아한　pattern ⓜ 패턴; *무늬　mix ⓜ 혼합체[섞인 것]　in particular 특히　Muslim ⓜ 이슬람교도, 회교도　depict ⓥ 묘사하다, 그리다　artwork ⓜ 미술품　pentagon ⓜ 오각형　rotate ⓥ 회전하다, 회전시키다　degree ⓜ (각도의 단위인) 도　combine ⓥ 결합하다　complex ⓗ 복잡한　repeat ⓥ 반복하다 (repetitive ⓗ 반복적인, 반복되는)　lay ⓥ 놓다[두다]　side by side 나란히　compass ⓜ 나침반; *(제도용) 컴퍼스　geometric ⓗ 기하학적인　describe ⓥ 말하다; *묘사하다　infinite ⓗ 무한한　nature ⓜ 자연; *본성, 본질　represent ⓥ 대표하다; *나타내다　[문제] element ⓜ 요소, 성분　origin ⓜ 기원[근원]

구문　　**1행** In Islamic countries such as Türkiye, you'll find **ceilings *and* floors of mosques *and* palaces** [covered in elegant patterns].
　　→ [ ]는 앞의 ceilings ... palaces를 수식하는 과거분사구이다.
　　→ 첫 번째 and는 ceilings와 floors를, 두 번째 and는 mosques와 palaces를 병렬 연결한다.

[5행] **Since** Muslims believe that only Allah, their god, can create life, … .
→ since는 〈이유〉를 나타내는 접속사로 '~ 때문에'의 의미이다.

[11행] Then Islamic artists make repeating patterns of the stars, [laying thousands of shapes side by side].
→ [ ]는 '~하면서'라는 의미의 〈동시동작〉을 나타내는 분사구문이다.

[15행] **Repeating geometric shapes** in Islamic art **have** a deep meaning.
→ Repeating은 주어인 geometric shapes를 수식하는 현재분사이며, 동사는 have이다.

[18행] Islamic art shows that art is **a great way** [to represent *how* people see the world].
→ [ ]는 앞의 a great way를 수식하는 형용사적 용법의 to부정사구이다.
→ how는 〈방법〉을 나타내는 관계부사로, 선행사 the way와 함께 쓰지 않는다.

READING 2 Lake Balls

Mini Quiz
1 they float during the day and sink at night 2 Japan

▶ Reading Comprehension
1 b 2 c 3 d 4 The use of fertilizers, block out the light for photosynthesis

▶ Grammar Inside LEVEL 3
[Check Up] 나는 카페에 내 우산을 놓고 왔을지도 모른다.

해석 민물 수족관에 방문해 본 적이 있는가? 만약 그렇다면, 당신은 녹색 벨벳 같은 공들이 물속에 떠다니는 것을 봤을지도 모른다. 이 작은 특이한 공들은 마리모 모스볼로 알려져 있는데, (이것들은) 사실상 이끼가 아니다. 사실 그것들은 일종의 민물 식물인 조류로 만들어졌다. 조류가 자라면서, 그것들은 가는 실을 생산한다. 이것들은 호수나 강바닥에서 뒤엉키게 된다. 시간이 지나면서, 그것들은 공 모양이 된다.

그 물속의 공들을 자세히 보라. 당신은 그것들이 낮에는 떠 있고 밤에는 가라앉는다는 것을 알아챘을지도 모른다. 이 동작의 비밀은 광합성이다. 그 공들은 햇빛을 받으면, 작은 산소 방울들을 내뿜는다. 이 방울들이 가는 실에 갇히게 되고, 공을 표면으로 밀어 올린다. 빛이 사라지면서 (산소) 방울들은 곧 사라지고, 공은 가라앉게 된다.

마리모 볼은 수십 년 전에는 찾아보기 쉬웠다. 하지만 그들의 개체 수가 감소했다. 농업에서 비료의 사용이 조류와 경쟁 관계에 있는 조류의 수를 증가시켰다. 이 식물들은 수면을 뒤덮고 광합성에 필요한 빛을 차단한다. 그 결과, 오늘날 마리모는 일본에서만 발견된다.

어휘 freshwater [형] 민물의[담수의] aquarium [명] 수족관 velvety [형] 벨벳 같은, 아주 부드러운 moss [명] 이끼 unusual [형] 특이한 actually [부] 사실상 algae [명] 조류(藻類), 말 produce [동] 생산하다 tangled [형] 헝클어진, 뒤얽힌 form [동] 형성하다 closely [부] 긴밀하게; *자세히 sink [동] 가라앉다 behavior [명] 행동 give off 내뿜다, 발산하다 oxygen [명] 산소 disappear [동] 사라지다 fade [동] (색깔이) 바래다; *서서히 사라지다 several [형] 몇몇의 decade [명] 10년 population [명] 인구; *개체 수 decrease [동] 감소하다 fertilizer [명] 비료 agriculture [명] 농업 rival [형] 경쟁하는 species [명] 종(種) block out (빛·소리를) 차단하다

구문 [2행] **(Being) Known** as Marimo moss balls, these small unusual balls are not actually moss.
→ Known은 앞에 Being이 생략된 분사구문이다.

3행 In fact, they **are made of** *algae, a kind of freshwater plant*.
- → 「be made of」는 '~으로 만들어지다'의 의미이다.
- → algae와 a kind of freshwater plant는 동격 관계이다.

7행 You *might have noticed* [*that* they float during the day and sink at night].
- → 「might have v-ed」는 '~이었을지도 모른다'는 의미로, 과거의 일에 대한 약한 추측을 나타낸다.
- → that은 명사절을 이끄는 접속사로, [ ]는 might have noticed의 목적어 역할을 한다.

10행 The bubbles soon disappear **as** the light fades, [*causing the balls to sink*].
- → as는 '~하면서'의 의미로, 〈때〉를 나타내는 접속사이다.
- → [ ]는 '그리고 ~하다'라는 의미의 〈연속동작〉을 나타내는 분사구문이다. 「cause+목적어+to-v」는 '~가 …하도록 하다'의 의미이고, to sink는 causing의 목적격 보어이다.

12행 Marimo balls were **easy to find** several decades ago.
- → to find는 형용사(easy)를 수식하는 to부정사의 부사적 용법이다.

15행 These plants **cover** the surface of the water and **block out** the light for photosynthesis.
- → cover와 block out이 접속사 and로 병렬 연결되어 있다.

● VOCABULARY INSIDE

Check Up	1 Combine	2 sink	3 agriculture	4 complex
	5 rotate	6 depicts	7 behavior	8 decreased

UNIT 04 | Nature

pp. 25-30

READING 1   Iceland

◐ Mini Quiz
1 ancient   2 the beautiful fjords and valleys

▶ Reading Comprehension
1 a   2 d   3 a   4 a battlefield of the gods

▶ Grammar Inside LEVEL 3
Check Up had worked

해석   아이슬란드는 모든 방문객들을 이곳의 숨 막히는 풍경과 사랑에 빠지게 만드는 나라이다. 전설에 따르면, 한 마법사가 자신의 마법으로 아이슬란드를 지배하기 위해 고래로 변한 후 그곳을 향해 헤엄쳤다. 그러나 그는 그 섬의 요정들에 의해 저지되었는데, 그 요정들은 용감하게 고국을 보호했다. 오늘날 당신은 그와 같은 요정들을 만나지는 못할 것이다. 하지만, 아이슬란드의 거대한 화산과 웅장한 빙하는 분명 당신이 마법을 믿도록 할 것이다.

그 섬은 대서양 중앙 해령을 따라 마그마가 끓어올랐던 2천만 년 전에 형성되었다. 그 연기 나는 땅과 용암은 신들의 싸움터로 보여서, 아이슬란드의 초창기 거주민들은 자신들이 고대의 땅을 발견했다고 믿었다.

　심지어 지금도, 그 땅은 여전히 형성되고 있는 중이다. 130여 개의 화산이 10년마다 두 번씩 분화가 일어나면서, 섬 전역에 펼쳐져 있다. 몇몇 분화는 그렇게 크지 (A) 않지만, 다른 것들은 엄청난 양의 용암을 분출한다. 모든 화산들 중, 그림스뵈튼 화산이 가장 활발하다. 2011년에 그 분화 (B) 때문에, 900편의 항공이 취소되었다.

　얼음은 아이슬란드를 형성하는 또 다른 자연의 힘이다. 지난 7천 년 동안, 섬을 덮은 빙하들은 차츰 녹아내려 아이슬란드의 아름다운 피오르드 지형과 계곡을 형성했다. 이러한 빙하들은 여전히 그 나라의 약 10퍼센트를 덮고 있다.

어휘　fall in love with ~와 사랑에 빠지다　breathtaking 혱 숨이 막히는　landscape 몡 풍경　according to ~에 의하면[따르면]　legend 몡 전설　wizard 몡 마법사　turn into ~으로 변하다　control 통 지배하다　spirit 몡 영혼; *정령, 요정　bravely 뷔 용감하게　homeland 몡 고국[조국]　huge 혱 거대한　volcano 몡 화산　grand 혱 웅장한　glacier 몡 빙하　magma 몡 마그마　bubble up 콸콸 솟다; *끓어오르다　lava 몡 용암　battlefield 몡 싸움터, 전쟁터　resident 몡 거주자　form 통 형성하다　spread 통 퍼지다; 펼쳐지다 (spread-spread)　erupt 통 분출하다 (eruption 몡 (화산의) 폭발, 분화)　active 혱 활동적인, 활발한　cancel 통 취소하다　shape 통 형성하다　melt 통 녹다　cover 통 씌우다; *(언급된 지역에) 걸치다

구문　1행 Iceland is **a country** [that makes every visitor fall in love with its breathtaking landscapes].
　→ [ ]는 선행사 a country를 수식하는 주격 관계대명사절이다.

　3행 But he was stopped by **the island's spirits, who** bravely protected their homeland.
　→ 「, who」는 선행사 the island's spirits를 부연 설명하는 계속적 용법의 주격 관계대명사이다.

　11행 Even now, the land **is** still **being formed**.
　→ is being formed는 '형성되고 있다'라는 의미로, 「be being v-ed」형태의 진행형 수동태이다.

　11행 About 130 volcanoes are spread across the island, **erupting** twice every ten years.
　→ erupting은 '분화하면서'의 의미로, 〈동시동작〉을 나타내는 분사구문이다.

　12행 Though **some** eruptions are not that big, **others** release large amounts of lava.
　→ 「some ~ others ...」은 '어떤 것들은 ~, 다른 어떤 것들은 …'의 의미이다.

READING 2　Living near Volcanoes

Ⓥ Mini Quiz
　1 T　2 T

▶ Reading Comprehension
　1 b　2 c　3 drives engines, produces electricity　4 b

해석　인도네시아에 위치한 메라피 산은 세계적으로 가장 활발한 화산들 중 하나이다. 놀랍게도, 이곳에서 20마일 내에 사는 사람들이 약 백만 명이다. 그리고 지역 인구는 증가하고 있다. 왜 그렇게 많은 사람들이 그토록 위험한 곳 근처에 거주하는 것일까? 믿거나 말거나 화산 근처에 사는 것에는 많은 혜택이 있다.

　첫째, 화산 주변의 토양은 미네랄이 풍부해서, 식물에 영양분을 제공해준다. 또한, 많은 화산 분출물들이 실제로 꽤 유용하다. 예를 들어, 유황은 약이나 성냥의 재료로 사용될 수 있다. 금, 은, 다이아몬드를 포함한 다른 귀중한 물질도 화산 근처에서 발견된다. 이러한 이유로, 광산촌이 종종 화산 근처에 지어진다.

아이슬란드와 뉴질랜드 같은 국가에서, 화산은 지열 에너지원으로 사용된다. 사람들은 지하 마그마로 데워진 증기를 사용해 발전소의 엔진을 돌린다. 이것은 가정과 공장에서 사용될 수 있는 전력을 생산한다.

게다가, 화산은 관광객들을 많이 끌어모으는데, 이들은 온천처럼 화산에 의해 만들어진 특징을 보러 온다. 하와이에서, 관광객들은 심지어 검은 모래가 화산암으로 만들어진 이국적인 해변을 방문할 수 있다. 그리고 이러한 모든 명소들은 현지인들을 위한 일자리를 창출해낸다. 이제 왜 그렇게 많은 사람들이 화산 근처에서 사는지 알겠는가?

어휘

volcano 명 화산 (volcanic 형 화산의)   local 형 지역의, 현지의   population 명 인구   believe it or not 믿거나 말거나   mineral 명 광물(질); 미네랄   nutrient 명 영양분   product 명 제품; *산물   ingredient 명 재료[성분]   match 명 성냥   valuable 형 귀중한[소중한]   material 명 재료, 물질   mining 명 채굴, 광산(업)   source 명 원천, 근원   steam 명 김, 증기   heat 통 가열하다   underground 형 지하의   drive 통 몰다; *(기계에) 동력을 공급하다   engine 명 엔진   power station 발전소   electricity 명 전기, 전력   factory 명 공장   draw 통 그리다; *(마음을) 끌다   hot spring 온천   exotic 형 이국적인   attraction 명 끌림; *명소   [문제] emergency 형 비상(사태)   erupt 통 분출하다   benefit 명 혜택, 이득 통 (~에서) 득을 보다   overcome 통 극복하다   fear 명 공포, 두려움

구문

1행 **Mount Merapi**, [located in Indonesia], is one of the world's most active volcanoes.
→ [ ]는 Mount Merapi를 수식하는 과거분사구로, 문장 중간에 삽입되었다.

3행 Why would so many people live near **something** so **dangerous**?
→ -thing, -body, -one으로 끝나는 명사는 형용사가 뒤에서 수식한다.

6행 ..., so it **provides** plants **with** nutrients.
→ 「provide A with B」는 'A에게 B를 제공하다'의 의미이다.

13행 People use **steam** [heated by underground magma] to drive engines in power stations.
→ [ ]는 steam을 수식하는 과거분사구이다.

16행 In addition, volcanoes draw **a lot of tourists, who** come to see volcanic features such as hot springs.
→ 「, who」는 선행사 a lot of tourists를 부연 설명하는 계속적 용법의 주격 관계대명사이다.

17행 In Hawaii, tourists can even visit **exotic beaches** [whose black sand *is made from* volcanic rocks].
→ [ ]는 선행사 exotic beaches를 수식하는 소유격 관계대명사절이다.
→ 「be made from」은 '~으로 만들어지다'의 의미이다.

19행 Now, do you see (**the reason**) **why** so many people live near volcanoes?
→ why는 이유를 나타내는 관계부사로, 앞에 선행사 the reason이 생략되었다.

● VOCABULARY INSIDE

Check Up	1 resident	2 electricity	3 erupt	4 population
	5 draw	6 spreads	7 melt	8 source

UNIT 05 | Buildings

READING 1   Svalbard Global Seed Vault

Mini Quiz
1 It is located in a mountain of the Arctic Circle.   2 in 2016

▶ **Reading Comprehension**
1 b   2 c   3 b   4 to help an agricultural research center[to help researchers continue their research]

해석   전 세계적인 재앙이 닥친다면 구해야 할 가장 중요한 것은 무엇일까? 놀랍게도 많은 과학자들은 우리가 종자를 저장해야 한다고 믿고 있는데, 그것들이 식량을 생산하는 데 필수적이기 때문이다. 이러한 이유로, 노르웨이 정부는 2008년에 세계에서 가장 큰 종자 저장고를 건설했다. 그것은 북극권의 산속에 위치해 있고, 스발바르 국제 종자 저장고라고 이름 지어졌다. 그 저장고의 주요 목적은 종자를 저장하고, 지구의 식물을 위협하는 지역적 또는 세계적 위기로부터 씨앗을 보호하는 것이다.

사실 전 세계에 다른 종자 저장고들이 있지만, 많은 곳들이 전쟁이나 자연재해에 의해 파괴되어 왔다. 그러나, 스발바르 저장고는 고립되고 추운 위치로 인해 보호된다. 산의 얼음과 바위는 저장고가 전기 없이도 종자들을 얼린 상태로 유지하기에 충분히 차갑도록 만들어준다. 게다가, 저장고는 해수면보다 상당히 위에 위치하여 홍수로부터 보호된다.

그 저장고는 시리아의 농업 연구 기관을 돕기 위해 2015년에 최초로 개방되었다. 내전 때문에 센터의 과학자들은 더 안전한 곳으로 옮겨야 했다. 연구를 계속하기 위해 그들은 스발바르 저장고에서 자신들이 필요로 하는 주요 종자들을 보내주기를 원했다. 이 사건은 저장고의 중요성을 보여주었다. 2016년에 또 다른 저장고가 한국에 건설되었다. 그곳은 4천 개가 넘는 야생 식물 종들에게서 나온 10만 개에 달하는 종자들을 가지고 있다.

어휘   catastrophe 몡 참사, 재앙   essential 혱 필수적인   Norwegian 혱 노르웨이의   government 몡 정부   locate 동 (특정한 위치에) 두다, 설치하다 (location 몡 장소, 위치)   primary 혱 주된, 주요한   store 동 저장[보관]하다   regional 혱 지방의, 지역의   crisis 몡 위기 ((pl.) crises)   threaten 동 위협하다   destroy 동 파괴하다   disaster 몡 참사, 재난, 재해   electricity 몡 전기, 전력   protect 동 보호하다   flooding 몡 홍수   place 동 놓다, 설치[배치]하다   sea level 해수면   agricultural 혱 농업의   due to ~ 때문에   incident 몡 일[사건]   importance 몡 중요성   [문제] isolated 혱 외딴, 고립된   chilly 혱 쌀쌀한, 추운

구문   **3행** ..., many scientists believe that they should save seeds, **as** they are essential for producing food.
→ as는 '~ 때문에'의 의미로, 〈이유〉를 나타내는 접속사이다.

7행 Its primary purpose is **to store** seeds, and **(to) protect** them from *regional or global crises* [that threaten the Earth's plants].
→ to store 이하는 보어 역할을 하는 명사적 용법의 to부정사구이며, to store와 (to) protect는 and로 병렬 연결되었다.
→ [ ]는 선행사 regional or global crises를 수식하는 주격 관계대명사절이다.

10행 Actually, there are other seed vaults around the world, but many **have been destroyed** by wars or natural disasters.
→ have been destroyed는 '파괴되어 왔다'의 의미로, 「have been v-ed」 형태의 〈계속〉을 나타내는 현재완료 수동태이다.

12 | Answer Key

[15행] The vault was opened for the first time in 2015 **to help** an agricultural research center in Syria.

→ to help는 '돕기 위하여'라는 의미로 〈목적〉을 나타내는 부사적 용법의 to부정사이다.

[20행] It has **nearly 100,000 seeds** [from over 4,000 different wild plant species].

→ [ ]는 nearly 100,000 seeds를 수식하는 전치사구이다.

READING 2 The Gherkin

Mini Quiz

1 T 2 F

▶ Reading Comprehension

1 d 2 it looks like a pickle 3 c 4 (1) c (2) a (3) b

해석 빅벤부터 런던아이까지, 런던은 수많은 위대한 건축술의 요람이다. 런던의 스카이라인에 가장 특이한 건물 중 하나는 2004년에 완공되었는데, 41층이며 높이가 180미터에 달한다. 그 건물은 피클처럼 생겨서 런던 사람들에 의해 '거킨(오이 피클)'이라는 별칭이 붙었다.

거킨의 색다른 형태에 더하여, 그것의 독특한 디자인은 많은 실용적인 특징들을 갖는다. 첫째, 그것의 곡선 형태는 바람이 건물 주변으로 부드럽게 불게 한다. 이것은 건물에 가해지는 압력을 줄이고 그 근처의 보행자들에게 부는 강풍의 양을 감소시킨다. 둘째, 바닥부터 천장까지 이어지는 창문은 자연 채광을 담아내서 인공조명의 필요성을 줄인다. 셋째, 거킨에 새로운 '녹색 벽'을 덧댈 계획이 있다. 시간이 지나면서, 잔디와 같은 식물이 건물 일부를 가로질러 자랄 것이다. 이 벽이 대기 오염을 줄이면서 건물에 그늘 및 단열 효과를 제공할 것이다. (35킬로미터가 넘는 철근이 거킨을 짓기 위해 사용될 것이다.) 거킨의 획기적인 설계로, 일반 사무실 건물보다 최대 50퍼센트까지의 에너지를 절감할 것으로 예상된다.

건축된 이래로, 거킨은 독특한 외관 때문에 많은 관심을 받아 오고 있다. 하지만 그 건물이 환경과 조화를 이루는 멋진 디자인적인 특징을 가진 것 또한 분명하다.

어휘 architecture [명] *건축학, 건축술; 건축물 unusual [형] 특이한, 색다른 skyline [명] 스카이라인(하늘이 배경인 산·건물의 윤곽) complete [동] 완료하다 floor [명] (건물의) 층 nickname [명] 별명 shape [명] 모양, 형태 practical [형] 현실적인; *실용적인 feature [명] 특색, 특징 curved [형] 곡선의, 약간 굽은 smoothly [부] 부드럽게 pressure [명] 압력 decrease [동] 줄이다 pedestrian [명] 보행자 capture [동] 포착하다, 담아내다 lessen [동] 줄이다 artificial [형] 인공의[인조의] add A to B A를 B에 덧붙이다 over time 시간이 지나면서 shade [명] 그늘 pollution [명] 오염, 공해 construct [동] 건설하다 (construction [명] 건설, 공사) innovative [형] 획기적인 ordinary [형] 보통의; 평범한 attention [명] 주목; 관심 appearance [명] (겉)모습, 외모 brilliant [형] 훌륭한, 멋진 in harmony with ~와 조화를 이루어 environment [명] 환경

구문 [2행] **One of the most unusual buildings** in London's skyline **was** completed in 2004, *standing* 180 meters tall with 41 floors.

→ 「one of the+형용사의 최상급+복수 명사」는 '가장 ~한 … 중 하나'의 의미로, 주어가 One이므로 단수 동사 was가 쓰였다.

→ standing은 '서 있으면서'의 의미로, 〈동시동작〉을 나타내는 분사구문이다.

[16행] This wall will **provide** shade and insulation **for** the building *while reducing* air pollution.

→ 「provide A for B」는 'B에게 A를 제공하다'의 의미이다.

→ while reducing 이하는 〈때〉를 나타내는 분사구문으로, 의미를 명확히 하거나 강조하기 위해 접속사를 생략하지 않았다.

18행 With its innovative design, the Gherkin is expected to use up to 50% **less energy than** ordinary office buildings.

→ 「less+명사+than ~」은 '~보다 더 적은 …'의 의미인 비교 표현이다.

21행 But **it**'s clear **that** the building also has *brilliant design features* [that work in harmony with its environment].

→ it은 가주어이고 that 이하가 진주어이다.

→ [ ]는 선행사 brilliant design features를 수식하는 주격 관계대명사절이다.

● **VOCABULARY INSIDE**

Check Up	1 pedestrian	2 artificial	3 primary	4 destroyed
	5 pressure	6 incident	7 flooding	8 government

UNIT 06 | Numbers

pp. 37-42

READING 1 42.195 Kilometers

◐ **Mini Quiz**
1 40 kilometers   2 Referees helped him up when he fell down.

▶ **Reading Comprehension**
1 c   2 b   3 received help   4 d

▶ **Grammar Inside LEVEL 3**
Check Up 1 What   2 that

해석   마라톤이라고 불리는 장거리 경주는 고대 이후로 계속되어 왔다. 그리스 역사학자들에 따르면, 한 전령(傳令)이 탈진으로 숨을 거두기 전에, 그리스 승리의 소식을 공유하기 위해 40킬로미터를 달렸다고 한다. 이 이야기는 현대 마라톤에 영감을 주었고, 이것이 처음에 (경주) 거리가 40킬로미터였던 이유이다. 그리고 나서 1908년 런던 올림픽에서 그 길이가 오늘날의 것인 42.195킬로미터로 늘어났다.

그렇다면 1908년에 무슨 일이 있었나? 어떤 사람들은 알렉산드라 여왕이 1908년 런던 올림픽에서 경기장이 아닌 윈저성의 잔디밭이 마라톤의 출발점이 되도록 요구했다고 말한다. (윈저성은 런던에서 가장 오래된 성들 중 하나이다.) 그녀는 왕실 자녀들이 집에서 경주를 보길 원했다. 그녀는 또한 경기장의 왕족을 위한 관람석 앞에서 경주가 끝나도록 요청했다. 이러한 요청들로 그 거리에 2.195킬로미터가 추가되었다.

하지만 그 거리가 어떻게 영구적인 것이 되었는지에 관한 또 다른 이야기가 있다. 런던 올림픽의 경주 중에, 이탈리아 주자인 Dorando Pietri는 경주를 마치려고 고군분투했다. 그는 계속해서 넘어졌지만, 절대 포기하지 않았다. 그의 노력에 감명받은 나머지, 심판들이 그가 넘어졌을 때 일으켜주었다. 마침내, Pietri는 경주에서 우승하였다. 하지만 그가 도움을 받았기 때문에, 그는 실격되었고 다른 주자가 우승자로 지명되었다. 그럼에도 불구하고, 언론은 Pietri의 강한 의지에 초점을 맞추었고, 그를 국제적인 스타로 만들었다. 사람들은 이 이야기가 거리를 42.195킬로미터로 유지하는 공식 위원들의 결정에 영향을 끼쳤을지도 모른다고 이야기한다.

어휘 historian 몡 역사학자 messenger 몡 전달자, 전령(傳令) share 동 함께 쓰다, 공유하다 victory 몡 승리 exhaustion 몡 탈진, 기진맥진 inspire 동 고무하다; *영감을 주다 distance 몡 거리 initially 뷔 처음에 length 몡 길이 increase 동 증가시키다 demand 동 요구하다 lawn 몡 잔디밭 stadium 몡 경기장 royal 혱 왕의, 왕실의 (royalty 몡 왕족) request 동 요청하다 몡 요청, 요구 add 동 추가하다 permanent 혱 영구적인 struggle to-v ~하려고 애쓰다 repeatedly 뷔 되풀이하여 give up 포기하다 impress 동 깊은 인상을 주다, 감명[감동]을 주다 referee 몡 심판 eventually 뷔 결국 receive 동 받다 disqualified 혱 자격을 잃은, 실격된 media 몡 대중 매체 [미디어] will 몡 의지 international 혱 국제적인 official 몡 (고위) 공무원[관리] [문제] political 혱 정치적인

구문

4행 This tale inspired the modern marathon, **which** is (*the reason*) *why* the distance was initially 40 kilometers.
→ 「, which」는 앞 절 전체를 선행사로 하는 계속적 용법의 주격 관계대명사이다.
→ why는 〈이유〉를 나타내는 관계부사로, 앞에 the reason이 생략되었다.

7행 Some **say (that)** Queen Alexandra *demanded* **that** Windsor Castle's lawn (*should*) *be* the starting line of the marathon, ... in London.
→ 두 개의 that 모두 명사절을 이끄는 접속사로 첫 번째 that은 동사 say의 목적어 역할을, 두 번째 that은 동사 demanded의 목적어 역할을 한다.
→ 〈제안·명령·요구·주장〉 등의 의미를 지닌 동사 뒤에 that이 이끄는 명사절이 나오는 경우, 명사절에는 「(should +)동사원형」을 쓰며, should는 흔히 생략된다.

14행 But there's another story **about** [how this distance became permanent].
→ [ ]는 「의문사+주어+동사」 어순의 간접의문문으로, 전치사 about의 목적어 역할을 한다.

17행 (**Being**) **Impressed** with his efforts, referees helped him up when he fell down.
→ Impressed는 '감동받았기 때문에'라는 의미로 〈이유〉를 나타내는 분사구문이며, 앞에 Being이 생략되었다.

20행 Nevertheless, the media focused on Pietri's strong will, [making him an international star].
→ [ ]는 〈연속동작〉을 나타내는 분사구문으로, and made him an international star로 바꿀 수 있다.

21행 People say that this story **might have influenced** *the officials' decision* [to keep the distance at 42.195 kilometers].
→ 「might have v-ed」는 '~이었을지도 모른다'는 의미로 과거 사실에 대한 약한 추측을 나타낸다.
→ [ ]는 the officials' decision을 수식하는 형용사적 용법의 to부정사구이다.

READING 2 Lunar Calendars

ⓥ Mini Quiz
1 F 2 T

▶ Reading Comprehension
1 d 2 b 3 (1) 365 (2) 4 (3) 12 (4) 3 4 leap day, February 29

해석

전 세계적으로, 대부분의 사람들은 한 해를 추적하기 위해 양력을 사용한다. 이 달력은 태양 주위를 도는 지구의 움직임에 기초한다. 그러나, 달의 움직임을 따르는 또 다른 달력이 있다. 그것은 음력이라고 불린다.

지구가 태양 주위를 도는 데 걸리는 시간은 태양년으로 알려져 있다. 태양월은 매 태양년의 12분의 1이다. 비슷하게 태음년에도 12개월이 있다. 그러나, 각 태음월은 달의 상(相)이 한 주기를 완료하는 데 걸리는 시간으로 정의된다. 이러한 상은 초승달, 반달, 보름달을 포함한다. 비록 그 기간이 매달 정확히 같지는 않지만, 전 과정은 대개 약 29.5일이 소요된다. 태음년은 이러한 주기가 12번 있다.

태양년이 약 365일 지속되는 반면, 태음년은 354일로 약간 더 짧다. 'epact'라는 용어는 이 11일간의 차이를 설명하기 위해 사용되었다. 두 달력의 균형을 맞추기 위해, 3년마다 음력에 여분의 한 달이 추가된다. 양력에는 4년마다 2월에 추가된 '윤일(閏日)'이 있다. 이날은 매 '윤년(閏年)'의 2월 29일에 해당한다.

어휘

lunar [형] 달의　calendar [명] 달력　solar [형] 태양의　track [동] 추적하다　be based on ~에 기초하다　movement [명] 움직임　follow [동] 따라가다　be known as ~으로 알려져 있다　similarly [부] 비슷하게　define [동] 정의하다　complete [동] 완료하다　cycle [명] 주기　include [동] 포함하다　whole [형] 전체의　process [명] 과정　typically [부] 보통, 일반적으로　period [명] 기간　exactly [부] 정확히　last [동] 지속되다　slightly [부] 약간　term [명] 용어　balance [동] 균형을 맞추다　extra [형] 추가의, 여분의　leap day 윤일(閏日)　fall [동] 떨어지다; *(날짜가) ~이다　leap year 윤년(閏年)　[문제] closely [부] 가까이, 밀접하게; 꼭　come up with (해답·아이디어를) 떠올리다, 내놓다　exact [형] 정확한

구문

[3행] However, there is **another calendar** [that follows the movements of the moon].
→ [ ]는 선행사 another calendar를 수식하는 주격 관계대명사절이다.

[5행] ***The time*** [(**which/that**) *it takes the Earth to move* around the Sun] **is** known as a solar year.
→ [ ]는 선행사 The time을 수식하는 목적격 관계대명사절로, 목적격 관계대명사(which/that)가 생략되었다. 이때 The time이 문장의 주어이고, is가 동사이다.
→ 「it takes+사람[사물]+시간+to-v」는 '~가 …하는 데 (시간이) 걸리다'의 의미이다.

[13행] **While** a solar year lasts around 365 days, a lunar year is slightly shorter at 354 days.
→ while은 '~인 반면에'의 의미로, 〈대조〉를 나타내는 접속사이다.

[15행] **In order to balance** the two calendars, an extra month *is added to* the lunar calendar every three years.
→ 「in order to-v」는 '~하기 위하여'의 의미이다.
→ 「A is added to B」는 'A가 B에 추가되었다'는 의미로, 「add A to B」의 수동형이다.

● VOCABULARY INSIDE

Check Up

1 balance	2 Typically	3 initially	4 permanent
5 exactly	6 cycle	7 international	8 receive

UNIT 07 | Sports

pp. 43-48

READING 1 Kabaddi

Mini Quiz

1 to practice village defense and group hunting 2 Whenever a player leaves the game, the other team gets a point.

▶ **Reading Comprehension**

1 d 2 b 3 d 4 to show the attacker is not inhaling

해석

언젠가 카바디를 본다면, 그것이 정말로 당신의 숨을 멎게 한다는 것을 알게 될 것이다! 카바디는 인도 남부에서 유래했는데, 그곳에서 카바디는 마을의 방어와 집단 사냥을 연습하는 데 이용되었다. 이후에, 이 경기는 팀워크와 폐활량을 시험하는 국제적인 경기로 발전했다.

카바디에서, 일곱 명으로 이루어진 두 팀이 각각 작은 코트의 절반을 차지한다. 그들은 교대로 공격수를 상대편 쪽으로 보낸다. 공격수는 상대 팀 선수를 터치하고 자신의 편으로 다시 돌아가야 한다. 만약 공격수가 성공하면, 터치된 상대는 아웃된다. 수비수들은 공격수가 그들 쪽에서 달아나는 것을 막기 위해 그 선수를 잡으려고 한다. 만약 공격수가 땅에 넘어뜨려지거나 상대를 치는 것에 실패하면, 그 사람은 경기에서 아웃된다. 한 선수가 경기에서 나갈 때마다, 상대 팀이 득점한다.

그런데 특별한 규칙이 있다. 바로 자기 팀으로 돌아오기 전에 공격수는 숨을 쉬어서는 안 되는 것이다! 공격수가 숨을 들이마시지 않는다는 것을 보여주기 위해, 그 선수는 "카바디, 카바디, 카바디"라고 계속해서 말해야 한다. 만약 공격수가 되풀이하기를 멈추거나 잠깐 쉬면, 그 사람은 경기에서 나가야 한다.

카바디는 이제 중국과 일본 같은 다른 국가에서도 경기 되며, 1990년 이래로 아시안 게임에 있어 왔다. 당신은 조국을 위해 금메달을 딸 수 있겠나?

어휘

breathless [형] 숨이 가쁜; *숨이 막히는 originate [동] 비롯되다, 유래하다 southern [형] 남쪽의[남향의] defense [명] 방어, 수비 (defender [명] 수비수) hunting [명] 사냥 evolve [동] 발달하다 test [동] 시험하다 lung [명] 폐 occupy [동] 차지하다 half [명] 반[절반] take turns 교대로 ~하다 attacker [명] 공격자[공격수] opponent [명] 상대 (opposing [형] 서로 겨루는, 상대방의) get back to ~으로 돌아가다 succeed [동] 성공하다 tag [동] ~을 달다; *터치하다 catch [동] 잡다, 받다 escape [동] 달아나다 side [명] 쪽, 편 take a breath 숨을 쉬다 inhale [동] 숨을 들이마시다 chant [동] 부르다; *(단조로운 어조로) 되풀이하다 continuously [부] 계속해서, 연속적으로 take a break (잠시) 휴식을 취하다

구문

[2행] Kabaddi originated in **southern India, where** it was used to practice village defense and group hunting.

→ 「, where」는 southern India를 부연 설명하는 계속적 용법의 관계부사로, and there로 바꿀 수 있다.

[3행] Later, the game evolved into **an international game** [testing teamwork and lung power].

→ [ ]는 앞의 an international game을 수식하는 현재분사구이다.

[8행] **If** the attacker succeeds, the tagged opponent is out.

→ if는 '만약 ~한다면'의 의미로 〈조건〉을 나타내는 접속사이다.

[11행] **Whenever** a player leaves the game, the other team gets a point.

→ whenever는 '~할 때마다'의 의미인 복합관계부사로, 시간의 부사절을 이끈다.

[14행] **To *show*** [(*that*) the attacker is not inhaling], the player must chant "kabaddi, kabaddi, kabaddi" continuously.

→ To show는 '보여주기 위해'라는 의미로, 〈목적〉을 나타내는 부사적 용법의 to부정사이다.

→ [ ]는 show의 목적어 역할을 하는 명사절로 접속사 that이 생략되었다.

READING 2 Snorkeling

Mini Quiz

1 F 2 T

▶ **Reading Comprehension**

1 b 2 d 3 d 4 two lengths without swimming

▶ **Grammar Inside LEVEL 3**

[Check Up] could he decide

해석

매년 여름, 사람들은 재미로 스노클링을 하러 간다. 스노클링은 수중 세계를 경험하고 그곳의 놀라운 야생 동물을 발견하는 좋은 방법이다. 그것은 특히 열대 지역에서 인기가 있다. 그것은 사람들이 산호초를 탐험하고 매우 다양한 바다 생물들을 볼 수 있게 해준다. 스쿠버 다이빙에 비해 스노클링은 많은 장비가 필요하지 않다. 스쿠버 다이버들은 특별한 옷을 입고 바다 깊은 곳으로 가기 위해 산소 탱크를 사용한다. 하지만 스노클러는 보통 바다 표면에서 떠다니므로 스노클링 마스크와 오리발만 있으면 된다.

수천 년 전, 스노클링은 단순한 수상 스포츠가 아니었다. 사실 최초의 스노클러는 그리스의 농부들이었다. 그들은 바다 수세미를 채집하는 동안 물속에서 숨을 쉬기 위해 속이 빈 갈대를 사용했다. 고맙게도, 현대의 스노클 장비는 훨씬 더 효과적이 되었다.

매년, 전 세계에서 열리는 스노클링 행사들이 있다. 하지만 가장 인기 있는 행사는 웨일스에서 열리는 밥 스노클링 세계 선수권 대회이다. 그것은 세계에서 가장 큰 스노클링 행사일 뿐만 아니라, 경쟁을 하는 유일한 행사이기도 하다. 그 행사에서, 참가자들은 습지에 판 도랑을 따라 서로 경주한다. 이기기 위해 그들은 수영하지 않고 두 번을 완주해야 한다. 첫 번째 선수권 대회는 1976년에 열렸고, 인기 있는 세계적인 행사가 되었다.

어휘

snorkeling [명] 스노클링 (snorkel [동] 스노클링을 하다 [명] 스노클[잠수 중에 호흡하기 위해 물 밖으로 연결한 관] snorkeler [명] 스노클러) experience [동] 경험하다 underwater [형] 물속의 [부] 물속에(서) discover [동] 발견하다 wildlife [명] 야생 동물 especially [부] 특히 popular [형] 인기 있는 tropical [형] 열대의 area [명] 지역 explore [동] 탐험하다 coral reef 산호초 a wide variety of 매우 다양한 ~ creature [명] 생물, 생명체 compared to ~와 비교하여 equipment [명] 장비 oxygen [명] 산소 surface [명] 표면 hollow [형] 속이 빈 reed [명] 갈대 breathe [동] 숨을 쉬다 collect [동] 수집하다, 모으다 sponge [명] 수세미 modern [형] 현대의 effective [형] 효과적인 championship [명] 선수권 대회 competitive [형] 경쟁을 하는 participant [명] 참가자 length [명] 길이; *(수영장 등의 끝에서 끝까지의) 길이[거리] take place (일·사건이) 일어나다, 개최되다 global [형] 세계적인

[문제] characteristic [명] 특징

구문

[1행] Snorkeling is **a great way** [*to experience* the underwater world and (*to*) *discover* its amazing wildlife].

→ [ ]는 a great way를 수식하는 형용사적 용법의 to부정사구로, to experience와 (to) discover가 접속사 and로 병렬 연결되어 있다.

It **allows people** *to explore* coral reefs and (**to**) *see* a wide variety of sea creatures.

→ 「allow+목적어+to-v」는 '~가 …하게 하다'의 의미로, to explore와 (to) see가 접속사 and로 병렬 연결되어 있다.

10행 They used hollow reeds **to breathe** underwater *while collecting* sea sponges.

→ to breathe는 '숨쉬기 위해'의 의미로, 〈목적〉을 나타내는 부사적 용법의 to부정사이다.

→ while collecting 이하는 〈때〉를 나타내는 분사구문으로, 의미를 명확하게 하기 위해 접속사를 생략하지 않았다.

11행 Thankfully, modern snorkel equipment **has become** *much* more effective.

→ has become은 '되어 왔다'의 의미로 〈계속〉을 나타내는 현재완료이다.

→ much는 '훨씬'의 의미로 비교급을 강조하는 부사이며, a lot, even, far 등으로 바꿀 수 있다.

15행 ***Not only*** **is it** the largest snorkeling event in the world, *but* it is *also* the only competitive one.

→ 부정어구 Not only가 문장 맨 앞에 위치하여 주어(it)와 동사(is)가 도치되었다.

→ 「not only A but also B」는 'A뿐만 아니라 B도'의 의미이다.

● VOCABULARY INSIDE

| ***Check Up*** | 1 collect | 2 escaped | 3 tropical | 4 succeed |
| | 5 opponents | 6 especially | 7 inhale | 8 length |

UNIT 08 | Future

pp. 49-54

READING 1   Future Batteries

✔ Mini Quiz
1 a lithium-ion battery   2 less than 20 minutes

▶ Reading Comprehension
1 d   2 d   3 c   4 (1) firm[solid] (2) varying (3) space (4) explosions

해석   전기 자동차와 가전제품이 점점 더 인기를 끌면서, 더 많은 리튬 이온 전지가 기계를 작동시키기 위해 기업들에 의해 사용되고 있다. 리튬 이온 전지는 에너지의 흐름을 관리하기 위해 액체로 된 전해질을 사용한다. 리튬 이온 전지를 사용하는 것에는 많은 이점이 있다. 그중 일부는 다양한 온도에서의 향상된 성능과 긴 배터리 수명을 포함한다. 그것들은 부정적인 측면도 있다. 예를 들어, 그 안의 액체는 그것들을 상당히 무겁게 만드는 경향이 있다. 게다가, 그것들 안의 전해질은 배터리가 손상되면 폭발을 일으키기 쉽다.

전고체 전지가 리튬 이온 배터리의 전도유망한 대체품이 될 수 있다. 주요 차이점은 리튬 이온 전지는 유동적인 반면, 전고체 전지는 단단한 전해질을 포함하고 있다는 것이다. 전고체 전지의 어떤 특징들이 그것들을 강력하게 만든다.

우선, 전고체 전지는 자주 충전될 필요가 없다. 그리고 그것들은 20분 이내에 완전히 충전될 수 있다. 그것들은 또한 손상 없이 오랫동안 사용될 수 있다. 게다가 그것들은 손상되어도 화재를 일으키지 않을 것이다. 따라서 안전을 위한 추가 부품이 설치될 필요가 없다. 이는 전고체 전지가 배터리 수명을 늘릴 물질을 위한 공간이 더 많다는 것을 의미한다.

어휘 battery 명 배터리, 전지   electric 형 전기의   consumer electronics 가전제품   increasingly 부 점점 더   power 동 동력을 공급하다, 작동시키다 (powerful 형 강력한)   liquid 명 액체   manage 동 관리하다   flow 명 흐름   benefit 명 이득   include 동 포함하다   improved 형 향상된   performance 명 성능   varying 형 변화하는 [바뀌는]   temperature 명 온도   negative 형 부정적인   aspect 명 측면   explosion 명 폭발   promising 형 전도유망한   substitute 명 대체품   fluid 형 유동성의   contain 동 함유하다, ~이 들어 있다   firm 형 단단한   first of all 우선   recharge 동 충전하다   frequently 부 자주   fully 부 완전히   charge 동 청구하다; *충전하다   additionally 부 게다가   extra 형 여분의, 추가의   install 동 설치하다   space 명 공간   material 명 재료

구문

1행 **As** electric cars and consumer electronics become increasingly popular, more lithium-ion batteries *are being used by* companies for powering our machines.
→ as는 '~함에 따라, ~하면서'의 의미로, 〈때〉를 나타내는 접속사이다.
→ are being used by는 '~에 의해 사용되고 있다'의 의미인 진행형 수동태이다.
→ for powering은 '작동시키기 위해'의 의미로 for는 〈목적·용도〉를 나타내는 전치사이며, powering은 for의 목적어로 쓰인 동명사이다.

9행 For instance, the liquid inside of them **tends to** *make* them *quite heavy*.
→ 「tend to-v」는 '~하는 경향이 있다'의 의미이다.
→ 「make+목적어+형용사」는 '~을 …하게 만들다'의 의미이며, 이때 quite heavy는 형용사구로 make의 목적격 보어이다.

14행 **The main difference** is [**that** a lithium-ion battery is fluid], *while* a solid-state battery contains a firm electrolyte.
→ that은 명사절을 이끄는 접속사로, [ ]는 주어 The main difference의 보어 역할을 한다.
→ while은 '~인 반면에'의 의미로, 〈대조〉를 나타내는 접속사이다.

18행 They can also be used for a long time **without being damaged**.
→ being damaged는 전치사 without의 목적어로 문장의 시제(can)와 동일하여 단순형 수동태로 쓰였다.

19행 Additionally, they **are** not **likely to cause** a fire **if** they are damaged.
→ 「be likely to-v」는 '~할 것 같다, ~할 가능성이 있다'의 의미이다.
→ if는 '만약 ~한다면'의 의미로 〈조건〉을 나타내는 접속사이다.

21행 This means solid-state batteries have more space for **materials** [that increase battery life].
→ [ ]는 선행사 materials를 수식하는 주격 관계대명사절이다.

READING 2 E-Sports

Mini Quiz
1 involve 2 The popularity of e-sports seems to grow every year.

▶ **Reading Comprehension**
1 a 2 d 3 a 4 a gaming system, a place where you can connect to the internet

해석

1990년대 후반까지 비디오 게임을 하는 것은 가벼운 취미로 여겨졌다. 그러나 1997년, 그것은 조직적인 경쟁 스포츠가 되었다. 이 연도는 첫 주요 e스포츠 토너먼트가 열린 해였다. e스포츠는 '전자 스포츠'의 줄임말이며, 그것은 전형적으로 치열한 경기에서 경쟁하는 선수팀들을 포함한다. e스포츠와 다른 스포츠의 유일한 차이점은 e스포츠가 물리적인 장소 대신 가상 환경 내 공간에서 일어난다는 것이다.

e스포츠의 인기는 매년 증가하는 것으로 보인다. 이러한 현상의 주된 이유는 그것이 광범위한 참여가 가능하도록 하기 때문이다. 게이머들은 신체적으로 강하거나 빠를 필요가 없으며, 연령이나 성별에 의해 제한받지 않는다. 또 다른 이유는 비디오 게임이 다른 스포츠보다 연습하기 쉽기 때문이다. 당신은 게임 시스템과 인터넷에 연결할 수 있는 장소만 있으면 된다. 스트리밍은 e스포츠가 매우 접근하기 쉬운 세 번째 이유이다. 스트리밍 웹사이트들은 팬들에게 세계 어디에서든 주요 토너먼트를 관람할 수 있는 방법을 제공한다.

요즘 e스포츠 산업은 마땅히 받을 만한 인정을 받기 시작하고 있다. 그것의 시장 가치는 10억 달러가 넘고, 곧 올림픽 경기의 일부가 될지도 모른다. 확실히, e스포츠는 주요 경쟁 스포츠가 되었다!

어휘

consider [동] 여기다 casual [형] 격식을 차리지 않는 organized [형] 조직적인 competitive [형] 경쟁을 하는 (compete [동] 경쟁하다, competition [명] 경쟁; *경기) major [형] 주요한 tournament [명] 토너먼트 hold [동] 잡고 있다; *(시합 등을) 열다 electronic [형] 전자의; *전자 장비와 관련된 typically [부] 전형적으로 involve [동] 포함하다 intense [형] 극심한; *치열한 take place 열리다, 일어나다 virtual [형] (컴퓨터를 이용한) 가상의 environment [명] 환경 rather than ~보다는 physical [형] 신체의; *물리적인 (physically [부] 신체적으로) popularity [명] 인기 phenomenon [명] 현상 gamer [명] 게임하는 사람, 게이머 (gaming [명] 비디오[컴퓨터] 게임하는 것) limit [동] 제한하다, 한정하다 gender [명] 성별 practice [동] 연습하다 connect [동] 연결하다; *접속하다 streaming [명] 스트리밍 (음성·동영상 등을 온라인상에서 실시간으로 재생하는 기술) accessible [형] 접근할 수 있는 industry [명] 산업 recognition [명] 인식; *인정 deserve [동] 받을 만하다 value [명] 가치 billion [명] 10억 [문제] flourishing [형] 번영하는, 융성한 comparison [명] 비교, 대조 official [형] 공식적인 broad [형] 폭넓은 participation [명] 참여 entertainment [명] 오락(거리) keep in shape 건강을 유지하다

구문

[1행] Until the late 1990s, [playing video games] ***was*** *considered to be a casual hobby*.
→ [ ]는 주어 역할을 하는 동명사구이며, 동명사구 주어는 단수 취급하므로 단수 동사 was가 쓰였다.
→ was considered는 '여겨졌다'의 의미로, 「be v-ed」의 수동태이다. to be a casual hobby는 5형식 문장의 목적격 보어인 to부정사구가 수동태 문장에서 was considered 뒤에 그대로 쓰인 형태이다.

[3행] This was **the year** [when the first major e-sports tournament was held].
→ [ ]는 선행사 the year를 수식하는 관계부사절이다.

[5행] **The only difference** [between e-sports and other sports] **is** {*that* e-sports takes place in a virtual environment rather than a physical place}.
→ [ ]는 주어 The only difference를 수식하는 전치사구이며, 동사는 is이다.
→ that은 명사절을 이끄는 접속사로, { }는 문장의 보어이다.

[14행] Streaming websites **give fans *a way* [to view major tournaments from anywhere in the world]**.

→ give는 4형식 동사로 간접목적어(fans)와 직접목적어(a way ... the world)를 취한다.

→ [ ]는 a way를 수식하는 형용사적 용법의 to부정사구이다.

[17행] These days, the e-sports industry is starting to get **the recognition** [(**that**) it deserves].

→ [ ]는 선행사 the recognition을 수식하는 목적격 관계대명사절로, 관계대명사 that이 생략되었다.

● VOCABULARY INSIDE

Check Up 1 billion 2 limit 3 physical 4 negative 5 improved 6 takes place 7 industry 8 contain

UNIT 09 | Animals

pp. 55-60

READING 1 Whale Poop

Mini Quiz

1 T 2 F

▶ Reading Comprehension

1 b 2 c 3 c 4 phytoplankton, CO_2[carbon dioxide]

▶ Grammar Inside LEVEL 3

[Check Up] walking her dog

해석 우리는 모두 지구가 많은 생태계적 위협에 직면해 있다는 것을 안다. 그러나, 그것들 중의 하나가 고래 배설물의 부족임을 아는 사람은 거의 없다. 해양 생물학자들에 의하면, 고래의 배설물은 기후 변화에 맞서 싸우는 데 필수적이다.

대부분의 해양 동물과 달리, 고래는 배설하기 위해 수면 위로 헤엄쳐 오른다. 그들의 배설물은 철분과 같은 주요한 영양소를 포함하고 있다. 그 배설물이 해저로 떨어질 때, 배설물 내 철분은 식물성 플랑크톤이라고 불리는 아주 작은 미생물의 성장을 돕는다. 다시 말해서, 고래 배설물은 식물성 플랑크톤에 천연 비료의 역할을 한다.

그런데 고래 배설물이 어떻게 기후 변화에 영향을 미칠까? 광합성을 하는 동안, 식물성 플랑크톤은 공기 중에서 엄청난 양의 이산화탄소를 흡수한다. 최근의 한 연구에 따르면, 고래 배설물은 매년 대기로부터 40만 톤의 이산화탄소를 취할 만큼 충분한 식물성 플랑크톤을 부양한다.

이 사실은 고래 포획에 대한 우려를 증가시키고 있다. 고래를 포획함으로써, 인간은 바다에서 철분이 풍부한 고래 배설물의 양을 감소시킨다. 결과적으로, 우리는 이산화탄소를 제거할 수 있는 식물성 플랑크톤의 양을 줄여 왔다. 이 관계는 생태계가 어떻게 작용하는지를 보여준다. 어떤 한 부분이 위험에 처하게 되면, 생태계 전체가 위협을 받는다. 이제 고래를 보호할 필요성이 그 어느 때보다 더 명백해 보인다!

어휘 poop [명] 똥 [동] 똥을 싸다 face [동] ~에 직면하다 ecological [형] 생태계의 threat [명] 위협 (threaten [동] 위태롭게

하다, 위협하다) lack 몡 부족, 결핍 marine 톙 바다의[해양의] biologist 몡 생물학자 surface 몡 표면[표층]
nutrient 몡 영양소 iron 몡 철; *철분 affect 통 영향을 미치다 absorb 통 (액체·가스 등을) 흡수하다 amount 몡
양 carbon dioxide 이산화탄소 increase 통 증가하다, 증가시키다 concern 몡 우려, 걱정 decrease 통 줄다
[감소하다] reduce 통 (규모·크기·양 등을) 줄이다 available 톙 이용할 수 있는 remove 통 제거하다
relationship 몡 관계 ecosystem 몡 생태계 endangered 톙 멸종 위기에 처한 protect 통 보호하다 clear
톙 분명한, 확실한   [문제] generate 통 발생시키다, 만들어 내다 chemical 몡 화학 물질 fertilizer 몡 비료 cozy 톙
아늑한

구문

1행 However, **few people** *know* [*that* one of them is a lack of whale poop].
→ few는 '거의 없는'의 의미로, 뒤에 셀 수 있는 복수 명사(people)가 온다.
→ that은 명사절을 이끄는 접속사로, [ ]는 동사 know의 목적어 역할을 한다.
→ 「one of+복수 명사」는 '~ 중의 하나'라는 의미로, 주어가 단수(one)이므로 단수 동사 is가 쓰였다.

3행 ..., whale poop **is essential to fighting** climate change.
→ 「be essential to」는 '~에 필수적이다'라는 의미로, fighting은 전치사 to의 목적어로 쓰인 동명사이다.

4행 Unlike most marine animals, whales swim up to the surface **to poop**.
→ to poop는 '배설하기 위해'의 의미로, 〈목적〉을 나타내는 to부정사의 부사적 용법이다.

11행 According to a recent study, whale poop supports **enough phytoplankton to take**
400,000 tons of CO2 from the air every year.
→ 「enough+명사+to-v」는 '~할 만큼 충분한 …'이라는 의미이다.

15행 ..., humans **have decreased** the amount of iron-rich whale poop in oceans.
→ have decreased는 '줄여 왔다'의 의미로 〈계속〉을 나타내는 현재완료이다.

16행 As a result, we have reduced **the amount of phytoplankton** [available to remove CO2].
→ [ ]는 the amount of phytoplankton을 수식하는 형용사구이다.

17행 This relationship **shows** [how ecosystems work].
→ [ ]는 「의문사+주어+동사」 어순의 간접의문문으로, 동사 shows의 목적어 역할을 한다.

READING 2 The Tragedy of White Tigers

⊙ Mini Quiz
1 normal   2 They trick the public into believing that they are helping white tigers.

▶ Reading Comprehension
1 a   2 d   3 (1) b (2) a (3) c   4 stay away from zoos

▶ Grammar Inside LEVEL 3
Check Up as if she were my sister

해석 Q: 백호 케니의 이야기를 해 주시겠습니까?
A: 케니는 한 개인 소유주로부터 2000년에 구조되었습니다. 그의 짧은 코, 넓은 얼굴, 못생긴 이빨 때문에 그는 거의 호
랑이처럼 보이지 않았습니다. 그의 주인은 케니가 종종 자신의 얼굴을 벽에 부딪혀서 이렇게 생겼다고 말했습니다. 하
지만 사실 그는 동족 교배로 인한 유전적 문제들로 고통받았습니다.

Q: 동족 교배의 원인과 결과는 무엇인가요?

A: 자연에서 백호는 매 일만 번의 출생 중 한 번 정도로만 발생합니다. 백호는 1951년 이후 야생에서 보이지 않고 있습니다. 그러나 이상하게도, 여전히 백호는 많습니다. 이것은 흰색 털을 생기게 하는 유전자를 만들어내기 위해 호랑이들이 계속해서 교배되고 있기 때문입니다. 안타깝게도, 이런 종류의 동족 교배는 그들에게 많은 유전적 문제를 가져다줍니다. 거의 모든 백호는 케니가 갖고 있던 문제점들을 지니고 있습니다. 이것은 수명을 단축시키기도 합니다. 보통, 서른 마리의 백호들 중 오직 한 마리 정도만 '정상적으로' 보이며, 나머지는 버려집니다.

Q: 동물원은 왜 여전히 백호를 번식시키나요?

A: 일부 사육사들은 마치 백호가 멸종 위기에 있는 것처럼 말합니다. 그들은 대중들을 속여서 자신들이 백호를 돕고 있다고 믿게 합니다. 그러나, 그들은 동물원이 더 인기 있도록 호랑이를 이용하는 것일 뿐입니다. 저는 사람들이 백호가 있는 동물원을 멀리해야 한다고 강력히 제안합니다. 그들은 이러한 동물들을 마케팅 목적으로 사용하지 않아야 합니다.

어휘 tragedy 몡 비극   rescue 통 구하다[구조하다]   private 혱 사유의[개인 소유의]   barely 閉 거의 ~ 아니게   suffer from ~으로 고통받다   genetic 혱 유전의 (gene 몡 유전자)   occur 통 발생하다   birth 몡 탄생, 출생   wild 혱 (야생 상태의) 자연   breed 통 새끼를 낳다; *번식시키다   over and over (again) 반복해서   coat 몡 외투; *(동물의) 털, 가죽   a number of 얼마간의; *많은 ~   life span 수명   normal 혱 보통의, 정상적인   rest 몡 나머지; *(남은) 다른 사람들[것들]   abandon 통 버리다   zookeeper 몡 (동물원) 사육사   endangered 혱 위기에 처한; *멸종 위기에 처한   trick 통 속이다   stay away (~에게) 접근하지 않다   marketing 몡 마케팅   purpose 몡 목적   [문제] fool 통 속이다   inform A of B A에게 B를 알려주다   cause and effect 원인과 결과

구문

5행 ... he suffered from **genetic problems** [caused by inbreeding].

→ [ ]는 genetic problems를 수식하는 과거분사구이다.

9행 White tigers **haven't been seen** in the wild **since** 1951.

→ haven't been seen은 '보이지 않아 왔다'의 의미로 〈계속〉을 나타내는 현재완료이며, 주로 since나 for와 함께 쓰인다.

10행 This is because tigers **are being bred** over and over *to produce* the gene [that creates a white coat].

→ 「be being v-ed」는 진행형 수동태로, '~되고 있다'의 의미이다.

→ to produce는 '만들어 내기 위해'의 의미로, 〈목적〉을 나타내는 to부정사의 부사적 용법이다.

→ [ ]는 선행사 the gene을 수식하는 주격 관계대명사절이다.

18행 They **trick** the public *into* believing [that they are helping white tigers].

→ 「trick A into B」는 'A를 속여서 B하게 하다'의 의미이다.

→ believing은 전치사 into의 목적어로 쓰인 동명사이며, [ ]은 believing의 목적어 역할을 한다.

21행 I strongly **suggest** (that) people (should) **stay** away from zoos with white tigers.

→ 〈제안·명령·요구·주장〉 등의 의미를 지닌 동사 뒤에 that이 이끄는 명사절이 나오는 경우, 명사절에는 「(should+)동사원형」을 쓰며, should는 흔히 생략된다.

● VOCABULARY INSIDE

Check Up	1 rescue	2 increase	3 occurred	4 absorb
	5 endangered	6 surface	7 rest	8 barely

UNIT 10 | Stories

READING 1   The Tell-Tale Heart

◐ Mini Quiz
1 F   2 F

▶ **Reading Comprehension**
1 a   2 c   3 d   4 hear the old man's heartbeat

▶ **Grammar Inside LEVEL 3**
Check Up   1 현재분사   2 동명사

해석
　　「고자질하는 심장」은 자신의 감정을 아주 상세하게 묘사하는 살인자에 관한 것이다. 이야기의 시작에서, 살인자는 자신이 미치지 않았다는 것을 독자에게 확신시키려고 한다. 그는 한 노인을 죽인 것을 자백하지만, 노인의 사악한 눈 때문에 필요했다고 말한다.

(C) 매일 밤, 그는 노인이 자는 것을 몰래 지켜보았다. 이렇게 하는 한 주 후, 그는 노인을 죽이지 못했다. 그러나 여덟 번째 밤에, 그는 마침내 성공할 거라고 느꼈다. 불행히도, 그는 소리를 내서 노인을 깨웠다. 그 남자는 비명을 질렀지만, 살인범은 재빨리 그를 공격하여 죽였다. 그러고 나서 그는 시신을 바닥 판자 밑에 숨겼다.

(A) 이윽고, 그는 경찰이 문을 두드리는 것을 들었다. 누군가가 비명을 들었기 때문에 그들은 거기에 있었다. 살인범은 자신 있게 경찰관들에게 노인의 방을 보여주었다. 방바닥 밑에 시신을 감춘 채, 그들은 이야기를 계속했다. 경찰은 아무것도 눈치채지 못했다. 살인범은 그들을 속이는 것을 즐겼다.

(B) 그러나 곧 살인자는 어떤 소리를 들었다. 그것은 그 노인의 심장 박동 소리처럼 들렸고, 점점 더 커졌다. 그는 경찰관들도 그것을 들을 수 있다고 생각했지만, 그들은 어떤 것도 전혀 듣지 못했다. 겁에 질린 나머지, 살인범은 경찰에게 시체를 어디서 찾을지 보여주었다.

어휘
murderer 명 살인범   describe 동 묘사하다   emotion 명 감정   detail 명 세부 사항   beginning 명 시작, 초(반)   convince 동 확신시키다   reader 명 독자   mad 형 화난; *미친 (madness 명 정신 이상, 광기)   necessary 형 필요한   evil 형 사악한   knock 동 (문을) 두드리다, 노크하다   scream 명 비명 동 비명을 지르다   confidently 부 자신 있게   (police) officer 명 경찰관   body 명 몸; *시체   continue to-v 계속하여 ~하다   notice 동 알아채다   fool 동 속이다   heartbeat 명 심장 박동   panic 동 겁에 질려 어쩔 줄 모르다 (panicked 형 겁에 질린)   secretly 부 비밀히, 몰래   make a noise 소리를 내다   attack 동 공격하다   board 명 판자   [문제] commit 동 (범죄를) 저지르다   crime 명 범죄   criminal 명 범인   confession 명 자백, 고백   case 명 경우; *사건   unsolved 형 해결되지[풀리지] 않은   stalker 명 스토커   defend A against B A를 B로부터 지키다

구문
4행 He **confesses to killing** an old man, but he *says* [*that* it was necessary because of the old man's evil eye].
→ confess to는 '~을 자백하다'의 의미로, 이때 killing은 전치사 to의 목적어인 동명사이다.
→ that은 명사절을 이끄는 접속사로, [ ]는 동사 says의 목적어 역할을 한다.
→ it은 앞의 killing an old man을 지칭하는 대명사이다.

9행 The murderer confidently **showed the officers the old man's room**.
→ show는 4형식 동사로 간접목적어(the officers)와 직접목적어(the old man's room)를 취한다.

10행 **With the dead body hidden** under the floor of the room, they continued to talk.
→ 「with+목적어+분사」는 '~가 …인 채로'의 의미이다.

13행 It **sounded like** the old man's heartbeat, and it *kept* [getting louder and louder].

→ sound like는 '~처럼 들리다'의 의미이다.

→ [ ]는 동사 kept의 목적어인 동명사구이다.

→ 「비교급+and+비교급」은 '점점 더 ~한[하게]'의 의미이다.

18행 Every night, he secretly **watched the old man sleep**.

→ 「watch+목적어+동사원형」은 '~가 …하고 있는 것을 지켜보다'라는 의미이다. 지각동사(watch)의 목적격 보어로는 동사원형이나 분사가 온다.

READING 2   The Elf-King

▼ Mini Quiz

1 the boy   2 The father realizes his son is dead.

▶ Reading Comprehension

1 d   2 d   3 b   4 to clearly distinguish each of the characters

▶ Grammar Inside LEVEL 3

Check Up why he didn't call me

해석　프란츠 슈베르트의 가장 잘 알려진 작품 중 하나인 「마왕」은 같은 제목의 괴테의 시에 기반을 두고 있다. 슈베르트는 괴테를 존경했기 때문에, 그는 그 시인의 전설적인 시를 빌려와서 그것을 음악으로 바꾸었다.

그 시의 이야기를 활용하여, 슈베르트는 성악가와 피아노 곡을 작곡했다. 등장인물들 각각을 확실히 구별하기 위해, 그는 각자 다른 목소리를 사용했다. 해설자에게는 중간 음역의 목소리, 아버지에게는 저음, 소년에게는 고음, 마왕에게는 부드럽고 매력적인 음성이었다.

초반에, 아버지와 그의 아들이 밤에 말을 타고 숲을 가로질러 갈 때, 피아노는 달리는 말을 흉내 낸다. 아버지는 그의 아들이 두려움에 떨고 있는 것을 보고, 소년에게 왜 두려워하는지 묻는다. 그러자 아들은 그의 아버지에게 마왕이 두렵다고 이야기한다. 곧, 피아노는 마왕의 목소리와 함께 부드러운 멜로디로 은은해진다. 그는 소년을 꾀어내려 하면서 상냥하게 말을 건넨다. 하지만 소년은 두려움에 소리를 지른다. 갑자기 피아니스트는 마왕이 고통으로 비명을 지르는 소년을 붙잡으려고 할 때 강렬한 화음을 연주한다. 피아니스트는 말이 숲에서 달아나는 동안 빠르게 연주한다. 마침내 아버지가 그의 아들이 죽은 것을 알게 될 때 음악은 슬퍼진다.

어휘　best-known 가장 잘 알려진   piece 몡 한 조각; *작품   poem 몡 시(詩)   admire 동 존경하다   legendary 혱 전설적인 (legend 몡 전설)   change A into B A를 B로 바꾸다   compose 동 구성하다; *작곡하다   distinguish 동 구별하다   character 몡 성격; *등장인물   medium 혱 중간의   narrator 몡 서술자, 내레이터   smooth 혱 매끄러운; *부드러운[감미로운]   attractive 혱 매력적인   imitate 동 흉내 내다   tremble 동 (몸이) 떨다, 떨리다   fear 몡 공포   be terrified of ~을 두려워하다   soften 동 부드러워지다, 은은해지다   gentle 혱 온화한, 부드러운   sweetly 閉 상냥하게[다정하게]   lure 동 꾀다, 유혹하다   intense 혱 극심한, 강렬한   grab 동 붙잡다[움켜잡다]   scream 동 비명을 지르다   sorrowful 혱 슬픈   realize 동 깨닫다, 알아차리다   [문제] companion 몡 친구, 벗   literary 혱 문학의, 문학적인   analysis 몡 분석   impressive 혱 감명 깊은   tragic 혱 비극적인   thrilling 혱 흥분되는, 짜릿한   miserable 혱 비참한

구문　**9행** In the beginning, the piano imitates a **running horse** *as* the father and his son ride through the forest at night.

→ running은 horse를 수식하는 현재분사이다.

→ as는 '~할 때'의 의미로 〈때〉를 나타내는 접속사이다.

10행 When the father **sees his son trembling** with fear, … .

→ 「see+목적어+현재분사」는 '~가 …하고 있는 것을 보다'라는 의미이며, 이때 trembling은 지각동사 see의 목적격 보어로 쓰였다.

13행 He speaks sweetly to the boy, **trying** to lure him away.

→ trying 이하는 〈동시동작〉을 나타내는 분사구문으로, '~하면서'로 해석한다.

15행 Suddenly, the pianist plays intense chords as the Elf-King tries to grab **the boy, who** screams out in pain.

→ 「, who」는 선행사 the boy를 부연 설명하는 계속적 용법의 주격 관계대명사이다.

16행 The pianist plays fast **while** the horse runs out of the forest.

→ while은 '~하는 동안'의 의미로 〈때〉를 나타내는 접속사이다.

● **VOCABULARY INSIDE**

Check Up	1 murderer	2 describe	3 necessary	4 notice
	5 imitates	6 scream[screaming]	7 admired	8 evil

UNIT 11 | Psychology

pp. 67-72

READING 1   Interview with an Author

Ⓥ Mini Quiz
1 homesickness   2 From the 1100s to the 1600s, looking at something in wonder was a natural part of human experience. People thought our world was filled with magical animals and objects.

▶ **Reading Comprehension**
1 d   2 c   3 d   4 consider science more important than magic

해석   **인터뷰 진행자:** 오늘 저희는 베스트셀러인 「어떻게 감정이 변해 왔는가」의 저자인 브라운 박사님을 모셨습니다. 브라운 박사님, 당신의 책에 따르면, 우리가 감정을 보는 방식은 시간이 지남에 따라 변해 왔습니다. 좀 더 말씀해 주시겠습니까?

브라운 박사: 물론입니다. 향수병을 예로 들어보죠. 그것은 1700년대 후반에 심각한 병으로 여겨졌고 '향수(鄕愁)'라고 불렸어요. 환자들은 집에 가고 싶은 생각이 간절할 때는 매우 지치고 우울해졌습니다. 그들은 또한 심한 종기와 열이 나곤 했습니다. 결국, 그들은 먹기를 중단했고, 이것은 그들을 죽음에 이르게 하곤 했습니다. 하지만 오늘날에는, 우리는 향수를 치명적으로 여기지 않습니다!

인터뷰 진행자: 무엇이 사람들에게 향수병을 그렇게 달리 보게 했나요?

브라운 박사: 음, 자동차와 비행기 같은 교통수단의 발전은 여행을 더 편리하게 만들었습니다. 전화기와 인터넷 또한 멀리 떨어져 사는 사람들이 연결되도록 도왔습니다. 하지만 그보다 더, 우리의 문화와 가치가 크게 변해왔습니다. 편안한 집에서 머무르기보다는, 우리는 이제 미지의 것들을 탐험하길 원하고, 이것은 향수병을 덜 심각하게 만듭니다.

인터뷰 진행자: 우리가 오늘날 다르게 생각하는 또 다른 감정에는 무엇이 있을까요?

브라운 박사: 1100년대에서 1600년대까지, 어떤 것을 경이롭게 바라보는 것은 인간의 경험에서 자연스러운 부분이었습니다. 사람들은 우리의 세계가 마법의 동물과 사물들로 가득 차 있다고 생각했습니다. 예를 들어, 악어 이빨은 보물로 여겨졌는데, 사람들은 그것이 용에서부터 나왔다고 생각했기 때문입니다. 그리고 결석은 약용으로 수집되었습니다. 그러나 상황이 18세기에 변했는데, 당시 사람들은 마법보다 과학을 더 중요하게 생각하기 시작했습니다. 그러자 지난날의 경이로움은 잊혀졌습니다.

어휘 author 몡 작가, 저자　interviewer 몡 면접관; *인터뷰 진행자　emotion 몡 감정 (emotional 휑 감정의; *감정적인)　view 통 보다　homesickness 몡 향수병　consider 통 여기다[생각하다]　illness 몡 병　nostalgia 몡 향수(鄕愁)　sufferer 몡 고통받는 사람, 환자　exhausted 휑 기진맥진한, 탈진한　depressed 휑 우울한　long to-v ~하기를 애타게 바라다　sore 몡 상처, 종기　fever 몡 열　eventually 튄 결국　lead to ~에 이르다[~하게 되다]　deadly 휑 치명적인　improvement 몡 향상, 발전　transportation 몡 수송[운송], 교통수단　convenient 휑 편리한　connect 통 연결하다　value 몡 가치　comfortable 휑 편안한　explore 통 탐험하다　unknown 휑 알려지지 않은, 미지의　wonder 몡 경탄, 경이　natural 휑 자연의; *정상적인, 당연한　experience 몡 경험　object 몡 물건, 물체　medicine 몡 약[약물]　[문제] die of ~으로 죽다

구문

2행 Dr. Brown, according to your book, **the way** [we view emotions] *has changed* over time.
→ [ ]는 선행사 the way를 수식하는 관계부사절이며, 선행사 the way와 관계부사 how는 함께 쓸 수 없다.
→ has changed는 '변해 왔다'의 의미로, 〈계속〉을 나타내는 현재완료이다.

5행 It *was considered* a serious illness and (*was*) *called* "nostalgia" during the late 1700s.
→ was considered와 (was) called는 접속사 and로 병렬 연결되었다.
→ a serious illness와 nostalgia는 5형식 문장의 목적격 보어가 수동태 문장에서 was considered와 (was) called 뒤에 그대로 쓰인 형태이다.

8행 They **would** also have bad sores and get fevers.
→ would는 '~하곤 했다'는 의미로 과거의 습성이나 경향을 나타낸다.

13행 Phones and the internet have also **helped connect** *people* [living far away].
→ help는 목적어 없이 바로 뒤에 to부정사나 동사원형을 쓸 수 있다.
→ [ ]는 people을 수식하는 현재분사구이다.

20행 ..., [looking at something in wonder] **was** a natural part of human experience.
→ [ ]는 주어 역할을 하는 동명사구로, 동명사구 주어는 단수 취급하여 단수 동사 was가 쓰였다.

21행 People thought our world **was filled with** magical animals and objects.
→ 「be filled with」는 '~으로 가득 차다'의 의미이다.

◎ Mini Quiz
1 T　2 F

▶ Reading Comprehension
1 a　2 c　3 b　4 improve their songwriting vocabulary

해석　치료사들은 감정을 표현하는 것이 감정을 다루고 치료하는 첫 번째 단계라고 말한다. 그러나, 일부 십 대들은 그들의 감정에 관해 이야기하는 것을 힘겨워한다. 열네 살의 엘리스는 그들 중 한 명이었다. 화가 날 때마다, 그는 싸움에 빠져들곤 했다. 그러나 이제 그는 자신의 분노를 다스리는 새로운 방법을 알아냈다. 바로 그것에 관해 랩을 하는 것이다. 인터뷰에서 엘리스는 "이제 저는 사람들을 때리는 대신에 제 감정에 관한 노래를 만들어요. 저는 가사를 쓰고 그것은 저를 진정시켜줘요."라고 말했다.

엘리스는 힙합을 이용하는 한 프로그램의 도움을 받았다. 그 프로그램은 전통적인 상담에 차도를 보이지 않는 십 대들에게 다가가기 위해 쓰인다. 힙합 요법은 새로운 것이 아니다. (A) 그러나, 그것은 힙합 음악의 올라가는 인기와 더불어 더 흔해지고 있다. 그것은 이제 많은 문제를 겪는 많은 십 대들이 자신들의 감정과 힘든 일을 표현하도록 돕고 있다. 힙합 요법 프로그램은 학생들에게 곡을 쓰고 녹음하며 온라인에 올릴 기회를 제공한다. 이 과정을 통해서, 그들은 부모와의 다툼, 가장 친한 친구를 잃는 것, 또는 성적에 관해 스트레스받는 것과 같은 개인적인 문제들에 대해서 터놓고 말하도록 권장된다.

치료의 직접적인 혜택(B)에 더해서, 십 대들은 많은 학습 기회도 얻게 된다. 그들은 자신의 작사 어휘를 향상시키기 위해 종종 사전을 이용한다. 그들은 또한 뮤직비디오를 제작하고 실제 녹음 및 편집 장비를 사용하는 방법을 배운다. 분명히 이 창의적인 프로그램은 오늘날의 십 대들에게 많은 방식으로 도움을 준다.

어휘　therapy 몡 치료, 요법 (therapist 몡 치료사)　express 통 나타내다, 표현하다　deal with ~을 다루다, 처리하다 heal 통 치유하다[낫게 하다]　struggle to-v 힘겹게 ~하다　punch 통 때리다　verse 몡 가사　cool down 진정하게 하다　respond to ~에게 대답하다[반응하다]　counseling 몡 상담　common 혱 일반적인, 흔한 popularity 몡 인기 (popular 혱 인기 많은)　troubled 혱 문제가 많은 (trouble 몡 문제)　struggle 몡 싸움; *힘든 일 offer 통 제의하다; *내놓다, 제공하다　process 몡 과정　personal 혱 개인의[개인적인]　grade 몡 등급; *성적 direct 혱 직접적인　benefit 몡 혜택, 이득 통 이득을 보다　opportunity 몡 기회　dictionary 몡 사전　improve 통 향상시키다[개선하다]　songwriting 몡 작사, 작곡　vocabulary 몡 어휘　editing 몡 편집　equipment 몡 장비, 장치　clearly 閉 분명히　creative 혱 창의적인　[문제] overcome 통 극복하다　refuse 통 거절하다, 거부하다 specialized 혱 전문적인, 전문화된

구문　**1행** Therapists **say** [**that** *expressing emotions is* the first step to dealing with them and healing].
→ [ ]는 접속사 that이 이끄는 명사절로 동사 say의 목적어 역할을 한다.
→ expressing emotions는 명사절에서 주어 역할을 하는 동명사구이며, 동명사구 주어는 단수 취급하므로 단수 동사 is가 쓰였다.

4행 But now he **has found** *a new way* [to deal with his anger]: ... .
→ has found는 〈완료〉를 나타내는 현재완료이다.
→ [ ]는 a new way를 수식하는 형용사적 용법의 to부정사구이다.

8행 Ellis was helped by **a program** [that uses hip-hop].
→ [ ]는 선행사 a program을 수식하는 주격 관계대명사절이다.

13행 Hip-hop therapy programs **offer students** *the chance* [*to write and record songs* and (*to*) *put them online*].

→ 4형식 동사 offer는 '～에게 …을 제공하다'의 의미로, 간접목적어(students)와 직접목적어(the chance … online)를 취한다.

→ [ ]는 the chance를 수식하는 형용사적 용법의 to부정사구이며, to write and record songs와 (to) put them online은 접속사 and로 병렬 연결되었다.

19행 They also **learn** [**how to make** music videos and (**how to**) **use** real recording and editing equipment].

→ [ ]는 동사 learn의 목적어 역할을 하며, 「how to-v」는 '어떻게 ～할지'의 의미로 how to make와 (how to) use가 and로 병렬 연결되었다.

● VOCABULARY INSIDE

Check Up
1 transportation 2 offered 3 opportunity 4 heal
5 emotion 6 explore 7 deadly 8 expressed

UNIT 12 | Business

pp. 73-78

READING 1 Crowdfunding

◎ Mini Quiz
1 T 2 F

▶ Reading Comprehension
1 b 2 c 3 (1) b (2) c (3) a 4 instantly share information about projects, reach their funding goals

▶ Grammar Inside LEVEL 3
Check Up was being repaired

해석 과거에는, 많은 사업 아이디어와 프로젝트들이 보통 은행에서 자금을 지원받았다. 이 모든 것은 크라우드펀딩의 도입으로 바뀌었다. 크라우드펀딩은 온라인에서 돈을 모으는 방법이다. 그것은 기업이 일반인들로부터 소액 투자를 모을 수 있게 해준다. 인터넷 덕분에, 기업들은 프로젝트에 관한 정보를 즉시 투자자들과 공유할 수 있다. 이는 기업의 자금 조달 목표에 더 쉽게 도달할 수 있도록 해준다.

크라우드펀딩은 일반적으로 세 가지 주요 방식으로 이루어진다. 기부형 크라우드펀딩은 특별한 대의명분을 위해 자선단체에 돈을 기부하는 것을 포함한다. 보상형 크라우드펀딩에 관한 한, 투자자들은 프로젝트의 총비용에 기부한다. 그 대가로, 그들은 이 활동으로부터 온 자금으로 개발될 제품이나 서비스를 약속 받는다. 투자형 크라우드펀딩을 통해서는 기업들이 자금을 조달하기 위해 주식을 판다. 주식을 산 투자자들은 회사의 부분적인 소유주가 되고 금전적인 보상을 받는다.

가장 큰 크라우드펀딩 캠페인 중 몇몇은 스마트워치와 전기 자동차와 같은 기술을 위한 것이었다. 그러나, 최근의 한 크라우드펀딩 성공 일화는 출판에 있었다. 브랜든 샌더슨은 그의 최신 소설을 출판하기 위해 온라인 활동을 시작했다. 그의 목표는 30일 안에 백만 달러를 모으는 것이었다. 놀랍게도, 그는 약 35분 만에 이를 달성했다. 그 캠페인은 24시간 만에 1,500만 달러 이상을 모금했다. 그것은 크라우드펀딩의 신기록이었다.

어휘 business 阅 사업; 사업체   fund 阁 자금을 대다 阅 자금   introduction 阅 도입   raise 阁 들어올리다; *(자금 등을) 모으다   investment 阅 투자, 투자금 (investor 阅 투자자)   ordinary 阅 보통의, 일상적인   instantly 阕 즉시   typically 阕 일반적으로   donation 阅 기부 (donate 阁 기부하다)   involve 阁 포함하다   charity 阅 자선 단체   reward 阅 보상   when it comes to ~에 관한 한   contribute 阁 기부하다, 기여하다   cost 阅 비용   in return 대신에, 답례로   equity 阅 주식   stock 阅 (상품 등의) 재고; *주식   capital 阅 수도; *자금   partial 阅 부분적인   campaign 阅 캠페인; (조직적인) 활동   technology 阅 기술   electric 阅 전기의   publishing 阅 출판 (publish 阁 출판하다)   latest 阅 최신의   million 阅 100만   record 阅 기록   [문제] efficient 阅 능률적인, 유효한   incredibly 阕 놀랍게도   achieve 阁 성취하다, 해내다

구문

3행 Crowdfunding is **a way** [to raise money online].
→ [ ]는 a way를 수식하는 형용사적 용법의 to부정사구이다.

6행 **This** makes *it* easier *to reach their funding goals*.
→ This는 바로 앞 문장 전체를 지칭하는 대명사이다.
→ it은 가목적어, to reach 이하는 진목적어이다.

10행 In return, they **are promised** *a product or service* [**that will be developed with money from the campaign**].
→ a product or service … the campaign은 4형식 동사의 직접목적어가 수동태 문장에서 are promised 뒤에 그대로 쓰인 형태이다.
→ [ ]는 선행사 a product or service를 수식하는 주격 관계대명사절이다.

13행 **Investors** [who buy the stocks] **become** partial owners of the company and **receive** financial rewards.
→ [ ]는 주어 Investors를 수식하는 주격 관계대명사절이고, 동사 become과 receive가 접속사 and로 병렬 연결되어 있다.

18행 Brandon Sanderson started an online campaign **to publish** his latest novels.
→ to publish는 '출판하기 위해'의 의미로, 〈목적〉을 나타내는 to부정사의 부사적 용법이다.

READING 2 Mobile Payments

Mini Quiz
1 I'm worried that my financial information could be stolen while using the app.
2 a one-time-use security code

▶ **Reading Comprehension**
1 d   2 a   3 b   4 steal financial data, retailers

▶ **Grammar Inside LEVEL 3**
Check Up   1 It was last night that   2 It was my sister that

해석 **Q:** 저는 스마트폰용 휴대 지갑 앱이 특징인 새 광고를 봤습니다. 그것은 굉장한 것 같았어요! 그것은 사용자들이 결제 기기에 자신의 전화기를 슬쩍 대는 것만으로 물건을 사도록 합니다. 하지만 그 앱을 받으려고 생각했을 때, 제 친구가 저에게 보안 문제 때문에 그것을 받아서는 안 된다고 말했습니다. 지금 저는 앱을 사용하는 도중에 제 금융 정보를 도난당할까 봐 걱정됩니다. 정말 안전한가요?

A: 네, 그렇습니다. 당신은 보안 문제에 관해 걱정할 필요는 없습니다. 대부분의 모바일 지갑은 토큰화 기술을 사용하는데, 당신의 정보를 안전하게 보호해주는 것이 바로 이 기술입니다. 당신의 앱으로 어떤 것을 사기 위해서는, 당신의 금융 정보를 앱에 저장해야 합니다. 그러나, 당신이 구매할 때마다, 그 앱은 당신의 정보를 무작위 숫자 혹은 디지털 토큰으로 대체합니다. 이 토큰은 당신의 실제 금융 데이터를 전혀 가지고 있지 않습니다. 대신에, 그것은 일회용 보안 코드를 가지고 있습니다. 이것은 소매업자가 당신의 금융 정보에 접근하도록 하는 열쇠입니다.

사실, 이 기술은 신용카드 범죄를 방지하는 데 있어서 전통적인 결제 방식보다 더 효과적입니다. 과거에는, 해커들이 소매업자들에게서 신용카드 번호와 같은 금융 정보를 훔칠 수 있었습니다. 하지만, 토큰화로 인해, 그들은 소매업자의 시스템 내에서 사용 불가한 디지털 토큰만 발견하게 될 것입니다. 이 기술 덕분에 당신의 실제 데이터는 은행에 안전하게 보관되어 당신은 모바일 기기를 이용해서 안심하고 쇼핑할 수 있습니다.

어휘 mobile 휑 휴대 전화 (= mobile phone)   payment 휑 지불   commercial 휑 광고 (방송)   feature 통 특징으로 삼다   stuff 휑 물건   slide 통 미끄러지다, 미끄러뜨리다   device 휑 장치[기구]   app 휑 응용 프로그램 (= application)   security 휑 보안 (secure 휑 안전한)   financial 휑 금융의, 재정의   steal 통 훔치다   save 통 구하다; 저축하다; *저장하다   make a purchase 구매하다   random 휑 무작위의   data 휑 (컴퓨터에 저장된) 자료, 정보   retailer 휑 소매업자, 소매상   access 통 접근하다   effective 휑 효과적인   prevent 통 막다[방지하다]   crime 휑 범죄   unusable 휑 사용할 수 없는   confidence 휑 신뢰; *확신

구문

4행 ..., my friend **told** me [**that** I shouldn't get it because of its security problems].
→ that은 명사절을 이끄는 접속사로, [ ]는 동사 told의 직접목적어 역할을 한다.

8행 You **don't have to worry** about security problems.
→ 「don't have to-v」는 '~할 필요가 없다'의 의미로, 「don't need to-v」로 바꿔 쓸 수 있다.

12행 However, **whenever** you make a purchase, the app *replaces* your information *with* a random number, or digital token.
→ whenever은 '~할 때마다'의 의미인 복합관계부사이며, 시간의 부사절을 이끈다.
→ 「replace A with B」는 'A를 B로 바꾸다, 대체하다'의 의미이다.

16행 This is **the key** [*allowing the retailer to access* your financial data].
→ [ ]는 the key를 수식하는 현재분사구이다.
→ 「allow+목적어+to-v」는 '~가 …하게 하다'의 의미이며, to access는 allowing의 목적격 보어이다.

18행 Actually, this technology is **more effective than** the traditional payment system *in preventing* credit card crimes.
→ 「비교급+than」은 '~보다 더 …한[하게]'의 의미이다.
→ 「in v-ing」는 '~하는 데 있어서'의 의미이며, 이때 preventing은 동명사로 전치사 in의 목적어이다.

● **VOCABULARY INSIDE**

Check Up   1 commercial   2 reward   3 prevent   4 achieve
5 random   6 contributed   7 security   8 raise

READING 1   Ambroise Paré

◊ Mini Quiz
1 T   2 F

▶ Reading Comprehension
1 d   2 b   3 b   4 read about his techniques, modern medical treatments

해석

중세 유럽에서, 모든 사람은 이발소를 바깥에 있는 빨간색과 흰색의 줄무늬 기둥으로 알아볼 수 있었다. 그 기둥은 오늘날 여전히 사용되고 있는데, 원래는 놀라운 의미를 지녔다. 붉은 줄무늬는 피를 상징했고, 흰 것은 붕대를 상징했다. 이것은 중세 시대에 이발사가 외과 의사이기도 했기 때문이다. 사실 그들은 이발사 겸 외과 의사라고 불렸다. 그들은 썩은 치아 뽑기와 수술 집도하기 같은 많은 일을 수행했다. 어떤 이발사 겸 외과 의사들은 의학 역사에서 또한 중요했다. 그들 중 한 명은 앙브루아즈 파레인데, 그는 현대의 수술을 향한 첫발을 내디뎠다.

앙브루아즈 파레는 1510년 프랑스에서 태어났다. 이발사 겸 외과 의사 밑에서 공부한 후에, 그는 30년을 군의관으로 보냈다. 그때, 군의관들은 끓는 기름으로 상처를 달구어 총상을 치료했다. 하지만 파레는 이 위험한 방법이 환자에게 큰 고통을 가하는 것을 관찰했다. 그리하여 그는 달걀노른자와 장미 기름의 순한 혼합물로 상처를 치료했다. 그의 치료법은 환자의 고통을 줄이는 데 더 나았을 뿐만 아니라, 몸에 덜 해로웠다.

파레는 그가 발견한 모든 것을 신중히 기록했고 그것들을 일련의 책으로 출간했다. 라틴어로 쓰인 다른 의학 서적과는 달리, 파레의 것들은 불어로 쓰였다. 이것은 더 많은 이발사 겸 외과 의사들이 그의 기법에 관해 읽도록 했다. 게다가, 파레의 책은 자신의 수술 경험만을 바탕으로 하였는데, 이것은 유럽에서 현대 의료의 기반을 마련했다.

어휘

medieval 휑 중세의   recognize 동 알아보다   barber 명 이발사   striped 형 줄무늬가 있는   pole 명 막대기, 기둥   symbolize 동 상징하다   bandage 명 붕대   surgeon 명 외과 의사   perform 동 (일·과제 등을) 수행하다   task 명 일, 과업   rotten 형 썩은, 부패한   surgery 명 수술 (surgical 형 수술의)   military 형 군사의   treat 동 대하다; *치료하다, 처치하다 (treatment 명 치료)   gunshot 명 사격, 발포   wound 명 상처   boil 동 끓이다   mild 형 가벼운[순한]   mixture 명 혼합물   egg yolk (계란) 노른자위   patient 명 환자   suffering 명 고통   damaging 형 (신체에) 손상을 주는, 해로운   write down ~을 적다   finding 명 연구 결과   a series of 일련의   technique 명 기법, 기술   foundation 명 토대[기초] [문제]   innovative 형 획기적인   observe 동 보다; *관찰하다   approach 명 접근법, 처리 방법   pain 명 통증, 고통

구문

5행 The red stripes symbolized blood, and **the white (stripes)** symbolized bandages.
→ 반복을 피하기 위해 the white 다음에 stripes가 생략되었다.

10행 One of them was **Ambroise Paré, who** took the first steps towards modern surgery.
→ 「, who」는 선행사 Ambroise Paré를 부연 설명하는 계속적 용법의 주격 관계대명사이다.

12행 **After studying** under a barber-surgeon, he spent 30 years *as* a military surgeon.
→ After studying은 '공부한 후에'라는 의미의 〈때〉를 나타내는 분사구문으로, 의미를 명확하게 하기 위해 접속사를 생략하지 않았다.
→ as는 '~로서'의 의미인 전치사이다.

15행 Paré, however, **observed** [**that** this dangerous approach *caused patients great pain*].
→ that은 명사절을 이끄는 접속사로, [ ]는 동사 observed의 목적어 역할을 한다.

→ 「cause A B」는 'A에게 B를 야기하다[초래하다]'의 의미이다.

[18행] Paré carefully **wrote down** all his findings and **published** them in a series of books.

→ wrote down과 published가 접속사 and로 병렬 연결되어 있다.

[19행] Unlike **other medical texts**[, which were written in Latin], *Paré's* (*medical texts*) were written in French.

→ [ ]는 선행사인 other medical texts를 부연 설명하는 계속적 용법의 주격 관계대명사절로, 문장 중간에 삽입되었다.

→ 반복을 피하기 위해 Paré's 뒤에 medical texts가 생략되었다.

READING 2 Raoul Wallenberg

Mini Quiz

1 rescue 2 Swedish people

▶ **Reading Comprehension**

1 c 2 b 3 b 4 Swedish territories, could not take any of the Jewish people

▶ **Grammar Inside LEVEL 3**

[Check Up] taller than any other girl

해석 제2차 세계 대전 동안, 많은 사람들이 유대인들을 구하기 위해 자신의 목숨을 걸었다. 그러나, 아마 아무도 라울 발렌베리만큼 용감하지 않았을 것이다. 1944년에, 나치는 헝가리에 사는 약 70만 명의 유대인들을 독일의 강제 수용소로 수송하려고 했다. 그 유대인들을 도우려는 시도로, 발렌베리는 스웨덴 외교관으로 고용되어 헝가리로 파송되었다. 외교 경험이 전혀 없었음에도 불구하고, 발렌베리는 홀로코스트의 가장 성공적인 구출 작전을 이끌었다.

발렌베리가 헝가리 부다페스트에 도착했을 때, 그는 즉시 유대인 거주 지역 근처에 스웨덴 대사관을 열고 400명의 유대인을 고용했다. 발렌베리와 그의 팀은 수천 명의 유대인을 위한 은신처, 병원, 학교를 지었다. 그러고 나서 발렌베리는 사람들이 건물 위로 스웨덴 깃발을 올리도록 했다. 이는 그곳들이 스웨덴 영토이며 나치는 내부에 있는 어떠한 유대인도 데려갈 수 없음을 의미했다.

게다가, 발렌베리는 기차에서 유대인을 직접 구출했다. 기차가 유대인들을 부다페스트에서 독일 강제 수용소로 데려가려는 찰나, 발렌베리가 나타났다. 그는 창문에 손을 뻗어서 닿을 수 있는 모든 사람에게 스웨덴 여권을 나눠주었다. 그러고 나서 그는 여권을 가진 사람들은 법적으로 스웨덴 국민이기 때문에 기차에서 내려져야만 한다고 주장했다. 마침내 전쟁이 1945년에 끝났을 때, 발렌베리와 그의 팀 덕분에 10만 명이 넘는 유대인들이 부다페스트에서 살아남았다.

어휘 risk [동] 위태롭게 하다 Jewish [형] 유대인의 transport [동] 수송하다 Hungary [명] 헝가리 (Hungarian [명] 헝가리 사람) in an attempt to-v ~하려는 시도로, ~하기 위해 hire [동] 고용하다 Swedish [형] 스웨덴의 diplomat [명] 외교관 (diplomacy [명] 외교 diplomatic [형] 외교의) rescue [명] 구출, 구조 [동] 구출하다 Budapest [명] 부다페스트 (헝가리의 수도) immediately [부] 즉시 embassy [명] 대사관 flag [명] 깃발 territory [명] 지역, 영토 personally [부] 직접, 개인적으로 appear [동] 나타나다 reach [동] 손[발]을 뻗다 hand out 나눠 주다 passport [명] 여권 argue [동] 주장하다 legally [부] 법률[합법]적으로 finally [부] 마침내 remain [동] 계속[여전히] ~이다 alive [형] 살아 있는 thanks to ~ 덕분에 [문제] equally [부] 동등하게

구문

3행 In 1944, the Nazis tried to **transport** *around 700,000 Jewish people* [living in Hungary] **to** German concentration camps.

→ 「transport A to B」는 'A를 B로 수송하다'의 의미이다.

→ [ ]는 around 700,000 Jewish people을 수식하는 현재분사구이다.

6행 **Despite** [having no experience in diplomacy], Wallenberg led the most successful … .

→ despite는 '~에도 불구하고'라는 의미의 전치사로, in spite of로 바꿀 수 있다. 동명사구 [ ]가 Despite의 목적어로 쓰였다.

12행 Then Wallenberg **made people raise** the Swedish flag on the buildings.

→ 「make+목적어+동사원형」은 '~가 …하게 하다[만들다]'라는 의미이며, 이때 동사원형 raise는 사역동사 made의 목적격 보어로 쓰였다.

17행 **Just as** the train *was about to take* the Jewish people from Budapest to German concentration camps, … .

→ as는 〈때〉를 나타내는 접속사로, just와 함께 쓰여 '막 ~할 때'의 의미를 나타낸다.

→ 「be about to-v」는 '막 ~하려고 하다'의 의미이다.

→ 「from A to B」는 'A에서 B로'의 의미이다.

18행 He reached into the windows **to hand out** Swedish passports to *every person* [(that) he could reach].

→ to hand out은 '나눠 주기 위해'의 의미로, 〈목적〉을 나타내는 to부정사의 부사적 용법이다.

→ [ ]는 선행사 every person을 수식하는 목적격 관계대명사절로, 관계대명사 that이 생략되었다.

20행 Then he argued that **the people** [with the passports] had to *be let off* the train … .

→ [ ]는 the people을 수식하는 전치사구이다.

→ 「let A off B」는 'A를 B에서 내리게 하다'의 의미로, 여기서는 수동형(A be let off B)으로 쓰였다.

● **VOCABULARY INSIDE**

| *Check Up* | 1 transport | 2 territory | 3 foundation | 4 surgery |
| | 5 treated | 6 performing | 7 appear | 8 diplomat |

UNIT 14 | Space

pp. 85-90

READING 1 Space Junk

Mini Quiz

1 When a satellite crashes into a small piece of debris, it can break apart into thousands of new pieces. The resulting space debris can damage other satellites and spacecrafts.
2 remove

▶ Reading Comprehension

1 b 2 a 3 c 4 burn up, the Earth's atmosphere

해석 인간은 수천 개의 위성과 로켓을 우주로 쏘아 올렸다. 그 과정에서, 우리는 또한 우주에 엄청난 양의 쓰레기를 만들어 오고 있다. 우주 쓰레기는 우주 잔해라고 불린다. 어떤 것들은 거대한 반면, 다른 잔해는 감자칩만큼 작다.

약 23,000개의 잔해가 지구 궤도를 돌고 있다. 그중 대부분은 소프트볼보다 크고 시간당 18,000미터까지의 속도로 이동한다. 그들의 속도 때문에, 아주 작은 우주 쓰레기도 큰 문제를 일으킬 수 있다. 위성이 작은 잔해 조각에 충돌하면, 그것은 수천 개의 새로운 조각으로 부서질 수 있다. 그 결과로 생긴 우주 잔해는 다른 위성과 우주선들에 손상을 입힐 수 있다.

이 문제에 대응하여, 국제 연합은 기업들에게 그들의 위성을 궤도에서 제거할 것을 요청해 오고 있다. 만약 인공위성이 임무를 완수하면, 그것들은 25년 내에 우주 밖으로 옮겨져야 한다. 이를 실현하기 위해 몇 가지 해결책이 제시되었다. 예를 들어, 수명이 다한 인공위성은 자석이나 거대한 그물을 이용하여 궤도에서 꺼내질 수 있다. 그 잔해들이 대기권으로 물러나게 되면, 그것들은 완전히 연소된다. 불행하게도 이 방법은 규모가 더 큰 위성들에만 효과가 있을 것이다. 장기적인 관점에서 해결책을 찾기 위해서는 더 많은 연구가 필요하다.

어휘 space [명] 우주 junk [명] 쓰레기 human [명] 인간 launch [동] 발사하다 thousands of 수천의 satellite [명] (인공)위성 process [명] 과정 tons of 매우 많은 enormous [형] 거대한 tiny [형] 아주 작은[적은] orbit [동] (다른 천체의) 궤도를 돌다 [명] 궤도 up to ~까지 huge [형] 거대한 crash [동] 충돌하다 break apart 쪼개지다, 분리되다 resulting [형] 그 결과로 초래된 damage [동] 손상을 입히다 spacecraft [명] 우주선 in response to ~에 대응하여 remove [동] 제거하다 complete [동] 완료하다 mission [명] 임무 take A out of B B에서 A를 꺼내다 within [전] ~ 이내에 solution [명] 해결책 dead [형] 죽은, 수명이 다한 pull back 후퇴하다, 물러나다 atmosphere [명] (지구의) 대기 unfortunately [부] 불행하게도 method [명] 방법 research [명] 연구, 조사 in the long term 장기적으로 [문제] pollution [명] 오염, 공해 emphasize [동] 강조하다 exploration [명] 탐험, 탐사 weight [명] 무게 location [명] 위치 enter [동] 들어가다, 진입하다

구문 [3행] Some is enormous, **while** other debris is *as tiny as* a potato chip.
→ while은 '~인 반면에'의 의미로, 〈대조〉를 나타내는 접속사이다.
→ 「as+형용사[부사]의 원급+as」는 '~만큼 …한[하게]'의 의미이다.

[5행] Most of them **are** *larger than* a softball and **travel** at up to 18 thousand meters per hour.
→ are와 travel이 접속사 and로 병렬 연결되어 있다.
→ 「비교급+than」은 '~보다 더 …한[하게]'의 의미이다.

[11행] In response to this problem, the United Nations **has been *asking*** *companies to remove* their satellites from orbit.

→ has been asking은 '요청해 오고 있다'의 의미로, 〈계속〉을 나타내는 「have been v-ing」 형태의 현재완료 진행형이다.

→ 「ask+목적어+to-v」는 '~에게 …하도록 요청하다'의 의미로, 이때 to remove는 asking의 목적격 보어이다.

16행 **Once** they are pulled back into the Earth's atmosphere, they *would* burn up.

→ once는 '~하자마자, ~할 때'의 의미로, 〈때〉를 나타내는 접속사이다.

→ would는 '~할 것이다'의 의미로, 현재·미래에 대한 추측을 나타내는 조동사이다.

READING 2　A Beautiful View from HDEV

Ⓥ Mini Quiz
1 F　2 F

▶ **Reading Comprehension**
1 a　2 c　3 c　4 the quality of the cameras, how they perform in space

해석　우주에서 지구를 보고 싶다면 여러분은 영화를 볼 필요가 없다. 여러분은 이 장관을 스마트폰에서 생중계로 볼 수 있다! 고화질 지구 관찰 시스템(HDEV)이라고 불리는 한 NASA 프로젝트가 2014년 4월부터 운영되고 있다. 그것은 지구 주변의 궤도를 도는 네 대의 카메라에서 받은 실시간 영상을 인터넷으로 방송한다.

그 프로젝트는 미국의 존슨 우주 기지에서 공학자들에 의해 주도된다. 카메라는 국제 우주 정거장(ISS)의 외부에 설치되어 있고, 각각의 카메라는 다른 위치에서 지구를 촬영하도록 설치되어 있다. 그것들은 ISS와 함께 궤도를 따라 움직이면서 다른 각도에서 영상을 녹화한다. 그 녹화 과정은 자동이며 작동하는 데는 오직 ISS의 전력만 필요하다. 카메라가 NASA로 영상을 보내면, 그것은 실시간으로 인터넷에 보여진다. 따라서, 누구나 언제든지 온라인에서 이 영상을 즐길 수 있다.

그런데 왜 NASA는 우리에게 이러한 지구의 영상을 보여주는가? 사실, HDEV 프로젝트의 목적은 카메라의 품질을 테스트하고 어떻게 그것이 우주에서 작동하는지를 관찰하는 것이다. 그 카메라들은 강한 방사선과 극한의 온도와 같은 거친 우주의 환경에 노출된다. 그것들이 이 어려움들을 견딜 수 있다면, 나중에 우주 탐사 임무에 사용될 것이다. 이제 당신의 스마트폰을 집어 들고 NASA의 공식 웹사이트로 가라. 지구를 즐길 시간이다!

어휘　view 몡 경관, 전망 통 보다　spectacular 혱 장관을 이루는　sight 몡 시야; *광경[모습]　live 뿐 생방송으로 혱 생방송의　run 통 달리다; *운영하다　broadcast 통 방송하다 (broadcast-broadcast)　engineer 몡 기술자, 공학자　install 통 설치하다　set up 설치하다　film 통 촬영하다　position 몡 위치　angle 몡 각도, 각　automatic 혱 자동의　at any time 언제든지　purpose 몡 목적　test 통 시험하다　quality 몡 품질　observe 통 관찰하다　perform 통 수행하다; *(작동하며) 돌아가다　expose 통 노출시키다　tough 혱 힘든, 어려운　condition 몡 상태; *환경　harsh 혱 가혹한; *너무 강한　extreme 혱 극심한　temperature 몡 온도, 기온　endure 통 견디다, 참다　challenge 몡 도전　official 혱 공식적인　[문제] fixed 혱 고정된　withstand 통 견뎌 내다

구문　1행 You **don't have to watch** a movie if you want to view the Earth from space.

→ 「don't have to-v」는 '~할 필요가 없다'의 의미이며, 「don't need to-v」로 바꿔 쓸 수 있다.

3행 **A NASA project** [called High Definition Earth Viewing (HDEV)] *has been running* since April 2014.

→ [ ]는 A NASA project를 수식하는 과거분사구이다.

→ has been running은 '운영되어 오고 있다'의 의미로, 〈계속〉을 나타내는 「have been v-ing」 형태의 현재완료 진행형이다.

9행 They record videos from different angles **while moving** with the ISS in its orbit.
→ while moving은 '움직일 동안'의 의미로 〈동시동작〉을 나타내는 분사구문이며, 의미를 명확히 하기 위해 접속사를 생략하지 않았다.

13행 Actually, the purpose of the HDEV project is **to test** the quality of the cameras and (**to**) *observe* [how they perform in space].
→ to test와 (to) observe는 문장의 보어 역할을 하는 명사적 용법의 to부정사로, 접속사 and로 병렬 연결되어 있다.
→ [ ]는 「의문사+주어+동사」 어순의 간접의문문으로, observe의 목적어 역할을 한다.

18행 Now **pick** up your smartphone and **go** to NASA's official website.
→ 명령문으로, 동사원형 pick과 go가 접속사 and로 병렬 연결되어 있다.

19행 **It's time to enjoy** the Earth!
→ 「it's time to-v」는 '~할 시간이다'라는 의미이다.

● **VOCABULARY INSIDE**

Check Up	1 launched	2 quality	3 extreme	4 broadcast
	5 automatic	6 Unfortunately	7 solution	8 damaged

UNIT 15 | Fiction   pp. 91-96

READING 1   Following Folktales

❷ **Mini Quiz**
  1 T   2 F

▶ **Reading Comprehension**
  1 b   2 d   3 c   4 tiger, wolf

해석 유럽과 중동에서 인기 있는 전래 동화 '늑대와 일곱 아기 염소'에서, 엄마 염소는 먹이를 찾는 동안 아이들을 집에 남겨둔다. 그동안에, 늑대는 아이들을 속여서 집 안으로 들어오려고 한다. 이와 유사하게, '빨간 모자'에는 소녀의 할머니인 척하여 어린 소녀를 속이는 늑대가 포함된다. 이 이야기는 중국, 일본, 한국의 '호랑이 할머니'와 같은 많은 다른 버전이 있다.

Jamie Tehrani 박사는 이렇게 다르지만 유사한 전래 동화에 관심을 가지게 되었다. 그는 생물학적 종이 각기 다른 환경에 적응하는 것과 같은 방식으로 전래 동화가 각기 다른 문화에서 변화한다고 생각했다. 그는 이야기의 어떤 부분이 특정 문화에서 발달하는 반면, 다른 부분들은 사라진다는 것을 알아냈다. (C) 그 이야기들이 어떻게 진화했는지 알아내기 위해, Tehrani 박사는 58개의 이야기를 검토하고 차이점을 열거하였다. (B) 그것에는 아이들의 수 및 악당의 종류와 속임수가 포함되었다. (A) 그는 그런 다음 그 이야기들이 시간이 지나면서 어떻게 변하였는지 살펴보았다.

그 결과는 매우 흥미로웠다. 그의 연구에서, 그는 '빨간 모자'가 '늑대와 일곱 아기 염소'의 초기 버전에서 진화했을 뿐만 아니라, 이후 버전에도 영감을 주었음을 시사했다. 또한, 그는 유럽 버전의 '빨간 모자'가 아시아 버전에 영감을 주었음을 시사했다. 그러나, 아시아권의 이야기에서는 늑대가 호랑이로 바뀌었다!

어휘 follow [동] 따르다[따라가다] folktale [명] 민간 설화, 전래 동화 goat [명] 염소 meanwhile [부] 그동안에 trick [동] 속이다 [명] 속임수 similarly [부] 비슷하게, 유사하게 (similarity [명] 유사성) include [동] 포함하다 pretend [동] ~인 척하다 tale [명] (허구의) 이야기 biological [형] 생물학의 adapt to ~에 적응하다 environment [명] 환경 disappear [동] 사라지다 character [명] 성격; *(책·영화의) 등장인물 find out ~을 알아내다 evolve [동] 발달하다; *진화하다 review [동] 재검토하다 list [동] (목록을) 작성하다 difference [명] 차이(점) result [명] 결과 pretty [부] 아주[매우] suggest [동] 제안하다; *시사하다 inspire [동] 고무하다; *영감을 주다 [문제] defend [동] 방어하다

구문

[2행] ..., a mother goat leaves her kids at home **while** she searches for food.
→ while은 '~하는 동안'의 의미인 〈때〉를 나타내는 접속사이다.

[3행] Meanwhile, a wolf **tries to *trick*** the kids *into* [letting him into the house].
→ 「try to-v」는 '~하려고 노력하다'의 의미이다.
→ 「trick A into B」는 'A를 속여 B하게 하다'의 의미이며, [ ]는 동명사구로 전치사 into의 목적어이다.

[4행] Similarly, "Little Red Riding Hood" includes **a wolf** [**who** tricks a little girl *by pretending* to be her grandmother].
→ [ ]는 선행사 a wolf를 수식하는 주격 관계대명사절이다. 이때 늑대는 동화 속 등장인물 중 하나이므로 관계대명사 who를 썼다.
→ 「by v-ing」은 '~함으로써'의 의미이다.

[9행] He **believed** [(**that**) folktales change in different cultures in the same way biological species adapt to different environments].
→ [ ]는 동사 believed의 목적어 역할을 하는 명사절로, 명사절을 이끄는 접속사 that이 생략되었다.

[10행] He found that some parts of stories developed in certain cultures, **while** others disappeared.
→ while은 '~하는 반면에'의 의미인 〈대조〉를 나타내는 접속사이다.

[12행] He then *looked* at **how** the stories *had changed* over time.
→ how는 〈방법〉을 나타내는 관계부사로, 선행사 the way와 함께 쓰지 않는다.
→ had changed는 과거완료(had v-ed)로, 과거의 어느 시점(looked)까지 지속되었던 일을 나타낸다.

[13행] They included **the number of children** *and* the type *and* (the) trick of the bad character.
→ 「the number of+복수 명사」는 '~의 수'라는 의미이다.
→ 첫 번째 and는 the number of children과 the type 이하를 병렬 연결하는 접속사이며, 두 번째 and는 the type과 (the) trick을 병렬 연결하는 접속사이다.

READING 2 The Ransom of Red Chief

[V] Mini Quiz
1 Red Chief 2 Mr. Dorset[Johnny's father]

▶ **Reading Comprehension**
1 b 2 b 3 c 4 take Johnny back, pay him $250

▶ **Grammar Inside LEVEL 3**
[Check Up] Considering her age

해석 두 명의 악당인 빌과 샘은 한 아이를 납치하고 2,000달러의 몸값을 요구할 계획이다. 그들은 부자인 도셋 씨의 외동 아들인 아홉 살 된 조니를 택한다.

그러나 그 소년은 굉장한 장난꾸러기이기 때문에 그를 납치하기는 쉽지 않다. 빌과 샘이 소년에게 가까이 다가가자, 조니는 빌의 눈에 벽돌 조각을 던진다. 빌과 샘은 조니를 붙잡고 그를 산속의 동굴로 태워 간다. 샘이 마을에 차를 돌려주고 돌아왔을 때, 빌은 소년과 함께 카우보이와 인디언 게임을 하도록 강요받고 있었다. 조니는 이제 '붉은 추장'이고, 빌은 멍투성이이다. 그들은 곧 조니가 학교를 싫어하고 산에서 야영하기를 좋아한다는 것을 알게 된다. 다음 날 아침, 어린 붉은 추장은 빌이 말인 것처럼 그 위에 뛰어 올라타고 심지어 그의 셔츠 아래에 뜨거운 감자를 넣는다.

빌과 샘은 도셋 씨에게 아들을 되돌려주는 데 1,500달러만 내라고 요청하며 재빨리 편지를 쓴다. 놀랍게도, 도셋 씨는 그들이 자신에게 250달러를 줄 때만 조니를 데려가겠다고 답한다! 조니의 지난 행동들을 고려해 보았을 때, 그들은 차라리 돈을 잃는 것이 더 낫다고 판단한다. 빌과 샘은 조니를 그의 아버지에게 돌려보내고 돈을 지불한다. 그러나, 조니는 그의 모험이 끝나는 것을 원하지 않았고, 빌의 다리에 매달린다. 마침내, 빌과 샘은 도셋 씨가 그의 아들을 잡고 있는 동안 달아날 수 있게 된다.

어휘 chief [명] 최고위자; *추장, 족장 villain [명] 악당 kidnap [동] 납치하다 demand [동] 요구하다 select [동] 선발[선택]하다 naughty [형] 버릇없는, 말을 안 듣는 brick [명] 벽돌 grab [동] 붙잡다[움켜잡다] cave [명] 동굴 return [동] 돌아오다; 돌려주다 [명] 돌아옴, 귀환 force [동] 강요하다 bruise [명] 멍 realize [동] 깨닫다, 알아차리다 leap [동] 뛰다, 뛰어오르다 surprisingly [부] 놀랍게도 reply [동] 대답하다, 답장하다 past [형] 지난 behavior [명] 행동 decide [동] 결정하다 adventure [명] 모험 cling to ~에 매달리다 escape [동] 탈출하다 [문제] cruel [형] 잔혹한, 잔인한 courageous [형] 용감한 regretful [형] 유감스러워하는 ashamed [형] 부끄러워하는 determined [형] 단호한, 완강한 embarrassed [형] 당혹스러운

구문 [1행] **Two villains, Bill and Sam,** *plan to kidnap* a child and (*to*) *demand* a $2,000 ransom.
→ Two villains와 Bill and Sam은 동격 관계이다.
→ 「plan to-v」는 '~할 것을 계획하다'의 의미이며, to kidnap과 (to) demand가 접속사 and로 병렬 연결되어 있다.

[4행] However, **it**'s not easy **to kidnap the boy**, because he is very naughty.
→ it은 가주어이고, to kidnap the boy는 진주어이다.

[8행] ..., Bill **has been forced** [to play a game of cowboys and Indians with the boy].
→ 「have been v-ed」는 '~되어 왔다'의 의미로, 〈계속〉을 나타내는 현재완료 수동태이다.
→ [ ]는 5형식 문장의 목적격 보어인 to부정사구가 현재완료 수동태인 have been forced 뒤에 그대로 쓰인 형태이다.

9행 Johnny is now "Red Chief," and Bill **is covered with** bruises.
　　→ 「be covered with」는 '~으로 덮여 있다'는 의미이다.

13행 Bill and Sam quickly write a letter, **asking** Mr. Dorset to pay only $1,500 … .
　　→ asking은 '부탁하면서'의 의미로, 〈동시동작〉을 나타내는 분사구문이다.

16행 …, they decide they**'d rather lose** some money.
　　→ 「would rather+동사원형」은 '차라리 ~하는 것이 낫다'의 의미이다.

● VOCABULARY INSIDE

Check Up	1 select	2 environment	3 adventure	4 character
	5 naughty	6 reviewing	7 forced	8 pretended

UNIT 16 | Food
pp. 97-102

READING 1　Swedish Candies

✔ Mini Quiz
1 F　2 T

▶ Reading Comprehension
1 c　2 prevent children from getting (so many) cavities　3 c　4 d

▶ Grammar Inside LEVEL 3
Check Up　1 접속사　2 관계대명사

해석　　아마도 세계에서 스웨덴만큼 사탕을 많이 먹는 나라는 없을 것이다. 사실 대부분의 스웨덴 사람들은 매년 대략 16킬로그램의 사탕을 먹는다. 세계 보건 기구는 이것이 평균 권장량의 세 배라고 한다. 스웨덴 정부는 아이들에게 충치가 너무 많이 생기는 것을 예방하기를 바랐다. 그래서 1950년대 후반에 정부는 토요일에만 사탕을 먹도록 장려하는 운동을 홍보했다. 이렇게 해서 로다구디스가 탄생했다. 로다구디스는 '토요일 단 것' 또는 '토요일 사탕'을 의미한다. 그것은 주말마다 일어나는 가족 활동이다.

　　스웨덴 사람들은 픽앤믹스 사탕 가게에서 가장 좋아하는 사탕을 고르는 것을 아주 좋아한다. 픽앤믹스 사탕 가게는 사람들이 많은 종류의 단 것들 중에 고를 수 있는 가게이다. 그 가게들은 셀 수 없이 많은 젤리, 초콜릿, 그리고 그 밖의 알록달록한 사탕들을 보유하고 있다. 그것들은 슈퍼마켓, 약국, 심지어 주유소에서도 흔히 볼 수 있다.

　　사탕에 대한 이 국민적인 열정 때문에, 스웨덴의 사탕 산업은 더 건강해지도록 발전해 오고 있다. 회사들은 점점 더 많은 유기농 재료와 천연 향료를 사용하고 있다. 채식주의자들은 심지어 그들만을 위한 단 것들을 찾을 수도 있다! (사탕은 여전히 체중을 감량하는 데 바람직하지 않은 선택으로 여겨진다.) 그래서, 건강을 의식하는 스웨덴 사람들은 재료 라벨을 더 자세히 살펴봐야 한다.

어휘 Swedish ⓗ 스웨덴의 (Sweden ⓘ 스웨덴 Swede ⓘ 스웨덴 사람) in fact 사실 roughly ⓟ 대략 average ⓗ 평균의 recommend ⓥ 추천하다; *권장하다 amount ⓘ 총액; *양 cavity ⓘ 충치 promote ⓥ 홍보하다 campaign ⓘ 캠페인, (조직적인) 운동 encourage ⓥ 격려하다; 장려하다 sweet ⓘ 단 것 activity ⓘ 활동 happen ⓥ 일어나다, 발생하다 countless ⓗ 셀 수 없이 많은 commonly ⓟ 흔히 national ⓗ 국가의, 전국민의 passion ⓘ 열정 industry ⓘ 산업 evolve ⓥ 발전하다 increasingly ⓟ 점점 더 ingredient ⓘ 재료[성분] natural ⓗ 자연의, 천연의 flavor ⓘ 맛; *향료 vegetarian ⓘ 채식주의자 be regarded as ~으로 여겨지다 undesirable ⓗ 바람직하지 않은 option ⓘ 선택 (사항) weight ⓘ 체중, 무게 conscious ⓗ 의식하는 take a closer look at ~을 자세히 살펴보다 label ⓘ 라벨, 상표 [문제] dessert ⓘ 디저트, 후식 nutritious ⓗ 영양분이 많은

구문

3행 The World Health Organization **says** [**that** this is three times the average recommended amount].
→ that은 명사절을 이끄는 접속사로, [ ]는 동사 says의 목적어 역할을 한다.

4행 The Swedish government hoped to **prevent children from getting** so many cavities.
→ 「prevent+목적어+from v-ing」는 '~가 …하는 것을 막다'의 의미이다.

8행 It is **a family activity** [that happens every weekend].
→ [ ]는 선행사 a family activity를 수식하는 주격 관계대명사절이다.

11행 A pick-n-mix candy shop is **a store** [**in which** people can choose from many kinds of sweets].
→ [ ]는 선행사 a store를 수식하는 목적격 관계대명사절이다. 관계대명사 which가 전치사 in의 목적어로 쓰였다.

15행 **Due to** this national passion for sweets, the Swedish candy industry *has been evolving* to be healthier.
→ 「due to」는 '~ 때문에'의 의미로, 뒤에 명사(구)가 온다.
→ has been evolving은 '발전해 오고 있다'의 의미이며, 〈계속〉을 나타내는 「have been v-ing」 형태의 현재완료 진행형이다.

READING 2 The History of Breakfast

♡ Mini Quiz
1 the Industrial Revolution 2 cereal with milk

▶ **Reading Comprehension**
1 b 2 eating, sin 3 c 4 d

▶ **Grammar Inside LEVEL 3**
Check Up Having left

해석 아침을 먹는 것은 많은 사람들이 아침에 하는 첫 번째 일이다. 하지만, 그것은 서양 사람들에게는 비교적 최근의 관습이다. 중세 유럽에서는 하루에 두 번의 식사가 있었는데, 정오에 한 번 그리고 초저녁에 한 번이었다. 놀랍게도, 어떤 사람들은 아침에 먹는 것을 죄라고 여겼다. 이러한 믿음 때문에, 농부와 노동자들 같은 하층 계급의 사람들만이 아침을 먹었다. 이들은 아침에 일하기 위해 에너지가 필요했던 사람들이었다. 역사학자들은 '아침 식사'라는 단어가 이 시기 즈음에 유래했다고 생각한다. 그들은 이 용어가 밤의 단식을 깬다는 것을 지칭한다고 제안한다.

아침 식사의 이러한 개념은 19세기 중반 산업 혁명과 함께 바뀌었다. 그 당시, 모든 계급의 사람들이 아침에 일하기 위해 집을 나서기 시작했다. 그 결과, 점점 더 많은 사람들이 출근하기 전에 치즈와 빵 같은 음식을 먹는 것으로 하루를 시작했다.

또 다른 변화가 20세기 초반쯤에 발생했다. (C) 존 하비 켈로그라는 이름의 한 미국인은 밀로 요리하다가 우연히 아침 식사용 시리얼을 만들었다. (A) 시리얼이 얼마나 맛있는지 알아낸 후, 그는 그것을 비타민과 미네랄이 함유된 건강에 좋은 아침 식사라고 광고했다. (B) 그 이후로 계속, 우유를 곁들인 시리얼을 아침으로 먹는 것이 세계적으로 사람들에게 인기를 끌어오고 있다.

어휘 relatively ⓟ 비교적   Westerner ⓔ 서양인   medieval ⓗ 중세의   daily ⓗ 매일 일어나는, 나날의   midday ⓔ 정오, 한낮   sin ⓔ 죄   belief ⓔ 신념, 믿음   lower class 하층 계급   laborer ⓔ 노동자   historian ⓔ 역사가   originate ⓥ 비롯되다, 유래하다   around ⓟ 약, ~쯤   term ⓔ 용어, 말   refer to ~을 지칭하다   breaking ⓔ 파괴, 절단   consequently ⓟ 그 결과, 따라서   shift ⓔ 변화   discover ⓥ 발견하다; *알아내다   tasty ⓗ 맛있는   advertise ⓥ 광고하다   healthy ⓗ 건강한; *건강에 좋은   contain ⓥ ~이 들어 있다, 함유하다   accidentally ⓟ 우연히, 뜻하지 않게

구문

1행 **Having breakfast is** *the first thing* [(that) many people do in the morning].
→ Having breakfast는 주어 역할을 하는 동명사구이며, is가 동사이다. 동명사구 주어는 단수 취급한다.
→ [ ]는 선행사 the first thing을 수식하는 목적격 관계대명사절로, 관계대명사 that이 생략되었다.

4행 Surprisingly, some people considered **it a sin to eat in the morning**.
→ it은 가목적어, to eat 이하는 진목적어이며, a sin은 동사 considered의 목적격 보어이다.

6행 These were **people** [who needed the energy *to work* in the morning].
→ [ ]는 선행사 people을 수식하는 주격 관계대명사절이다.
→ to work는 '일하기 위해'의 의미로, 〈목적〉을 나타내는 to부정사의 부사적 용법이다.

12행 Consequently, **more and more** people began the day by eating food such as cheese and bread *before going* to work.
→ 「비교급+and+비교급」은 '점점 더 ~한[하게]'의 의미이다.
→ before going은 '가기 전에'의 의미로, 〈때〉를 나타내는 분사구문이다. 의미를 명확히 하기 위해 접속사를 생략하지 않았다.

16행 ..., he advertised it as **a healthy breakfast** [containing vitamins and minerals].
→ [ ]는 a healthy breakfast를 수식하는 현재분사구이다.

19행 **An American** [named John Harvey Kellogg] accidentally **created** breakfast cereal *by cooking* wheat.
→ [ ]는 주어인 An American을 수식하는 과거분사구이며, 동사는 created이다.
→ 「by v-ing」는 '~함으로써'의 의미이다.

● **VOCABULARY INSIDE**

Check Up	1 accidentally	2 ingredients	3 relatively	4 recommend
	5 flavor	6 advertise	7 vegetarian	8 originated

READING
Inside
Workbook

LEVEL 3

UNIT 01 | Culture

VOCABULARY TEST 1

01 적응   02 세기, 100년   03 주민, 지역 사회; 공동체
04 산호초   05 창의력   06 시(詩)   07 깊이
08 발달시키다   09 (물·공기에) 떠가다, 표류하다
10 환경   11 유산   12 존경하다; 기리다   13 의도하다
14 불을 붙이다   15 보호   16 좁은   17 거의
18 유목민   19 평화롭게   20 육체의[신체의]
21 준비하다   22 비교적   23 대표하다; 나타내다,
상징하다   24 책임(감)   25 종(種)   26 전통적으로
27 신뢰   28 연합하다; 통합하다[결속하다]   29 통합
30 시력   31 discuss   32 celebrate
33 marine   34 ethnic   35 scholar
36 principle   37 prefer   38 generation
39 describe   40 value   41 ~에 관심을 가지다
42 ~에 적응하다   43 ~을 자랑스러워하다
44 또한[역시]

VOCABULARY TEST 2

A 1 ⓐ   2 ⓔ   3 ⓓ   4 ⓒ   5 ⓑ
B 1 ⓔ   2 ⓑ   3 ⓓ
C 1 be proud of   2 adapt to
3 care about   4 as well

GRAMMAR TEST

A 1 It, to plan   2 It, to go   3 It, to read
4 It, to swim
B 1 to build a boat in a week, 그녀는 일주일 안에
배를 만드는 것을 불가능하다고 생각한다.
2 to help the poor, 로이는 가난한 사람들을 돕는
것을 가치 있다고 믿는다.
3 to exercise every day, 그 남자는 매일 운동하는
것을 규칙으로 만들었다.
4 to take care of my family, 나는 우리 가족을
보살피는 것을 내 의무라고 생각한다.
C 1 to listen[listening]   2 it[it is]
3 to play   4 to give[giving]

WRITING TEST

A 1 celebrate a holiday called
2 wanted people to care about
3 named the holiday with a Swahili word

---

4 call the ocean their home
5 When hunting for fish
B 1 floating   2 have, developed
3 find it, to live   4 After researching
5 has become, to help

UNIT 02 | Wealth

VOCABULARY TEST 1

01 연금술사   02 마음을 끌다; (사람을) 끌어들이다
03 화학   04 건설하다   05 치료하다, 치유하다
06 발달, 성장   07 요소, 성분   08 필수적인; 극히 중요한
09 설립하다   10 영원한   11 재정의, 금전적인
12 질병   13 영향을 주다   14 관심[흥미]   15 철
16 전설   17 중세의   18 현대의   19 신화, 근거 없는
믿음   20 보통의   21 주인, 소유주   22 기간; 시대
23 철학자   24 가능한   25 실행; 관행   26 비율
27 상승, 성장   28 후원하다   29 후원자
30 변형시키다   31 text   32 ancient   33 metal
34 beginning   35 master   36 universe
37 decrease   38 wealthy   39 early
40 earn   41 ~으로 구성되다   42 ~에 주력하다,
초점을 맞추다   43 절정에 이르다   44 A를 B로 바꾸다

VOCABULARY TEST 2

A 1 ⓔ   2 ⓐ   3 ⓓ   4 ⓑ   5 ⓒ
B 1 attract   2 financial   3 sponsored
4 constructed
C 1 focus on   2 turned, into
3 reached her peak   4 is composed of

GRAMMAR TEST

A 1 What I want to do, 내가 하고 싶은 것은 저
쇼핑몰에서 쇼핑하는 것이다.
2 Drinking coffee, 커피를 마시는 것은 내가 아침에
제일 먼저 하는 일이다.
3 The girl on the bench, 벤치 위의 소녀는 나의
언니이다.
4 Reading books to kids, 아이들에게 책을
읽어주는 것은 내가 가장 좋아하는 것들 중 하나이다.
5 The woman wearing a yellow dress, 노란
원피스를 입은 저 여성은 우리 엄마이다.

6 Playing soccer with my friends, 내 친구들과 축구하는 것은 신난다.

7 The boy that talked to me, 나에게 말했던 그 소년은 마이크의 아들이었다.

B 1 that we will go camping without her, 그녀는 우리가 그녀 없이 캠핑 갈 것을 알고 있니?

2 whether Sam is interested in movies, 나는 샘이 영화에 관심이 있는지 없는지 궁금하다.

3 the cake that was made by her husband, 그 여성은 그녀의 남편이 만든 케이크를 좋아했다.

4 where you put your keys, 너는 네 열쇠를 어디에 두었는지 기억하니?

5 collecting foreign coins, 나는 외국 동전을 수집하는 것을 좋아한다.

6 that I was at the beach, 우리 엄마는 내가 해변에 있다고 생각했다.

WRITING TEST

A 1 early scientists believed it was possible

2 It was believed that the stone had the power

3 Artists needed the help of

4 helped scholars study ancient texts

B 1 To make, happen

2 was able to change

3 without worrying about

4 Without, would be

5 Coming from

UNIT 03 | Shapes   pp. 10-13

VOCABULARY TEST 1

01 모스크, 회교 사원   02 우아한   03 혼합체[섞인 것]
04 묘사하다, 그리다   05 미술품   06 오각형
07 결합하다   08 수족관   09 경쟁하는   10 농업
11 비료   12 우아한   13 인구; 개체 수   14 10년
15 회전하다, 회전시키다   16 복잡한   17 놓다[두다]
18 기하학적인   19 말하다; 묘사하다   20 무한한
21 대표하다; 나타내다   22 몇몇의   23 (색깔이) 바래다; 서서히 사라지다   24 사라지다   25 산소   26 행동
27 생산하다   28 조류(藻類), 말   29 특이한   30 이끼
31 ceiling   32 palace   33 pattern   34 repeat
35 nature   36 freshwater   37 actually

38 tangled   39 form   40 sink   41 특히
42 나란히   43 내뿜다, 발산하다   44 (빛·소리를) 차단하다

VOCABULARY TEST 2

A 1 ⓒ   2 ⓐ   3 ⓓ   4 ⓑ
B 1 fade   2 infinite   3 repeat
   4 depicts   5 rival
C 1 in particular   2 side by side
   3 blocks out   4 gave off

GRAMMAR TEST

A 1 teaching[to teach]   2 meeting   3 to be
   4 to turn   5 exercising[to exercise]
B 1 might → should   2 should → can't
   3 can't → must   4 must → may[might]
   5 can't → shouldn't
C 1 to dance → dancing   2 to write → writing
   3 get → got[gotten]
   4 has went → have gone

WRITING TEST

A 1 find ceilings covered in elegant patterns
   2 Repeating geometric shapes
   3 try to show beauty by
   4 may have seen some green velvety balls
   5 Known as Marimo moss balls
B 1 are proud of developing
   2 how people see
   3 might have noticed that
   4 were easy to find

UNIT 04 | Nature   pp. 14-17

VOCABULARY TEST 1

01 화산   02 숨이 막히는   03 풍경   04 지역의, 현지의   05 전설   06 마법사   07 퍼지다; 펼쳐지다
08 지배하다   09 광물(질); 미네랄   10 영혼; 정령, 요정
11 용감하게   12 웅장한   13 재료, 물질   14 용암
15 재료[성분]   16 싸움터, 전쟁터   17 성냥
18 거주자   19 형성하다   20 분출하다   21 몰다;

(기계에) 전력을 공급하다 **22** 엔진 **23** 전기, 전력
24 공장 **25** 그리다; (마음을) 끌다 **26** 끌림; 명소
27 형성하다 **28** 극복하다 **29** 녹다 **30** 씌우다;
(언급된 지역에) 걸치다 **31** volcanic **32** nutrient
33 product **34** magma **35** valuable
36 glacier **37** eruption **38** underground
39 active **40** exotic **41** 콸콸 솟다; 끓어오르다
42 ~으로 변하다 **43** A에게 B를 제공하다 **44** ~와
사랑에 빠지다 **45** ~에 의하면[따르면]

VOCABULARY TEST 2

A 1 spread   2 underground   3 erupt
4 electricity   5 melt
B 1 ⓒ   2 ⓐ   3 ⓒ
C 1 According to   2 bubble up
3 provide, with   4 turn into

GRAMMAR TEST

A 1 healthiest   2 better   3 hot
4 dirtier, dirtier   5 funniest   6 earlier
B 1 완료   2 결과   3 계속   4 경험   5 결과
C 1 had never baked   2 had given[gave]
3 more   4 the most expensive desserts
5 had done[did]   6 as

WRITING TEST

A 1 that is shaping Iceland
2 will make you believe in
3 He was stopped by
4 is one of the world's most active volcanoes
5 live near something so dangerous
B 1 had found   2 the most active
3 heated by   4 is made from volcanic rocks

UNIT 05 | Buildings   pp. 18-21

VOCABULARY TEST 1

01 건축학, 건축술; 건축물 **02** 인공의[인조의] **03** 주목;
관심 **04** 훌륭한, 멋진 **05** 포착하다, 담아내다
06 완료하다 **07** 건설, 공사 **08** 위기 **09** 곡선의,
약간 굽은 **10** 일[사건] **11** 필수적인 **12** 특색, 특징

---

13 부드럽게 **14** 획기적인 **15** 줄이다 **16** 별명
17 보통의; 평범한 **18** 보행자 **19** 오염, 공해
20 현실적인; 실용적인 **21** 압력 **22** 주된, 주요한
23 참사, 재난, 재해 **24** (겉)모습, 외모 **25** 쌀쌀한, 추운
26 그늘 **27** 중요성 **28** 특이한, 색다른 **29** 정부
30 홍수 **31** store **32** floor **33** destroy
34 electricity **35** regional **36** threaten
37 isolated **38** shape **39** agricultural
40 protect **41** A를 B에 덧붙이다 **42** ~ 때문에
43 ~와 조화를 이루어 **44** 시간이 지나면서

VOCABULARY TEST 2

A 1 ⓐ   2 ⓔ   3 ⓓ   4 ⓒ   5 ⓑ
B 1 ⓓ   2 ⓒ   3 ⓐ
C 1 in harmony with   2 Over time
3 add, to   4 Due to

GRAMMAR TEST

A 1 singing   2 to cook   3 to be
4 yelling   5 to pick   6 to stop
B 1 play   2 to give   3 call[calling]
4 to become   5 work[working]   6 to pick
C 1 score[scoring]   2 pulled out
3 lie   4 remodeled
5 to use   6 to clean

WRITING TEST

A 1 is protected from flooding
2 was opened for the first time
3 while reducing air pollution
4 was given the nickname by Londoners
5 wanted the vault to send them
B 1 One of the most unusual buildings
2 cold enough to keep
3 It is expected to
4 has received
5 It's clear that[It is clear]

UNIT 06 | Numbers pp. 22-25

VOCABULARY TEST 1

01 전달자, 전령(傳令)   02 국제적인   03 탈진, 기진맥진
04 고무하다; 영감을 주다   05 처음에   06 증가시키다
07 요구하다   08 태양의   09 추적하다   10 움직임
11 따라가다   12 비슷하게   13 정의하다
14 완료하다   15 경기장   16 왕의, 왕실의
17 요청하다; 요청, 요구   18 떨어지다; (날짜가) ~이다
19 깊은 인상을 주다, 감명[감동]을 주다   20 심판
21 자격을 잃은, 실격된   22 대중 매체[미디어]
23 (고위) 공무원[관리]   24 함께 쓰다, 공유하다
25 전체의   26 과정   27 기간   28 정확히   29 약간
30 여분의, 추가의   31 distance   32 historian
33 victory   34 length   35 permanent
36 calendar   37 lunar   38 cycle   39 term
40 balance   41 ~하려고 애쓰다   42 포기하다
43 ~으로 알려져 있다   44 ~하기 위하여

VOCABULARY TEST 2

A 1 exactly   2 permanent   3 international
4 cycle
B 1 ⓒ   2 ⓔ   3 ⓓ
C 1 gave up   2 is known as   3 struggled to
4 in order to

GRAMMAR TEST

A 1 O   2 O   3 X   4 O   5 X   6 O
B 1 what   2 that   3 What   4 what
5 what   6 that
C 1 그녀는 자신의 친구들이 말한 것을 믿을 수 없었다.
2 에디는 과학 프로젝트에 필요한 것을 주문했다.
3 어제 내가 산 책은 브라이언을 위한 선물이었다.
4 그날 네가 말한 것이 내게 희망을 주었다.
5 그녀는 내게 제이슨이 그린 그림 몇 점을 보여주었다.
6 그것은 우리가 추구하는 가치를 대표하는 것이 아니다.

WRITING TEST

A 1 wanted the royal kids to watch the race
2 requested that the race end in front of
3 about how the distance became
permanent
4 it takes the Earth to move around

5 the time the moon takes to complete
B 1 was named
2 was increased to what
3 was used to describe   4 added to

UNIT 07 | Sports pp. 26-29

VOCABULARY TEST 1

01 숨이 가쁜; 숨이 막히는   02 비롯되다, 유래하다
03 사냥   04 발달하다   05 차지하다
06 공격자[공격수]   07 상대   08 스노클링
09 물속의; 물속에(서)   10 발견하다   11 특히
12 인기 있는   13 지역   14 생물, 생명체
15 달아나다   16 ~을 달다; 터치하다   17 부르다;
(단조로운 어조로) 되풀이하다   18 계속해서, 연속적으로
19 장비   20 표면   21 숨을 쉬다   22 효과적인
23 선수권 대회   24 경쟁을 하는   25 참가자
26 길이; (수영장 등의 끝에서 끝까지의) 길이[거리]
27 세계적인   28 쪽, 편   29 속이 빈   30 특징
31 defense   32 lung   33 half   34 inhale
35 experience   36 wildlife   37 tropical
38 explore   39 oxygen   40 modern
41 교대로 ~하다   42 숨을 쉬다   43 (잠시) 휴식을
취하다   44 매우 다양한 ~   45 ~와 비교하여

VOCABULARY TEST 2

A 1 ⓑ   2 ⓐ   3 ⓔ   4 ⓒ   5 ⓓ
B 1 occupied   2 evolve   3 surface
4 inhaled   5 effective
C 1 take a breath   2 take turns
3 take a break   4 compared to

GRAMMAR TEST

A 1 flew the birds   2 do we   3 did I
4 has she   5 comes the bus   6 is the store
B 1 was worth waiting
2 looking forward to having
3 am used to traveling
4 prevent the accident from occurring
C 1 was busy reading
2 couldn't help laughing
3 kept me from talking

4 have I heard   5 stood my friend

5 having been served

A 1 take a breath before getting back to
  2 If the attacker stops chanting or takes a break
  3 is a great way to experience
  4 It allows people to explore
  5 to breathe underwater while collecting
B 1 take turns sending 2 has been
  3 from escaping   4 is it, it is

A 1 This was the year when
  2 is a third reason why e-sports
  3 are being used by companies
  4 tends to make them quite heavy
  5 materials that increase battery life
B 1 don't have to be recharged
  2 without being damaged
  3 are easier, than
  4 a place where you can

UNIT 08 | Future   pp. 30-33

VOCABULARY TEST 1

01 재료   02 설치하다   03 여분의, 추가의   04 완전히
05 자주   06 유동성의   07 대체품   08 10억
09 가치   10 받을 만하다   11 인식; 인정   12 산업
13 접근할 수 있는   14 성별   15 전도유망한   16 폭발
17 측면   18 온도   19 성능   20 포함하다
21 관리하다   22 전기의   23 참여   24 폭넓은
25 환경   26 극심한; 치열한   27 전형적으로
28 주요한   29 경쟁; 경기   30 여기다   31 liquid
32 flow   33 benefit   34 negative   35 space
36 practice   37 popularity   38 phenomenon
39 electronic   40 connect   41 우선   42 ~할 것 같다   43 ~보다는   44 열리다, 일어나다

VOCABULARY TEST 2

A 1 ⓓ   2 ⓒ   3 ⓐ   4 ⓑ
B 1 extra   2 electric   3 include
  4 deserves   5 accessible
C 1 are likely to   2 rather than
  3 First of all   4 take place

GRAMMAR TEST

A 1 where   2 why   3 being scolded
  4 having been invited
B 1 where   2 why   3 when   4 how
C 1 being called   2 having been educated
  3 having been treated   4 being laughed

UNIT 09 | Animals   pp. 34-37

VOCABULARY TEST 1

01 생태계의   02 위협   03 생물학자   04 화학 물질
05 표면[표층]   06 버리다   07 영향을 미치다
08 구하다[구조하다]   09 거의 ~ 아니게   10 유전자
11 발생하다   12 (야생 상태의) 자연   13 새끼를 낳다; 번식시키다   14 나머지; (남은) 다른 사람들[것들]
15 (액체·가스 등을) 흡수하다   16 양   17 증가하다, 증가시키다   18 우려, 걱정   19 줄다[감소하다]
20 (규모·크기·양 등을) 줄이다   21 이용할 수 있는
22 관계   23 멸종 위기에 처한   24 보호하다
25 분명한, 확실한   26 속이다   27 마케팅   28 목적
29 외투; (동물의) 털, 가죽   30 탄생, 출생   31 face
32 lack   33 iron   34 marine   35 ecosystem
36 private   37 genetic   38 normal
39 zookeeper   40 remove   41 ~으로 고통받다
42 얼마간의; 많은 ~   43 (~에게) 접근하지 않다
44 ~에 필수적이다   45 반복해서

VOCABULARY TEST 2

A 1 ⓑ   2 ⓓ   3 ⓔ   4 ⓐ   5 ⓒ
B 1 endangered   2 reduce   3 trick
  4 private   5 lack
C 1 suffer from   2 stay away
  3 over and over   4 a number of

GRAMMAR TEST

A 1 Walking to school 2 Being angry
  3 finishing her homework
B 1 were   2 had entered
  3 had seen   4 knew
C 1 그녀는 마치 뉴욕에 가봤던 것처럼 말한다.
  2 그는 마치 그 소식을 듣지 못했던 것처럼 행동했다.
  3 그녀의 자리에 앉으면서, 그녀는 나에게 미소 지었다.
  4 그의 컴퓨터를 끄고 나서, 그는 저녁 식사를 위해
    외출했다.

WRITING TEST

A 1 one of them is a lack of
  2 swim up to the surface to poop
  3 being bred to produce the gene
  4 suffered from genetic problems caused by
  5 suggest people stay away from these zoos
B 1 is essential to fighting
  2 While photosynthesizing
  3 haven't been seen   4 talk as if, were

UNIT 10 | Stories   pp. 38-41

VOCABULARY TEST 1

01 겁에 질려 어쩔 줄 모르다   02 심장 박동   03 속이다
04 알아채다   05 시작, 초(반)   06 독자   07 자신 있게
08 한 조각; 작품   09 시(詩)   10 존경하다   11 서술자,
내레이터   12 매끄러운; 부드러운[감미로운]
13 매력적인   14 흉내 내다   15 판자   16 비명;
비명을 지르다   17 필요한   18 확신시키다   19 화난;
미친   20 상냥하게[다정하게]   21 살인범   22 몸; 시체
23 (몸이) 떨다, 떨리다   24 공포   25 부드러워지다,
은은해지다   26 온화한, 부드러운   27 꾀다, 유혹하다
28 극심한, 강렬한   29 슬픈   30 깨닫다, 알아차리다
31 (police) officer   32 evil   33 secretly
34 attack   35 detail   36 legendary
37 compose   38 character   39 grab
40 tragic   41 소리를 내다   42 ~을 자백하다
43 계속해서 ~하다   44 ~을 두려워하다

VOCABULARY TEST 2

A 1 poem   2 admire   3 describe
  4 murderer
B 1 tremble   2 legendary   3 emotions
  4 convince   5 necessary
C 1 continue to   2 were terrified of
  3 confess to   4 make a noise

GRAMMAR TEST

A 1 현재분사   2 동명사   3 현재분사   4 동명사
  5 동명사
B 1 what I was   2 he is[was]
  3 whether[if] I had gone
  4 that she had heard
C 1 제이크는 지난밤 그의 첫 소설 쓰기를 끝마쳤다.
  2 바이올린을 연주하는 소년은 겨우 여섯 살이다.
  3 나는 그에게 어떻게 그가 그렇게 일찍 집에 도착했는지
    물었다.
  4 그는 나에게 그가 내 숙제를 도와주겠다고 말했다.

WRITING TEST

A 1 confesses to killing an old man
  2 heard the police knocking on
  3 kept getting louder and louder
  4 He used a different voice
  5 tells his father that he is terrified of
B 1 convince the reader that
  2 enjoyed fooling them
  3 why he is afraid
  4 trying to lure

UNIT 11 | Psychology   pp. 42-45

VOCABULARY TEST 1

01 일반적인, 흔한   02 작가, 저자   03 혜택, 이득;
이득을 보다   04 연결하다   05 편리한   06 상담
07 치명적인   08 우울한   09 감정   10 기진맥진한,
탈진한   11 탐험하다   12 열   13 치유하다[낫게 하다]
14 향수병   15 향상, 발전   16 향수(鄕愁)   17 개인의
[개인적인]   18 인기   19 결국   20 때리다
21 문제가 많은   22 상처, 종기   23 싸움; 힘든 일
24 고통받는 사람, 환자   25 치료, 요법   26 수송[운송],

교통수단　　27 알려지지 않은, 미지의　　28 어휘
29 직접적인　　30 제의하다; 내놓다, 제공하다
31 opportunity　　32 improve　　33 editing
34 equipment　　35 dictionary　　36 clearly
37 express　　38 comfortable　　39 process
40 grade　　41 ~을 다루다, 처리하다　　42 ~하기를
애타게 바라다　　43 진정하게 하다　　44 ~으로 죽다

VOCABULARY TEST 2

A 1 ⓑ　　2 ⓒ　　3 ⓓ　　4 ⓔ　　5 ⓐ
B 1 ⓒ　　2 ⓑ　　3 ⓐ
C 1 cool, down　　　　2 deal with
　　3 longed to[been longing to]
　　4 die of

GRAMMAR TEST

A 1 Whenever　2 However　　　3 when
　　4 where　　　5 which
B 1 when　　　2 which　　　3 where
　　4 However　　5 Whenever
C 1 who　　　2 which　　　3 when
　　4 where　　　5 However

WRITING TEST

A 1 The way we view emotions
　　2 which would lead to their deaths
　　3 Whenever he got angry
　　4 offer students the chance to write songs
　　5 makes it easier to reach
B 1 was considered, called
　　2 connect, living　　　3 Expressing, healing
　　4 how to make　　　5 struggle to talk about

UNIT 12 | Business　　pp. 46-49

VOCABULARY TEST 1

01 들어올리다; (자금 등을) 모으다　　02 보통의, 일상적인
03 즉시　　04 투자자　　05 일반적으로　　06 기부하다
07 자선 단체　　08 광고 (방송)　　09 특징으로 삼다
10 물건　　11 지불　　12 장치[기구]　　13 금융의, 재정의
14 안전한　　15 기부하다, 기여하다　　16 놀랍게도

17 (상품 등의) 재고; 주식　　18 수도; 자금　　19 캠페인;
(조직적인) 활동　　20 기술　　21 전기의　　22 출판
23 기록　　24 소매업자, 소매상　　25 효과적인
26 막대[방지하다]　　27 사용할 수 없는　　28 신뢰; 확신
29 최신의　　30 100만　　31 business　　32 fund
33 introduction　　34 investment　　35 donation
36 security　　37 steal　　38 random
39 access　　40 crime　　41 ~에 관한 한
42 구매하다　　43 A를 B로 바꾸다, 대체하다

VOCABULARY TEST 2

A 1 achieve　　2 random　　3 commercial
　　4 security　　5 reward
B 1 incredibly　　　2 effective
　　3 capital　　　4 publishing
　　5 steal
C 1 replaced, with　　2 make a purchase
　　3 When it comes to

GRAMMAR TEST

A 1 Soccer is being played in the field by
　　some students.
　　2 The science homework has just been
　　finished by Fred.
　　3 Our shopping carts can be used by any of
　　our customers.
　　4 A new jacket will be bought by him.
B 1 was a ball that　　2 was Emma that
　　3 was this morning that
　　4 was in front of the shopping mall that
C 1 be → being　　2 deliver → be delivered
　　3 recognizing → recognized
　　4 She → It　　5 what → that[where]

WRITING TEST

A 1 were usually funded by banks
　　2 makes it easier to reach
　　3 don't have to worry about
　　4 allowing the retailer to access
　　5 shop with your mobile device
B 1 is more effective than　2 was to raise
　　3 It is, that　　　　　4 will be developed

UNIT 13 | People pp. 50-53

VOCABULARY TEST 1

01 살아있는　02 나타나다　03 주장하다　04 붕대
05 끓이다　06 상징하다　07 (신체에) 손상을 주는,
해로운　08 동등하게　09 외교관　10 대사관
11 고용하다　12 즉시　13 법률[합법]적으로
14 혼합물　15 보다; 관찰하다　16 통증, 고통
17 여권　18 환자　19 직접, 개인적으로　20 알아보다
21 구출, 구조; 구출하다　22 위태롭게 하다
23 줄무늬가 있는　24 수술　25 지역, 영토
26 수송하다　27 가벼운[순한]　28 막대기, 기둥
29 고통　30 획기적인　31 rotten　32 medieval
33 surgeon　34 perform　35 task　36 flag
37 military　38 wound　39 approach
40 technique　41 일련의　42 나눠 주다　43 막
～하려고 하다　44 ～을 적다　45 ～하려는 시도로,
～하기 위해

VOCABULARY TEST 2

A 1 ⓑ　2 ⓔ　3 ⓓ　4 ⓐ　5 ⓒ
B 1 ⓔ　2 ⓓ　3 ⓒ　4 ⓑ
C 1 hand out　　2 a series of
　3 Write down　　4 in an attempt to

GRAMMAR TEST

A 1 is　2 Is　3 has　4 seems
B 1 kind as　　2 kinder than
　3 kinder than any other student
　4 as long as　　5 longer than
　6 longer than any other river
C 1 has　　2 was　　3 boy
　4 nice　　5 faster

WRITING TEST

A 1 risked their lives to save Jewish people
　2 had to be let off the train
　3 dangerous approach caused patients
　　great pain
　4 His book was based on
　5 by burning the wound with boiling oil
B 1 as brave as　　2 was hired as
　3 made people raise　　4 not only, but, also

5 which were written

UNIT 14 | Space pp. 54-57

VOCABULARY TEST 1

01 인간　02 (인공)위성　03 거대한　04 (다른 천체의)
궤도를 돌다; 궤도　05 거대한　06 충돌하다
07 우주선　08 장관을 이루는　09 도전　10 ～ 이내에
11 촬영하다　12 위치　13 목적　14 관찰하다
15 제거하다　16 완료하다　17 견디다, 참다
18 불행하게도　19 방법　20 연구, 조사　21 해결책
22 수행하다; (작동하며) 돌아가다　23 노출시키다
24 힘든, 어려운　25 상태; 환경　26 가혹한; 너무 강한
27 기술자, 공학자　28 극심한　29 온도, 기온
30 공식적인　31 launch　32 space
33 resulting　34 damage　35 mission
36 broadcast　37 live　38 angle
39 automatic　40 quality　41 쪼개지다, 분리되다
42 ～에 대응하여　43 수천의　44 언제든지
45 ～까지

VOCABULARY TEST 2

A 1 ⓑ　2 ⓒ　3 ⓐ　4 ⓔ　5 ⓓ
B 1 endured　　2 install　　3 orbit
　4 solutions　　5 extreme
C 1 at any time　　2 breaks apart
　3 thousands of　　4 In response to

GRAMMAR TEST

A 1 has lived　2 have been eating　3 seen
　4 traveled　5 have just received
B 1 가정법, 내가 차를 갖고 있다면, 너를 집까지 차로
　　데려다 줄 텐데.
　2 가정법, 비가 오지 않으면, 우리는 밖에서 축구를 할 수
　　있을 텐데.
　3 조건문, 네가 지금 상점에 가면, 너는 50퍼센트 할인된
　　가격에 그 셔츠를 살 수 있어.
　4 가정법, 내가 일본어를 말할 줄 안다면, 그 일본인
　　관광객들을 도울 수 있을 텐데.
C 1 moved　　2 have known　3 been
　4 weren't　5 could

A 1 Humans have launched

  2 has been asking companies to remove

  3 Each camera is set up to film

  4 Why does NASA show us these images

  5 they will be used

B 1 have been creating

  2 have been suggested

  3 has been running

  4 is led by

B 1 전체 부정, 학생들 중 아무도 그의 의견에 동의하지 않는다.

  2 부분 부정, 내 친구들이 내 생일 파티에 모두 오지는 않았다.

  3 전체 부정, 우리 중 아무도 그림을 잘 그리지 못한다.

  4 부분 부정, 우리 엄마가 오후에 항상 집에 계시는 것은 아니다.

C 1 to speak → speaking

  2 To consider → Considering

  3 Judged → Judging

  4 to say → speaking

  5 speak → speaking

UNIT 15 | Fiction   pp. 58-61

VOCABULARY TEST 1

01 생물학의 **02** 벽돌 **03** 동굴 **04** 성격; (책·영화의) 등장인물 **05** 아주[매우] **06** 유사성 **07** 차이(점) **08** 사라지다 **09** 따르다[따라가다] **10** 발달하다; 진화하다 **11** 민간 설화, 전래 동화 **12** 강요하다 **13** 염소 **14** 고무하다; 영감을 주다 **15** 납치하다 **16** 뛰다, 뛰어오르다 **17** (목록을) 작성하다 **18** 그동안에 **19** 버릇없는, 말을 안 듣는 **20** 지난 **21** ~인 척하다 **22** 대답하다, 답장하다 **23** 결과 **24** 돌아오다, 돌려주다; 돌아옴, 귀환 **25** 재검토하다 **26** 용감한 **27** 놀랍게도 **28** 선발[선택]하다 **29** 속이다; 속임수 **30** 요구하다 **31** villain **32** chief **33** grab **34** bruise **35** realize **36** behavior **37** adventure **38** escape **39** similarly **40** include **41** ~으로 덮여 있다 **42** ~에 매달리다 **43** ~을 알아내다 **44** A를 속여 B하게 하다

VOCABULARY TEST 2

A 1 ⓔ **2** ⓑ **3** ⓒ **4** ⓓ **5** ⓐ

B 1 include **2** grab **3** kidnap

  4 select **5** review

C 1 are covered with **2** find out

  3 clinging to **4** tricks, into

GRAMMAR TEST

A 1 walk **2** funny **3** lost

  4 to bake **5** recommended

A 1 how the stories had changed

  2 It's not easy to kidnap

  3 plan to kidnap a child and demand

  4 her kids at home while she searches for

  5 would rather lose some money

B 1 been forced to play

  2 into letting

  3 asking, to pay

  4 pretending to be

  5 how the stories evolved

UNIT 16 | Food   pp. 62-65

VOCABULARY TEST 1

01 라벨, 상표 **02** 선택 (사항) **03** 바람직하지 않은 **04** 채식주의자 **05** 맛; 향료 **06** 자연의, 천연의 **07** 재료[성분] **08** 비교적 **09** 서양인 **10** 중세의 **11** 정오, 한낮 **12** 죄 **13** 노동자 **14** 그 결과, 따라서 **15** 발전하다 **16** 국가의, 전국민의 **17** 흔히 **18** 셀 수 없이 많은 **19** 일어나다, 발생하다 **20** 활동 **21** 총액; 양 **22** 대략 **23** 스웨덴의 **24** 역사가 **25** 변화 **26** 맛있는 **27** 광고하다 **28** 건강한; 건강에 좋은 **29** ~이 들어 있다, 함유하다 **30** 우연히, 뜻하지 않게 **31** average **32** recommend **33** cavity **34** promote **35** industry **36** belief **37** Sweden **38** originate **39** term **40** discover **41** 사실 **42** ~을 지칭하다 **43** ~으로 여겨지다 **44** ~을 자세히 살펴보다

VOCABULARY TEST 2

A 1 ⓔ   2 ⓓ   3 ⓑ   4 ⓒ   5 ⓐ

B 1 ⓒ   2 ⓓ   3 ⓑ

C 1 is regarded as   2 take a closer look at
   3 In fact   4 refer to

GRAMMAR TEST

A 1 Having walked   2 It being sunny
   3 Having left

B 1 목적어   2 형용사   3 보어   4 목적어   5 주어

C 1 사실은 그가 너보다 나이가 많다는 것이다.
   2 제니퍼는 할인 중인 자동차를 샀다.
   3 버스가 너무 붐벼서, 우리는 기차를 탔다.
   4 그녀가 내게 준 시계를 잃어버려서, 나는 우울해졌다.

WRITING TEST

A 1 promoted a campaign that encouraged
   2 It is a family activity that happens
   3 relatively recent tradition for Westerners
   4 considered it a sin to eat
   5 Having discovered how tasty the cereal
    was

B 1 says that   2 eats as much, as
   3 Having breakfast   4 More and more

READING
Inside

A 4-level curriculum
integration reading course

- **A thematic reading program that integrates with school curriculum**
  중등 교육과정이 지향하는 문이과 통합 및 타교과 연계 반영한 독해서

- **Informative content with well-designed comprehension questions**
  정보성 있는 지문과 질 높은 다양한 유형의 문항 그리고 서술형 평가도 대비

- **Grammar points directly related to the *Grammar Inside* series**
  베스트셀러 Grammar Inside와 직접적으로 연계된 문법 항목 및 문항 제공

- **Exercises with useful, essential, and academic vocabulary**
  중등 필수 어휘 학습 코너 제공

- **A workbook for more vocabulary, grammar, and reading exercises**
  풍부한 양의 어휘, 문법, 그리고 쓰기 추가 문제 등을 수록한 워크북

Level	Grade	Words Limit
Reading Inside Starter	Low-Intermediate	140-160
Reading Inside Level 1	Intermediate	160-180
Reading Inside Level 2	Intermediate	180-200
Reading Inside Level 3	**Low-Advanced**	**200-220**